Ünless Recalled Earlier

MAY 3 1 1991		
OCT 1 2 1992		
NOV 4 1992		

DEMCO 38-297

The Developer's Frontier

WILLIAM WYCKOFF

The Developer's Frontier
The Making of the Western
New York Landscape

YALE UNIVERSITY PRESS
NEW HAVEN AND LONDON

Designed by Nancy Ovedovitz and set in Berkeley Old
Style type by The Composing Room of Michigan, Inc.
Printed in the United States of America by Vail-Ballou
Press, Binghamton, N.Y.

Library of Congress Cataloging-in-Publication Data

Wyckoff, William.
The developer's frontier: the making of the western New
York landscape/William Wyckoff.

   p.   cm.
      Bibliography: p.
      Includes index.
      ISBN 0–300–04154–3 (alk. paper)
      1. New York (State)—Historical geography. 2.
Land settlement patterns—New York (State)—History.
3. Land use, Rural—New York (State)—History. 4.
Frontier and pioneer life—New York (State) 5. Cities
and towns—New York (State)—History. I. Title.
F128.44.W93 1988
974.7'03—dc19   87–21760
                                    CIP

The paper in this book meets the guidelines for
permanence and durability of the Committee on
Production Guidelines for Book Longevity of the Council
on Library Resources.

10   9   8   7   6   5   4   3   2   1

For LLW and DWM

Contents

Figures

Tables

Preface

The historical geographer is forever linked both to the archive and to the land itself. We are enriched by what others have recorded of the past and by what the past has left us on the modern landscape. Such was the case in my sojourn to the developer's frontier in early nineteenth-century New York. Everywhere I turned within the halls of historical society libraries and county clerk's offices I encountered clues to how the land was changed, and everywhere on the backroads and in the fields of the region I came to know, I saw the evidence, often in undramatic and everyday pose, that displayed the enduring nature of decisions and investments made almost two centuries ago.

I did not journey alone. From the project's inception I profited from my contacts with David Sopher, Mark Monmonier, John Thompson, Sally Kohlstedt, and Bill Stinchcombe. My greatest intellectual debt is owed to Donald Meinig, who provided me with the tools and patience to see the project through. More generally, his wisdom taught me to see the world whole and to appreciate that the legacy of human impact on the land was a story worth understanding and telling.

Numerous library and archival staffs saved hours if not days of wandering. Special thanks go to the staff of the Buffalo and Erie County Historical Society. In particular, Herman Sass and Art Detmers provided a congenial research environment that made my months there both pleasant and rewarding. In Amsterdam, the Municipal Archives staff was similarly generous with their time and resources. Dr. Wilhelmina Pieterse, Walter Hofman, Paul van den Brink, and Michael Menschaar deserve particular attention.

Generous grants from the National Science Foundation and Syracuse University made the thousands of miles of travel possible, and I heartily thank them for their generous support.

Cartographic services at Syracuse University, the University of Georgia, and Montana State University proved invaluable in assisting with the maps and diagrams. Typing chores of various drafts were shouldered by Sharon Dusenberry, Audrey Hawkins, and Ann Parker. I am forever indebted to their sure and fleet fingers. Thanks also to John Wilson for helping with word-processing bugs along the way. The manuscript also received much appreciated care and editorial assistance from Yale University Press.

Finally, a reminder that ultimately all landscapes are personally encountered as well as historically reconstructed. My own capacity for seeing and appreciating the beauty and significance of the western New York landscape was a function of the insight and devotion given me by my parents. My wife, Linda, was my constant companion researcher and traveler from the backroads of upstate New York to the archives of Amsterdam. Her love inspired every page of this volume, and without her dedication the manuscript surely would have remained unwritten.

CHAPTER 1

The Developer's Frontier: Background and Setting

Although the Speculation may appear to be of a lucrative nature, yet if a proper System is not devised having a liberal policy, and conducted with perseverance, industry economy and Circumspection, the very reverse may eventually happen. I shall therefore do myself the pleasure of addressing these ideas relative to this Great Object.

—Joseph Ellicott

The large-scale private land developer is a figure of conspicuous importance on the postrevolutionary American frontier. The institutions he created, the wilderness tracts he transformed, and the pioneer lives both enriched and impoverished through his policies form a distinctive chapter in American settlement history. When the developer engaged in the business of selling, promoting, and managing fron-

1

tier acreage, the landscape was changed forever and with it the fortunes and experiences of those who came to settle. These enduring relationships between developer, settler, and the land itself were displayed wherever company invest- ments molded survey patterns, village locations, road networks, or the place- ment of frontier services. Through such investments the developer shaped significant portions of the American landscape, and because his imprint was often made so early and so rapidly, much of his mark on the land is visible today—a clear display of his special role in making the American scene.

The operations of the Holland Land Company in western New York State in the years following the American Revolution offer an example of this dis- tinctive brand of frontier experience, both as a process of settlement and as an assemblage of landscape features. A group of Dutch investors headquartered in Amsterdam purchased over three million acres of wild land in western New York in 1792 and 1793, and after several years of preliminary planning and initial surveys they opened the acreage to settlement in 1800 (fig. 1.1).[1] The decade that followed was hardly one of vigorous sales and heady profits, howev- er. The Dutch persistently struggled to entice settlers to their tract, but easy success eluded them, and they were compelled to invest in the region in ways that would make their acreage appeal to potential buyers. Company-financed land surveys reshaped the wilderness landscape into an orderly geometry of townships and lots; company villages were established as centers of economic and social activity; company-constructed roads connected settlers with one another and with the outside world.

The resident land agent was a pivotal figure in this company-sponsored improvements plan on the developer's frontier. Joseph Ellicott served in that capacity for over two decades.[2] Beginning in 1800, he reshaped the wilderness landscape by laying out a grid of six-mile-square townships and lots across the region. Company villages at such centers as Batavia, Buffalo, and Mayville became focal points of economic activity on the Holland Purchase. Ellicott assisted in the construction of hundreds of miles of roads in the wilderness, opening up isolated tracts to settlers and offering at least the rudimentary avenues along which frontier products might find a commercial market. Partic- ularly in his first decade as agent, Ellicott believed that the company needed to manage carefully the spread of settlement across the region and to promote and guide the project according to some well-defined plan of action.

It was a comprehensive effort, requiring that Ellicott integrate different dimensions of his development strategy: land sales, for example, were coordi- nated with new road and lot surveys, and the establishment of villages was linked with incentives offered to millers, shopkeepers, and others. Many pol-

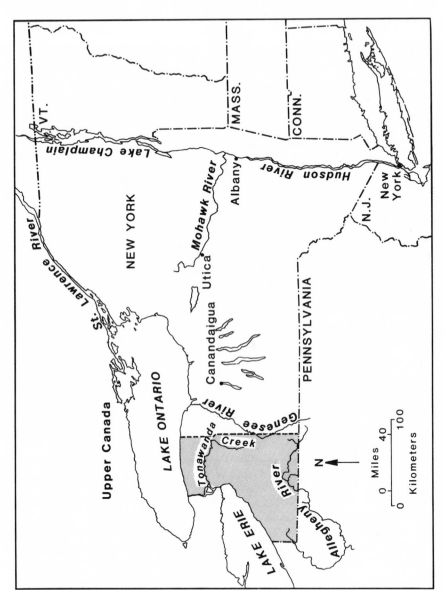

Figure 1.1 The Holland Purchase

icies directly effected the frontier settlement pattern, and Ellicott's early designs to spur regional growth ultimately became an enduring legacy on the landscape, especially in the form of surviving survey lines, village locations, and road networks. That palpable imprint on the land is largely unrecognized and uncelebrated; yet in a rich and dramatic way it displays a chapter in the course of American frontier settlement history that differs sharply from other frontier experiences and highlights the key role played by the land developer in creating many of the ordinary landscapes of our everyday lives.[3]

THEORIES OF FRONTIER SETTLEMENT

The developer's frontier was hardly unique to western New York's Holland Purchase. The Dutch company's project was set amid similar ventures in the region. Many individuals or private companies fostered long-term settlement and regional growth on large frontier land tracts by implementing carefully designed, comprehensive development plans and by making the sustained investments into settlement infrastructure necessary to attract prospective pioneers and support enduring economic growth (fig. 1.2). In subsequent periods of American history, the developer shaped other American landscapes in various guises and a multitude of ways. Later nineteenth-century examples include many of the better-financed and long-lived schemes of railroad companies that were compelled to foster settlement on their vast, isolated land tracts on the Great Plains and in the Far West.[4] No doubt the most familiar twentieth-century setting for the developer has been on the edge of the American city, where the creation of a constantly expanding suburban fringe has promoted the large-scale development and sale of planned residential subdivisions and outlying commercial centers. In such ventures, success, as in Ellicott's time, is predicated on the careful planning of entrepreneurs often acting in concert with other local political and financial figures.[5] Existing theories of frontier settlement, however, do little to interpret in any penetrating way the impact of these promoters, investors, and developers on the making of the American landscape or on the evolution of American culture.

The subject of intense scrutiny for almost a century, the American frontier remains an elusive entity, still likely to provoke from both scholars and amateur historians a never-ending debate over precisely what might be, as Frederick Jackson Turner pondered, "the significance of the frontier in American history." Turner's landmark essay by that title was presented before the American Historical Association at its annual meeting of 1893.[6] For Turner, the frontier, as a condition of settlement and as a crucible of social and political change, ex-

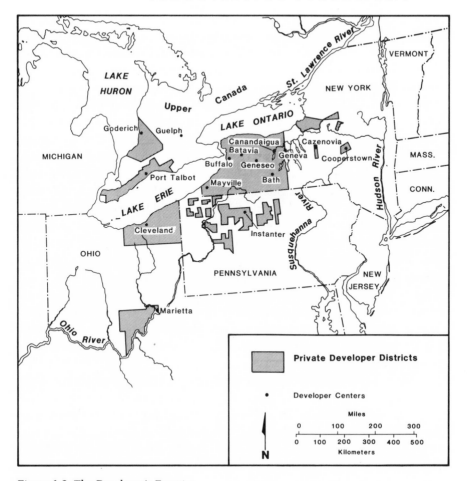

Figure 1.2 The Developer's Frontier

plained a great deal about a larger American character that was evolving in the nineteenth century and was expressing itself in the nation's political, economic, and social institutions. Turner argued that the "primitive conditions" of the frontier community helped to shape a social experience and a political reality that clearly evidenced an egalitarian bent, which Turner ultimately believed spurred the development of democracy in the nation as a whole.

To Turner, several key geographical and historical circumstances in the frontier setting contributed to these democratic predilections. Available cheap land on the American frontier was fundamental, according to Turner, because it continued to give settlers the opportunity to own their own farms and to create a frontier community isolated and distinct from that in Europe or the civilized East. Isolation further defined for Turner the significance of the frontier. Only in isolation, with its back turned from the conventions of civilization, could the frontier logically assume the special qualities Turner ascribed to it. Only there could a society, given the dearth of established institutions on the wilderness's edge, be expected to develop novel responses to social, economic, and political dilemmas. Only then could a new, more democratic, set of institutions be created—institutions that functioned well on the frontier and subsequently became an integral part of the larger national social and political machinery.

A second aspect of Turner's frontier model focused on the sequence of development as a frontier region was opened to settlement. Although Turner readily recognized and detailed regional or sectional differences in environment and history, he saw the archetypal frontier society as evolving in a regular fashion. This model of frontier development began with the game trails and Indian villages of the wilderness and proceeded to the era of the fur trader and hunter in which Europeans made their first fleeting forays into the interior. On their heels came the cattleman and then the subsistence pioneer farmer, who broke the frontier soil. Finally arrived more monied and permanent farmer-settlers to buy out the initial clearers of land and accompanying them, "men of capital and enterprise," who transformed the lonely frontier outpost into a bustling village or town.[7] This sequence of settlement gradually saw the isolation and subsistence economy of Turner's frontier replaced by a more commercial orientation that was increasingly well connected to Eastern markets.

Turner's ideas had a great impact on subsequent interpretations of the American frontier. Variations on his view of American settlement have been offered by second- and third-generation Turnerians such as Frederick Merk and Ray Allan Billington.[8] Others have rejected all or parts of Turner's frontier doctrine, however, pointing to conflicting evidence about the ability of frontier "democracy" to reshape national institutions and noting that the frontier described by Turner was hardly a generic phenomenon but was rather a specific and quite limited approximation of particular frontier experiences at particular times.[9]

In American history the closest approximation to Turner's frontier might be found in portions of the upland South; some areas of Kentucky and Tennessee just before and after the Revolution fit the model tolerably well. Here isolated pioneer communities persisted and in some cases fostered and aspired to various degrees of political autonomy. The Wautauga settlements of eastern Tennessee and their Articles of Association establishing local legislative and judicial powers as well as the attempted creation in the 1770s of the state of

Transylvania in present-day Kentucky illustrate Turner's argument.[10] Critics are quick to point out, however, that such cases hardly provide a suitable description of the process of settlement and of social, economic, and political change on many other American frontiers.[11] In particular, Turner's interpretation does little to enlighten us on the process of settlement undertaken on the developer's frontier in western New York and elsewhere. Here connections with the East were fostered from the beginning, and the "men of capital and enterprise" were the first and not the last figures to arrive on the scene.

Other historians who have assessed different chapters of American frontier history have departed from Turner's emphasis on isolation and from his sequential frontier thesis. The federally supported public lands system initiated in the Ohio Country during the 1780s certainly disputes some of Turner's arguments concerning the frontier's development in the pristine, primitive environment of an economic and political vacuum. In this "federal frontier," the national government was at the center of land-selling, town-founding, and road-building activities. The six-mile-square township grid is the most familiar legacy of that public lands system, but the government's policies toward granting free school and church lands also shaped the social fabric of the frontier, and the need for land offices spurred the development of key frontier villages and the roads that connected them.[12]

The "speculator's frontier" has also been examined carefully by such historians as Paul Wallace Gates, who argued that the land speculator on the frontier often "preceded the settler, selected the choice locations, purchased them with land warrants or cash, surveyed and located them, and then sought to turn immigration into his section."[13] Although Gates was a student of the Turnerian historian Frederick Merk, the speculator's frontier as Gates described it emphasizes the intimate connection of the American frontier to Eastern financial institutions. Gates limited most of his detailed research to the Midwest, where land speculators and railroad companies shaped much of the initial pattern of settlement.[14] An even broader, more comprehensive role for the land speculator is described by A. M. Sakolski, who began his work *The Great American Land Bubble* with the dramatic words, "America, from its inception, was a speculation."[15] From the colonial period to twentieth-century Florida land booms, Sakolski traced the presence and the impact of land-grabbers, jobbers, and speculators on the American scene.

Common to both Gates's and Sakolski's assessments of the speculator's frontier is a recognition that, although the speculator clearly bridged the gap between "savagery and civilization" and thus challenged portions of Turner's interpretation of the frontier, the speculator was less interested in substantive long-term development and regional growth than he was in seeing quick short-term profits, regardless of any development on the lands he held. Actual retail settlement, land clearing, and town founding were not critical elements of the speculator's frontier; it was a setting dominated by and focused around land promoting and land selling, which often saw the rapid turnover of a parcel with only a minimum impact on the land itself. Therefore, even though the presence of the land speculator complicates and to some extent contradicts aspects of the classic Turnerian model, the speculator's frontier is just as sharply distinguished from the developer's frontier, in which land agents were committed not only to promoting and selling land but also to reshaping and transforming the landscape in a manner that would attract settlers and would endure on the visible scene for decades.

The formative role of cities and commercial activities on the American frontier and the general question of subsequent regional economic growth offers another perspective that departs significantly from the Turnerian approach and adds more to our conception of the developer's frontier. Economic historian Douglass C. North directly challenged the Turnerian notion that economic isolation and subsistence-based agriculture necessarily characterized the frontier in its early stages.[16] North argued that connections with and not isolation from the national and world economy were fundamental in furthering the economic viability of a frontier region. Specifically, North noted the need for developing export commodities in frontier settings that could satisfy existing demand in accessible commercial markets. In a similar vein, R. D. Mitchell concluded that from the outset "commercialism" characterized the frontier economy in the Shenandoah Valley of Virginia and that most frontiers were not isolated for long initial periods but rather were "commercially oriented, although not commercially operative, from the beginning."[17]

Urban historians and geographers have placed the role of the city at the center of this debate. Among historians, Richard Wade and John Reps have been leading advocates of reevaluating Turner's frontier and the relatively late and secondary role he assigned to town founding in his sequential development scenario.[18] Much of the American frontier from the Ohio Valley to the Far West was an "urban frontier," and towns and villages "spearheaded" the advance rather than followed the course of settlement. These centers hardly conformed to Turner's theory of isolation; as James Vance has argued in his "mercantile model" of development, these early urban centers frequently grew on the strength of commercial investments and export-oriented long-distance trade.[19]

Clearly the "commercial" and "urban" frontiers challenge Turner's conceptions of frontier isolation and sequential frontier development. Still, these ways of looking at the frontier do not adequately encompass or describe the developer's frontier. A focus on commerce and urban growth helps to identify it, but the comprehensive nature of the developer's frontier—its impact on an entire region, rural and urban, over a sustained period—needs to be defined. Most important, the developer himself needs to be placed at the center of this definition because his decisions shaped the course of settlement and the subsequent look of the land.[20]

CHARACTERISTICS OF THE DEVELOPER'S FRONTIER

The land developer has created a distinctive chapter in American settlement history. But what were the antecedents of the developer's frontier in the context of postrevolutionary America? How did the Holland Land Company's agent, Joseph Ellicott, understand his role and what was expected of him? The developer appears to be an amalgam of earlier institutions, some dating well back into the colonial period, others quite specific to the era just following the Revolution.

The New England town system as it evolved in the seventeenth and eighteenth centuries seems to have anticipated important aspects of the developer's frontier. The New England town or village, whether it developed as a dispersed or a nucleated settlement, was founded as a social and economic entity and as an orderly way "to encourage settlement and establish political and religious institutions within clearly-defined geographic boundaries."[21] A congregation or association of settlers, sharing a common social purpose acted as developers in laying out lots, encouraging millers and innkeepers to locate in the area, and in providing schools, churches, and town meetinghouses that helped cement community ideals and promote spiritual and earthly prosperity.[22] Such a venture was a long-term investment in land and people that often extended over generations and led to lasting changes on the landscape.

Another forerunner of the developer's frontier may have been the manorial land system in colonial New York's Hudson Valley. An outgrowth of the European feudal land tradition, the manor was a grant of land, often thousands of acres in size, bestowed by the colonial governor and the Crown on individuals who agreed to develop the tracts and to attract tenants willing to fulfill certain obligations and payments to their landlords in return for the right to settle in the area.[23] Unlike the Old World, however, the leasehold system in New York State hardly had the same potential to exploit a class of landless, poverty-stricken tenants. The abundance of land in the New World meant, in fact, that the manor landlords were obliged to attract tenants, and they often had trouble convincing prospective farmers to lease acreage on a manor when land in the region was available to own outright.

To attract tenants, the landlords in effect became land developers: they offered special incentives to new settlers by deferring initial rent payments; they established mills to provide critical frontier services to settlers; they financed and constructed roads across the manor.[24] These actions also increased the commercial viability of the manor as an economic unit, another orientation it shared with the developer's frontier after the Revolution. The landlord was thus a land agent, and at his best he was seen as a "moral influence" who "performed many of the basic leadership functions of [the] agrarian society."[25] This tradition of the slow fostering of development by a paternalistic and "enlightened" landed elite peculiarly stamped the colonial New York frontier, and it is not surprising that New York became the setting for numerous large private land developments in the postcolonial period. In fact, James Wadsworth, one developer in western New York, not only sold lands but also retained the colonial penchant for renting some of this acreage to lease-holding tenants.[26]

The developer's rise can also be traced to events that more immediately preceded and followed the Revolution. A series of land companies and land ventures sprouted in the late colonial period after the French were removed as a threat to the interior in 1763. The abortive Vandalia, Indiana, and Wabash land companies promoted the virtues of the interior Ohio and Mississippi valleys.[27] Often companies involved the leading political and financial figures of the period. Although the emphasis in such ventures was clearly land speculation rather than land development, they established a precedent for the all-important land rushes that followed the Revolution.

A rapid revival in land-selling schemes accompanied the end of the Revolution, and soon many investors in the United States and abroad were speculating in small and large ways in the wild lands of the American backcountry. The spirit of speculation was spurred by several Eastern state governments that attempted to finance state debts and obligations from the sale or disposal of wild lands. States also compensated war veterans by the issuance of scrips or warrants that could be redeemed for land, and these often fell into the hands of speculators as well. Sure profits were supposedly guaranteed by engaging in such ventures—did not the rapidly growing American population have an insatiable demand for land? When such demand failed to appear in the right places at the right times and at the right prices, however, the fortunes of the land market shifted rapidly, as was the case in the 1780s and 1790s.

Ultimately, the Dutch in western New York became enamored with the process of long-term comprehensive development of their acreage because they had little choice: the speculative fever that had run so high when they accumulated their acreage in the early 1790s sharply subsided later in the decade. The changing economic climate seemed to preclude the rapid wholesale disposal of their acreage, and their hope of selling the tract at a profit became directly linked to the ability of their agent—Ellicott—to develop the parcel and thereby make it attractive to small retail purchasers.

Ellicott's efforts were replicated in many other settings (see fig. 1.2). One of the most significant of the early postrevolutionary developer schemes was established near the headwaters of the Susquehanna at Cooperstown, New York, in 1785.[28] Judge William Cooper initially offered forty thousand acres of land for sale in and around his village, and soon he had even more land in the region on the market. Cooper hoped to profit from his venture, but he was hardly a speculator in the same sense as many of the others who were buying and selling land in his day. Cooper was most interested in fostering long-term development by investing in the tract of land he purchased and by seeing that actual pioneers settled on the acreage. He succeeded in making Cooperstown a bustling frontier village, and in 1806 he offered some of his ideas to other prospective developers.

Cooper's *Guide in the Wilderness,* designed to instruct those interested in developing American wild lands, provides a good description of many key characteristics of the developer's frontier.[29] Cooper believed in the careful planning and promotion of a prospective settlement. He argued that "a moderate price, long credit, a deed in fee, and a friendly landlord are infallible inducements to a numerous settlement."[30] The "landlord's" or developer's role was a key element in Cooper's plan, and he believed that a liberal sales strategy would appeal to the small retail purchaser not just the wholesale speculator interested in buying and holding wild acreage. Investments in stores, mills, and roads were also necessary expenditures to encourage settlement and growth. In addition, Cooper believed that the long-term success of a development effort might well depend on its ability to generate commercial trade and therefore that the developer needed to foster such economic connections. As he stated, "where there is much people there will be trade; and where there is trade there will be money; and where there is money the landlord will succeed; but he should ever be in the midst of the settlement, aiding and promoting every beneficial enterprise."[31]

Another early effort marking the developer's frontier was far to the southwest in the newly opened Ohio Country. In 1786 the Ohio Company was created to invest in western lands by applying for acreage directly from the federal government and by purchasing depreciated land warrants that had been issued to revolutionary war veterans.[32] Although the group became entangled with the speculative Scioto Company, the Ohio Company retained control over a 1.7-million-acre parcel in present-day southeastern Ohio. Settlement began in 1787, when a group of company officials, mostly from New England, arrived in the area to begin development. These agents carefully led the process, and the result was "a New England village transplanted bodily to the Ohio wilderness, with a paternalistic colonizing company playing the same valuable role that town proprietors played in seventeenth-century Massachusetts."[33] As in New England, a town or village was more than a geographical area: the company invested in frontier services at its village of Marietta; it raised sawmills and gristmills near important settlements; it gave aid to initial settlers, especially if they located in isolated areas. The Ohio Company hardly proved to be a model for other land ventures in the area, however. The Scioto Company lands and the Symmes Purchase nearby were characterized by speculation rather than development—owners of these tracts demonstrated less of a sustained interest in actual settlement than in the hope of swift, often unscrupulously garnered profits from the sale of frequently unseen and still wild lands.[34]

One other large and early-opened tract in the Ohio Country reflected the concerns of development over those of speculation, however, and, as with the Ohio Company, it represented a strong New England connection. The Western Reserve in the northeastern corner of the state was developed by the Connecticut Land Company in the 1790s.[35] The area was ceded to Connecticut by Congress when that state's interior land claims were settled. A group of investors bought the parcel in 1795 and began initial surveys the following year. The company founded the village of Cleveland at the mouth of the Cuyahoga River and proceeded to improve roads, invest in frontier services, and offer lands at reasonable prices to retail purchasers.

The 1790s also saw development in upstate New York. Although the state itself, along with numerous small speculators, shaped the early settlement of the New Military Tract in central New York, the lands that stretched between that parcel and the Holland Land Company's lands to the west were held by large privately controlled land companies. The Phelps and Gorham acreage near Canandaigua, the Wadsworth tract surrounding Geneseo, and the Pulteney Purchase focused on Bath and Geneva were all developer-inspired retail land sales ventures that took shape during the decade.[36] Each was accompanied by land surveys, town founding, and various inducements to attract settlers. The Dutch company itself managed other development projects in central New York. One venture was headquartered at Cazenovia and a second on the Oldenbarneveld tract to the northeast.[37] In addition, the Dutch owned wild lands in the vicinity of Instanter in the rugged reaches of northwestern Pennsylvania.

West of the Niagara River, the settlement systems of neighboring districts in Upper Canada were shaped largely through the efforts of the British government and its local colonial representatives. Individuals such as Lt. Gov. John Simcoe mandated the geometry of survey patterns, the placement of administrative centers, and the construction of a rudimentary regional road network.[38] Even on this frontier dominated largely by public figures and institutions, a number of significan private land development schemes characterized the period. Entrepreneur Thomas Talbot successfully developed approximately 500,000 acres north of Lake Erie in the early nineteenth century, and after 1825 the Canada Company, in a deal with the Crown, acquired the rights to develop an even larger parcel just east of Lake Huron.[39] Both projects displayed the same set of investments and landscape changes that typified the developer's frontier south of the border.

Although the relative success of these ventures varied, they shared several characteristics with the Holland Land Company's western New York project that, when taken together, define the essential and distinctive qualities of the developer's frontier:

An Orderly System of Land Disposal Although precise methods of land disposal varied, the private developer commonly opted for a simple, orderly way in which to survey and sell land. Prospective buyers needed to be able to find a parcel easily in the wilderness, but the developer avoided a policy of allowing the settler to locate and mark the boundaries of his desired lot. This tradition was common in such states as Pennsylvania, Virginia, and North Carolina, but it often led to confused claims and lengthy land disputes.[40] From the developer's point of view, a much more rational and manageable system would organize the wilderness landscape into an orderly lotted geometry in which prospective settlers could pinpoint a parcel defined by clearly surveyed and recorded boundaries. The developer commonly decided on some form of square or rectangular lots arranged in a repeating and easy-to-interpret pattern. From the outset, these lines on the land symbolized the developer's predilection to shape the evolution of his project in an orderly, rational fashion.

A Need for Planning The developer was the eighteenth- or nineteenth-century version of the regional planner. He needed to guide and anticipate change in newly opened areas of settlement in a comprehensive way. The developer recognized this need, and even before preliminary surveys were made or the first towns established, he had to envisage, to some degree, his long-term objectives. Success demanded an imaginative but practical blending of the varied dimensions of development policy. It required the careful coordination of lot and village surveys with sales policies, assistance to settlers, road-building activities, and other efforts. Furthermore, as development progressed, plans needed to be reevaluated and adopted to the changing requirements of a maturing settlement.

A Need for Promotion In one important respect, the developer resembled the speculator—to be successful, both needed to promote their lands and to spread the word about the character and potential of their wilderness tracts. The developer gave particular care to the initial stages of actual settlement, since the landscape shaped and managed during this early period of frontiering might well encourage or discourage future movements into the region. Developers also often made an early effort to appeal to potential buyers through advertisements in newspapers and broadsides. Maintaining an active and responsive correspondence with those writing to the land agency also convinced people already interested in the area to make the move. In sum, the developer saw that sales and profits were the product of favorable images and that to be successful such images had to appeal not just to the well-financed investor but to the common settler as well.

A Retail Sales Orientation The developer recognized that the small retail purchaser was the bread and butter of his venture. Whole townships and larger tracts typically were made available to the infrequent wholesale buyer, but the bulk of agency expenses and sales planning efforts were aimed at attracting the family farmer or craftsman who might buy a lot or a portion of a lot for a total purchase of perhaps 40 to 150 acres. The geometry of the lot surveys, the pricing of lands, and the terms of credit available to settlers were geared to this retail buyer. In this way the developer's frontier predated the evolution of the public lands system, which only gradually became oriented to selling smaller and smaller tracts of land.[41] It was not until 1832 that a standard 40-acre parcel was made available to settlers on the public lands frontier, but in many private development projects agents were more likely and more able to be flexible in surveying and subdividing various smaller lot sizes for purchase. They also had greater flexibility in shifting pricing and credit policies to meet the needs of settlers who arrived unable even to make initial down payments on their land.

Investments in Frontier Centers and Services The developer usually felt it wise to make a series of long-term investments in certain frontier services that would encourage sales and would eventually help to define the orientation of the region's entire settlement system and economy. There was a recognized need for platting village centers, and in this sense the developer's frontier was certainly an urban frontier. In addition, there was an understanding that to some degree the developer should subsidize the operations of early millers, tavernkeepers, artisans, storekeepers, and perhaps other key individuals in the frontier community. This assistance, although certainly most critical in the opening days of the settlement, often continued for years. The long-term impact of these company-sponsored imprints depended ironically on the relatively limited success of the entire project. If millers, tavernkeepers, and others swarmed to an area of their own accord, the developer did not need to attract them with special discounts or cash advances. Therefore, the longer sales languished, the more determining was the land developer's role. As sales increased, the economic geography of the area became less the product of the developer's policies and more the outgrowth of decisions and investments made by individual settlers and merchants.

The Role of Commerce The developer believed that fostering commerce was important in the economic growth of the frontier because commercial agriculture and small-scale export-oriented manufacturing generated scarce cash. The most obvious investment that fostered interaction and offered at least the opportunity for export-based economic expansion was the building of roads, especially networks of long-distance routes designed to fit into existing water and overland corridors of movement. Developer-assisted sawmills, gristmills, distilleries, and potash-refining operations can also be seen as direct investments into infant manufacturing industries. Trading ventures organized and coordinated by developers were another way in which commerce was encouraged. The goal of such initiatives was not to reap profits or to control the regional economy; rather it was to generate increased interest in the tract and thereby permit land prices and the volume of sales to rise.

A Legacy on the Landscape The frontier landscape reflected the developer's policies in direct and enduring ways. Through initial survey lines, village centers, mill site hamlets, and roads, the developer provided the critical early framework for settlement, the bare but essential skeleton of regional infrastructure and support. The detailed infilling that followed, the flesh and fiber of the local landscape that gave character to individual farmsteads and particular village streets, was not the developer's doing. It was transformed in texture and in substance by the pioneers themselves and by subsequent settlers. Still, much of the larger pattern of order on the land visible today reflects the developer's comprehensive early imprint, and it displays how he contributed to the making of the American landscape in ways clearly different from that of the isolated pioneer carving out his own niche in the wilderness or from the speculator hoping to sell undeveloped acreage at inflated prices.

THE WESTERN NEW YORK SETTING

Holland Land Company Acquisition

The developer's frontier advanced rapidly across upstate New York in the postrevolutionary period, and its institutions were firmly entrenched in the region when the Dutch bought their land in the early 1790s. The Pulteney Purchase, located just east of the Holland Land Company's acreage, was the largest land agency in the area before the Dutch acquired the Holland Purchase. Its enthusiastic promoter and agent, Charles Williamson, was headquartered on a tributary of the Susquehanna River at the village of Bath, a frontier burg complete with racetrack and commodious accommodations for potential buyers. Another smaller land agency run by the Wadsworth family peddled acreage amid rich, fertile farming country at Geneseo in the Genesee River Valley. Another hotbed of sales focused on Canandaigua, where entrepreneurs Oliver Phelps and Nathaniel Gorham offered additional acreage for sale.[42] Elsewhere across upstate New York other land agencies extolled the virtues of development projects ranging in size from a few thousand to 100,000 acres.

This complex mosaic of large, privately controlled land parcels resulted from a series of transactions that began in the 1780s.[43] Following the Revolution, the states of New York and Massachusetts both claimed over six million acres of upstate New York that included all of the land in the state west of a line through Seneca Lake. Massachusetts based its assertions on the "sea to sea" provisions in the Plymouth Charter of 1620. New York's claim was based on grants made in 1664 by King Charles II to his brother, James. At a convention in Hartford, Connecticut, in late 1786, the two states came to an agreement regarding the disputed tract. West of a line surveyed through Seneca Lake, Massachusetts received the right to sell all of the land except for a narrow strip bordering on the Niagara River that was reserved for New York State. In exchange, Massachusetts agreed to give up all claims of political sovereignty over the region.

Massachusetts was anxious to sell its development rights in order to improve its financial situation, and in 1788 the state sold the six-million-acre tract to a group of Yankee investors led by Oliver Phelps and Nathaniel Gorham. The buyers offered approximately one million dollars for the entire parcel. A few months after the deal was struck, Phelps succeeded in securing Indian title to 2.6 million acres of land in the eastern portion of the tract. The group soon had financial difficulties, however, and failed to make its subsequent payments to Massachusetts. As a result, they were forced to give up control over much of the region. All of the acreage that included the Holland Purchase reverted to Massachusetts, while some acreage further east in areas cleared of Indian title was either sold to other investors or, in the vicinity of Canadaigua, subsequently developed by Phelps and Gorham.[44]

After reverting to Massachusetts for a short while, the western portions of the Phelps and Gorham tract soon fell into the hands of another private investor—Robert Morris, a major financier and speculator in America after the Revolution. He quickly sold, at a generous profit, a sizable portion of the land to a group of English capitalists led by Sir William Pulteney. Equally anxious to dispose of at least some portions of his remaining acreage, Morris sent his son, Robert, Jr., to Europe in 1792, hoping to spark interest in wild American lands among money-laden European investors and speculators. In December 1792, however, the elder Morris found a buyer for a good portion of his remaining upstate New York land. Theophile Cazenove, acting as agent for a group of Dutch bankers, secured the rights to purchase 1.5 million acres of western New York wilderness. The parcel bordered Lake Erie in the isolated westernmost part of the state. Pleased with the sale but now desiring to retain his remaining land in the valuable region east of the 1.5-million-acre tract, Morris wrote to his son, ordering him not to sell any more acreage. The message arrived too late, however; only several weeks after the elder Morris completed the sale in America, Robert, Jr., had sold much of the remaining acreage to virtually the same group of Dutch bankers in Holland.

This collection of Dutch investors included some of Amsterdam's most prestigious banking houses.[45] The firm of Pieter Stadnitski and Son had been investors in American ventures since 1786. The Van Staphorst family also had previous American financial connections. In 1789 these two banking interests united with the houses of Van Eeghen and Ten Cate and Vollenhoven to make further joint investments in promising American projects. These investors, along with W. and J. Willinks, were the principal purchasers of the western New York lands. They chose Theophile Cazenove to coordinate their American operations from Philadelphia. After 1800, Cazenove retired and was replaced by another trusted company employee, Paul Busti, who served as general agent until 1824.

The Dutch purchases amounted to 3.3 million acres of wild land, but the western New York tract was only one of several of the group's large land investments in New York and Pennsylvania.[46] Several sizable purchases of central New York acreage were negotiated in the early 1790s. John Lincklaen developed one tract of approximately 100,000 acres. He coordinated the generous investments that led to the inception and growth of the village of Cazenovia, still a distinctive settlement on the upstate landscape. The Dutch also purchased two other blocks of land near the Black River north of Cazenovia during the same period. In Pennsylvania, General Agent Cazenove obtained additional rights to buy approximately 1.4 million acres of land for his Dutch employers. The East Allegheny and West Allegheny land agencies were created to promote the tract, but the poor quality of land across much of the region precluded any substantive development. It soon became apparent that by far the most valuable of the Dutch company's lands were located in the western New York parcel purchased from Morris, and it was here that the Dutch concentrated their resources and development efforts in subsequent years.

Joseph Ellicott: Background and Experience

In western New York, Cazenove and other company officials selected Joseph Ellicott to be the chief surveyor and resident land agent for the parcel. Ellicott thus became the developer responsible for directing new company investments into the region, and it is his mark that has endured on the landscape since the early nineteenth century. Who was this pivotal frontier land surveyor, agent, and developer? Born in 1760 in Bucks County, Pennsylvania, Ellicott was the fifth child of a Quaker family (fig. 1.3).[47] Ellicott's grandfather was a textile manufacturer who migrated from County Devonshire, England, in 1730. Once in Pennsylvania, the family bought fifty acres of land and built a gristmill. Ellicott's father also repaired nearby mills to earn additional income for his large family. Above all, he was a tinkerer with a flair for mathematics, a talent he passed on to his several sons.

When Ellicott was fourteen, the entire family left Bucks County and moved to Maryland. Their new home was on the Patapsco River, about ten miles west of Baltimore. The family located on seven hundred acres of wilderness, and they soon built a new series of mills and a store to serve surrounding settlers. Their enterprise prospered, and the site became the nucleus for Ellicott City. In 1780, at the age of twenty, Ellicott left the mills and moved to Baltimore, where he taught school and studied mathematics and surveying.

Ellicott's field training as a surveyor began in 1785. In that year he joined his eldest brother, Andrew, in a federally funded survey to fix the western boundary of the state of Pennsylvania.[48] Brother Andrew was already a veteran of earlier Pennsylvania state surveys, and he acted as Joseph's mentor from 1785

Figure 1.3 Joseph Ellicott

to 1791. The younger Ellicott proved an especially promising and capable performer in the field. Four more seasons with Andrew, in 1786, 1787, 1789, and 1790, were devoted to laying out the southern and western boundaries of New York State. In those years, several of the Ellicott brothers worked together boundary surveying in summer and living in Philadelphia during the off-season. Between 1791 and 1793, Andrew, Joseph, and brother Benjamin did additional surveying in and near the new city of Washington, D.C.

A new phase of Joseph's career began in 1794 when he began to establish himself as a surveyor in his own right. In February of that year, he accepted a position with the Holland Land Company through its American representative, Theophile Cazenove.[49] This first assignment with the Dutch investors involved Ellicott in leading a detailed survey and land assessment project of company lands in north-central Pennsylvania. Although the surveying was completed in 1795, final maps and reports were not submitted until early 1796. Ellicott frankly informed the Dutch that much of the land in their Pennsylvania tract was of limited value.[50] Nevertheless, he did identify 900,000 acres for final company purchase and development.

Later in 1796 Ellicott was introduced to another dimension of frontier land development: he helped to build a state-financed road in Pennsylvania that stretched from the Susquehanna River to the shores of Lake Erie. Joseph soon found himself in charge of the entire project, leading the track through "one entire and uninterrupted wilderness."[51] On the completion of this assignment, Ellicott returned to Maryland and the family's milling operations.

When Ellicott was rehired by the company in 1797 to lead new surveys and development in western New York, a lifetime of family upbringing, training, and practical experience had prepared him for the job. Childhood years exposed him to the complexities of building and running frontier milling operations and the problems associated with relocating a family in the wilderness. His father and brother Andrew contributed to his training in practical mathematics. His Quaker heritage emphasized the simple and sober life, another useful trait for a land agent charged with the responsibility of surveying and managing a frontier district. The years spent working with Andrew and his own experiences in Pennsylvania added to his technical skills as a surveyor and exposed him to a variety of surveying operations. By 1797 he was familiar with the laying out of boundaries, wilderness lots, urban plats, and roads, and his training in the surveying of the Dutch company parcels in Pennsylvania honed his skills in assessing the potential of wilderness lands.

The Presurvey Landscape

When Ellicott arrived in the region in 1797 to begin surveying, much of the tract was only thinly populated by scattered bands of Indians and was still little known to American explorers and settlers. Whole streamcourses and drainage divides were yet to be charted, and before formal surveys the soils and vegetation of the tract had never been assessed in a systematic fashion.

The terrain of the purchase varied widely from extensive and sometimes poorly drained lowlands in the north to increasingly rugged mountains in the south.[52] Ellicott found that the areas bordering Lakes Erie and Ontario generally displayed little relief. Along Lake Erie, these plains formed a narrow strip of fertile lowlands in the southwestern purchase. The Ontario Lake plain was much broader and incorporated the entire northern third of the tract. In places low rolling hills and ridges indicated the location of glacial deposits and old beach shore lines, while elsewhere extensive swamps bordered a number of streamcourses in poorly drained sections. Most of the southern two-thirds of the purchase was part of the Appalachian Uplands that stretch across much of the interior East. In general, moderately rolling hills in the central purchase gave way to steeper and less accessible mountains near the Pennsylvania border. In fact, to Ellicott much of the upland acreage in the vicinity of the state line must have borne a striking and unwelcome resemblance to the Dutch company's rugged East and West Allegheny tracts in Pennsylvania.

The region's drainage patterns did little to link the purchase in any convenient network of navigable waterways. Ellicott discovered no single lake or stream system that united the region. This fragmented hydrography was also a potential advantage, however, because it connected western New York by water to a surprising variety of regions. In the north several small streams drained directly into Lake Ontario. Streams in the central purchase flowed into Buffalo and Tonawanda creeks and eventually to the east end of Lake Erie and the Niagara River. Toward the Pennsylvania border, a different system of waterways drained south and west, down the Connewongo and Allegheny rivers to the Ohio River. Just east of the purchase several other watercourses flowed into the Canisteo River and then down the Susquehanna toward Baltimore.

Soil types and soil fertility varied from north to south.[53] Soils of the northern lake plains were glacial tills generously endowed with limestone, which added to the potential agricultural fertility of the land. Small ridges of well-drained, coarsely textured sandy soils marked ancient lakeshores south of existing Lake Ontario. Toward the southern uplands, soils became increasingly acid, thin, and stony. Although these areas, too, were generally covered by glacial till, their overall lime content was lower. This pattern in the south was interrupted only occasionally by narrow strips of deep alluvial soils that bordered major creeks and rivers.

A northern hardwood forest clothed most of the purchase in a dense growth of sugar maple, beech, birch, and elm.[54] The hardwoods grew amid a tangled garden of undergrowth, nettles, and vines that slowed easy movement across the region. While such species as sugar maple thrived throughout the area, other trees grew only in limited sections of the purchase. Oak and white pine flourished mainly in the south, while black ash and cedar were concentrated in the northern swamps on the lake plains. Hemlock dominated sections of the southern and central hills, preferring the moist and shady slopes. Alluvial bottoms attracted their own assemblage of hardwoods; butternut, sycanore, and poplar did especially well in the deep streamside soils.

Surveyor Ellicott did not encounter a pristine "natural" landscape, however, when he commenced his surveys for the Dutch late in 1797. Indians had shaped the look of the land for thousands of years with their villages, fields, and trails.[55] Even these imprints were constantly changing: village sites were periodically abandoned and relocated, fields and paths were cleared and then fell into disuse, and trading relationships with neighboring tribes, as well as with Europeans and Americans, further altered the regional economy and society.

Europeans arriving in the area in the seventeenth century found the region settled by several Iroquois tribes. Seneca dominated the westernmost part of the state. The group was soon incorporated into British and French colonial spheres of influence, particularly in gathering and transporting pelts and furs. The American Revolution radically disrupted Seneca trade and settlement geography. East of the purchase whole villages were plundered, and the Indian refugees moved west, seeking the relative safety of the British settlements on the Niagara River.[56] After the war, the Indian population resettled, occupying some new areas and abandoning others. Thus, when Ellicott and his surveyors arrived in the late 1790s they hardly found a timeless culture in an unchanging setting; the newcomers were merely another element in a continually evolving cultural landscape.

In the 1790s the Indians concentrated their settlements in the region along several major creeks. Alluvial flats along the Genesee River provided sites for a number of villages. Other groups were situated further west, strung along winding Tonawanda and Buffalo creeks. In the southern and central purchase, settlement was confined to two main watercourses: several villages were located near Lake Erie not far from the mouth of Cattaraugus Creek, while other settlements lined the Allegheny River near the Pennsylvania border. Overall, the census of 1795 counted about 1,700 Indians in the region.[57]

Every village site was a focus of significant landscape change.[58] Acreage was cleared for the central settlement and for nearby agricultural fields. Fields typically were irregular in shape and variable in size, and they stretched for some distance along creek bottoms.[59] Demand for wood further reduced local forests. Evidence also suggests that the Indians purposely burned large areas to encourage the production of certain grasses and berries.[60] Another significant feature of the village settlement pattern was its dynamic migratory character. During initial surveys, Ellicott found evidence of several recently abandoned villages that were apparently occupied in the early 1790s and then relocated by 1800.[61]

A network of Indian paths connected these settlements. Many trails focused on the Niagara River and Buffalo Creek districts. West of the Niagara, these routes joined trails in Upper Canada.[62] Eastward, a number of paths passed through the Tonawanda Creek settlements to the Genesee River. Other trails led into the interior, branching southeast from villages on Buffalo and Cattaraugus creeks. The trails encouraged and were the product of trade among the Indians. Specialization enhanced a group's surplus store of goods to trade. Indians living on the fertile Genesee River flats, for example, grew more corn than they could consume and traded this grain for arrowheads, canoes, and other items.[63] They also maintained trade with Europeans and later with Americans, and by the time of Ellicott's arrival in 1797, the Indians were in "constant intercourse with white people."[64] By then, Indians had participated in the European pelt and fur trade for over a century. Americans continued the exchange, traveling to Buffalo Creek and bartering for furs and pelts with whiskey, tools, and trinkets.

Thus by 1797 a geography of Indian settlements had already altered the physical landscape of the region. It provided Ellicott with an initial framework of localities and connections that often suggested clues for subsequent development. Even with this tenuous imprint, however, much of the purchase was a rough, uncharted tract of wilderness when Ellicott arrived. His first task, therefore, was a careful reconnaissance of the entire region. Ellicott's initial township surveys, undertaken between 1797 and 1799, proved to be an excellent opportunity to complete a systematic assessment of the tract and to ponder the possibilities that future development might offer.

CHAPTER 2

The Township Surveys
of 1797–1799

*The Holland Land Company has submitted to
the great expense of . . . a survey in order a
perfect knowledge of the quality and
circumstances of their lands should guide all
their future sales and settlements.*
                        —Theophile Cazenove

After establishing a few initial boundaries in
the fall of 1797, Ellicott devoted much of the
following two summers to completing the
township surveys. The survey grid established
structure and order on the wilderness landscape and provided a framework in which to
sell acreage and develop settlements. The form
of that initial survey geometry shaped the scale
and character of subsequent development; its
central feature was to lay out the entire 3.3-
million-acre parcel in cardinally ordinated six-
mile-square townships. The decision on the
part of Surveyor Ellicott, General Agent
Cazenove, and their Dutch superiors to use a

system of township units was a logical response to the problem of organizing for sale a large parcel of land. It was grounded in well-known and widely accepted notions of land surveying and selling.

IMPOSING ORDER: FASHIONING THE TOWNSHIP GRID

Ellicott was familiar with a variety of solutions to the problem of surveying wild lands. Two quite different approaches to the task evolved in America during the colonial period. In Ellicott's home state of Pennsylvania and elsewhere across much of the mid-Atlantic and Southeast, land was traditionally divided into private holdings by the use of irregular natural boundaries.[1] Rivers, ridge lines, blazed trees, and boulders functioned as boundary markers under this system. Its flexibility and appeal to early settlers was its greatest advantage. It often allowed pioneers the freedom to avoid poor acreage and to select only premium parcels for ownership, even if the tracts were highly irregular in shape and size. This unsystematic surveying tradition resulted in an often intricate and complex cadastral landscape characterized by oddly shaped land units, little development of more marginal tracts, and constant land disputes between adjacent owners who might disagree on which creek, elm, or pile of rocks constituted the legitimate boundary between parcels.

These disadvantages of the unsystematic surveying tradition were anathema to the private land developer. Strangely shaped parcels meant additional survey costs and record-keeping problems. Giving settlers the right to locate parcels at their pleasure guaranteed that the land company would be left with thousands of isolated and inferior acres it could not peddle at any price. Confusions over land titles posed additional potential headaches and costs. It simply made little sense for the private developer to opt for such a system if his goal was the careful, planned development and sale of large wilderness parcels. A logical alternative, known to Ellicott and any other land peddler of the period, was the systematic survey system, well exemplified by the township grid, in which a regular and orderly method of land disposal was established before settlement.

This survey tradition also predated the Revolution and, for that matter, the settlement of North America.[2] Rectangular surveys in the classical world molded landscapes from Miletus in Asia Minor to Etruscan and Roman cities on the Italian peninsula. The planned grid was not unique to Western civilization either. Examples from the ancient cities of the Indus Valley and China and the use of the *jori* system of rectangular land units in Japan are convincing evidence that for centuries the cosmological and utilitarian allure of a regular, orderly survey system shaped the world's cultural landscapes.

Ellicott's experiences in late eighteenth-century North America placed him in a setting replete with examples of the rectangular survey system and its specific and common application in the form of the township grid. Clearly Ellicott and the Dutch borrowed the idea of the township from several well-known sources. New England traced its use of the township to the colonial period, when the grid represented not only a unit of orderly survey but often a unit of closely knit community as well. In practice, the dimensions and directional orientation of these New England towns varied appreciably, although they tended to become more regular and uniform as newer lands were opened in the Northeast's interior in the late colonial period.[3] In fact, the Dutch were familiar with the pattern directly because their own search for cheap, undeveloped acreage took them to a series of available Maine townships during the 1790s.[4]

The federal government's use of the township in the newly opened Ohio Country was another powerful influence on the private developer of the period.[5] National attention turned to the region after the Land Ordinance of 1785 opened a portion of the region to settlement. The ordinance stipulated the use of the township in preparing the region for sale and development. Furthermore, it mandated its regular size and placement by institutionalizing the tradition of the six-mile-square unit oriented cardinally on the wilderness landscape. In subsequent decades, that decision had enormous impact on federal lands from Ohio to California. Private land companies often were also persuaded to replicate the pattern. The Ohio Land Company along the Ohio River and the Connecticut Land Company in northeastern Ohio each adopted much of the detail and all of the spirit of the federal system as they opened their tracts to settlement in the 1780s and 1790s. The Dutch were aware of these ventures and collected information on them to guide their own investment strategy.[6]

Perhaps the most immediate and significant contemporary influence on Ellicott and the Dutch was the widespread use of the township in state-sponsored and privately funded land surveys in upstate New York. In central New York near modern-day Syracuse, the state government-controlled New Military Tract was opened to settlers in the early 1790s.[7] The state surveyed a township grid across the tract, and though some townships were larger than their counterparts in the Ohio Country and a few contained boundaries not cardinally oriented, the system echoed the structure and the virtues of the federal grid. Even closer to the Holland Purchase, the Phelps and Gorham tract also adopted the township system in its initial private land surveys. Almost the entire region was laid out in cardinally oriented six-mile-square townships.[8] To the west of the Holland Land Company's lands, the wilderness of British-controlled Upper Canada was also typically divided into township units, although their size varied considerably and their orientation was aligned less to cardinal directions than to important lakes and rivers.[9]

Aided by suggestions from Ellicott and their general agent, Theophile Cazenove, the Dutch made their final decision to adopt the township unit on their western New York lands less than one year before beginning the surveys. Before that, even with the widespread use of the township grid in nearby areas, it was unclear precisely how they would divide the western New York landscape for sales and settlement. Earlier Dutch company development projects in central New York and in Pennsylvania had not incorporated a township survey system. There was also a complicating stipulation in the original sales agreement made between the Dutch and Robert Morris that the latter pay for the survey costs for the entire tract "to be laid out into lots of not more than five hundred and fifty acres and not less than four hundred and fifty acres, each lot as nearly square as may be."[10] Morris's rapidly worsening financial situation by 1796, however, precluded the likely imposition of that surveying geometry across the region.

With Morris unable to finance a survey, Cazenove turned to Ellicott, other employees, and a number of land agents in the region for ideas on organizing and dividing the parcel for settlement. Suggestions offered to Cazenove confirmed the widespread appeal of the township grid. It seemed a desirable unit of survey for a variety of reasons. Overall, from a technical and financial point of view, the simplicity and regularity of the township were appealing.

Ellicott and others saw additional assets. The surveys would serve as an effective tool of landscape assessment, as an aid in gathering detailed information on potential land quality.[11] Surveying the township grid lines permitted a systematic and comprehensive reconnaissance of a region, and, while specific features might be overlooked, the overall quality of the land could be sampled by noting the character of terrain, soils, and vegetation in survey field books.[12] Such information became invaluable in guiding the spread of development once lands were opened for sale.

The township was valuable also because it could be used as a sales unit, a spatial mechanism designed to control and to channel development. This was a critical feature to the developer, who might see reasons for reserving some townships, selling others wholesale, and dividing still others into village and retail lots. Considering the large size of the purchase, it would be logical that initial development efforts might be restricted to a limited number of towns and then gradually expanded to incorporate more of the grid as actual settlement increased. The land agent could direct that spread of settlement through the number and location of the new townships opened.

Attractive social and political dimensions of the township were also suggested to Cazenove. Several nearby agents and company advisers noted that each township should have a central meetinghouse where school, church, and other social activities would take place. Townships defined in such a manner "would be extremely gratifying to the best kind of New England settlers . . . they would induce large families to emigrate, and they would be the means of perpetuating that attachment to and knowledge of government for which the New England settlers are so famous at home."[13] William Morris, an employee for the Dutch, argued along similar social grounds, noting that townships would be desirable because children in each town would have, at most, about three miles to travel to the central school.[14] James Wadsworth, land agent in nearby Geneseo, also reminded the Dutch of the potentially advantageous relationship between the surveyed township unit and the civil township unit. The latter was an important subcounty division of government in New York that maintained roads, collected taxes, and provided other local services. According to Wadsworth, equating the survey unit with an evolving political township framework would "unite all the advantages without the contention and party spirit generally attending larger towns."[15]

Cazenove placed great importance on the role such a survey would have in assessing the potential value of the tract. He informed Ellicott of his final decision in October 1797: "Considering how much a rational plan to settle and realizing such a vast tract of land will depend upon a just and precise notion of the several circumstances and quality of the land it appears to me, a general survey of the whole in townships of six miles square distinguished in several ranges will be the best means to that effect."[16]

As chief surveyor, Ellicott was responsible for taking the idea of the "six miles square" township and making it a part of the western New York landscape. This was no small task. After an initial lakeshore boundary reconnaissance in the fall of 1797, Ellicott planned for the hiring of laborers and for the purchasing of supplies. Finally, in May 1798, the complicated job began, as men, pack-horses, surveyors' chains, pork barrels, and whiskey made the trip from the Holland Land Company headquarters in Philadelphia to the wilderness of western New York.[17] For the next year and a half, Ellicott, along with over twenty trained surveyors and approximately one hundred laborers trudged through the swamps, forests, and hills of the vast tract.

Life on the survey was miserable.[18] The northern swamps meant wet shoes for survey teams. Late autumn snows and steep-wooded terrain slowed progress. Shortages of supplies frequently developed, and it was Ellicott's task to coordinate the flow of food and equipment to minimize such inconveniences. Many of the men contracted "ague," a debilitating illness that was often a combination of malaria and exhaustion. The crews were also a rowdy lot: whiskey was a staple in the woods, and fights frequently erupted between hands. Even with such perennial problems, Ellicott managed to complete the surveys by the end of the 1799 season.

The resulting township grid departed slightly from the ideal six-mile-square configuration (fig. 2.1). Some relatively minor problems involved

Figure 2.1 The Township Grid

slightly crooked or misplaced lines.[19] In several places, in order to complete the survey Ellicott had to plan for ranges of townships that were six miles from north to south but only four miles from east to west. Township boundaries also had to be extended or truncated along the major lakeshores of Erie and Ontario. By far the most significant interruption in the ideal grid was the series of Indian reservations across the purchase. These resulted from treaty negotiations held in western New York in September 1797. Ellicott, Indian leaders, and representatives of Robert Morris and the federal government attended the negotiations.[20] In return for $100,000 in United States Bank securities, the Indians agreed to relinquish their claims to all but about 200,000 acres of land west of the Genesee River. Most of their retained acreage was on the Holland Purchase, which necessitated the survey of a series of Indian reservations across the region.

Laying out the reserves was difficult, however, because several tracts were described only vaguely in the treaty. Nor was any effort made to incorporate the reserve boundaries into the planned township grid. Rather, the boundaries conformed to Indian settlement patterns, typically elongated along stream valleys. Near the Pennsylvania line, for example, the Allegheny River Reserve stretched for miles along the main watercourse, producing a forty-sided parcel that was expensive and time-consuming to survey. Other reservations were laid out and then had to be resurveyed after local Indians disagreed about the lines run. Finally, in 1799, the last of the reserves and the final township boundaries were established; with their completion, the necessary framework for settlement and planned development was in place.

ASSESSING THE LANDSCAPE

Assessing the potential agricultural value of wild acreage was a critical responsibility of the land developer. Such assessments shaped decisions on where to focus settlement and how to price agricultural parcels for purchase. Indeed, the surveys provided Ellicott with a wealth of information on the potential of western New York lands. The field books used by the surveyors served as an invaluable archive, a continuing reference that shaped Ellicott's development and sales policies. The notes contained extensive comments on terrain, soils, and vegetation that were used to gauge the agricultural value of the land. Clear images of desirable and undesirable acreage emerged.

The task of assessing land was not new for the surveyor of the late eighteenth century.[21] In Britain land surveyors were often responsible both for laying out boundary lines and for assessing the value of particular tracts. The

American colonial surveyor was a direct product of this British tradition, and his frequent role as explorer enhanced his powers as an evaluator of wilderness landscapes. The tradition of surveyor as land assessor continued following the Revolution and with the establishment of the public lands survey in the Northwest Territory. According to the Federal Land Act of 1796, each surveyor was to note in his field book "the true situations of all mines, salt licks, salt springs, and Mill seats, which shall come to his knowledge; all water courses . . . ; and also the quality of the lands."[22]

Ellicott was no doubt familiar with such procedures, and he had acquired considerable personal experience in assessing wild lands during his tenure as the company's surveyor in Pennsylvania.[23] He knew that along every surveyed line detailed information on specific location and on overall land quality would be recorded. On the western New York project, a survey line might begin in a corner of a planned township, where initial assessments would be made. As conditions changed along the line, new assessments were recorded: "Upland of the first quality" might be replaced by "Bottomland of the second quality." The length of the assessments varied: some descriptions pertained to only a limited distance along a survey line, perhaps 5 or 10 chains (1 chain = 66 feet), while other assessments sufficed to describe an entire 480-chain line (one side of a six-mile-square township) as being of one quality.

Ellicott asked his survey assistants to record a variety of specific observations relating to land quality. He needed their general descriptions of the lay of the land (upland, bottomland, intervale, plains, or swamps). To enhance the detail of these assessments, Ellicott also asked that the surveyor include sketch maps that would describe in visual terms the terrain features crossed. This surveying practice was not at all customary.[24] Ellicott believed that such a technique, even though it took added time and money, would provide important information in identifying landscapes too steep and rough for cultivation.[25]

From rough notes and sketches gathered in the field, Ellicott compiled a series of Range Books that organized all of the line descriptions and assessments for each township.[26] All of the relevant information regarding the four sides of any township perimeter could thus be readily evaluated. The completed Range Books were then used by Ellicott and his assistants to construct a preliminary general map of the purchase.[27] The books were also used to draw detailed individual maps that were designed to display graphically major features and variations in land quality found along the township perimeters. Major ridges and creeks were portrayed, and different colors along the town boundaries denoted the extent of first-, second-, and third-quality lands. Evaluating land in such a three-tiered manner was widely accepted during the period, and Ellicott had used this method in his earlier surveys.[28] Overall, the field notes described about 51 percent of the land as "first quality," 41 percent as "second quality," and only about 7 percent as "third quality."[29]

Terrain

Ellicott and his surveyors recorded all major terrain features, using a number of key terms to designate different landscapes. Bottomlands of the first quality were found along river flats. They appeared "from their richness to have been formed by a continual accumulation of the Soil deposited by the overflowing of the Rivers and Creeks" (fig. 2.2).[30] Bottomlands appearing to overflow less frequently were ranked as second quality. Intervale land was "of a moist nature; it is also that description of Swalely Land that some time lies below Hills without Any Water Course."[31] Uplands of the first quality contained rich soil and were excellent locations for growing grain, grass, roots, and vines. More rugged uplands were classified as second quality, or, if deemed unfit for any cultivation, as third quality. All distinctly swampy areas were also recorded.

Figure 2.2 Bottomland of the First Quality, Tonawanda Creek, Wyoming County

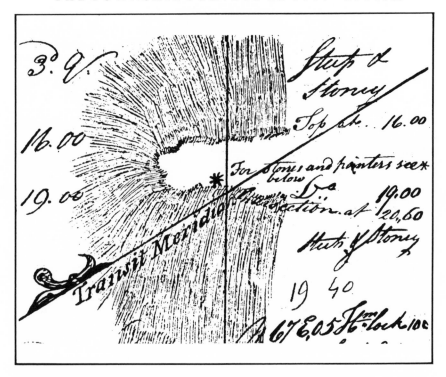

Figure 2.3 "Steep and Stony" Lands, Allegheny Mountains

Ellicott considered well-drained bottomlands to be the richest acreage on the purchase. He was hardly the first to place a premium value on such tracts—Indian settlement patterns also indicated an attachment to the fertile alluvial acreage bordering major watercourses. Distinguishing between uplands and bottomlands did not involve simply the difference between flat lands and hills. "Upland" meant drier, well-drained lands, both hilly and flat, and bottomland referred to alluvial valley bottoms that could be either well drained or swampy. "Upland," according to the contemporary definition, was both "high ground" and "land which is generally dry."[32] As a result, uplands of the first quality were found both in the high, rolling country of the central purchase and on the virtually flat lake plains to the north.

More detailed observations of terrain were made if they provided additional information of special importance. Many of these more specific comments concerned land on which excessive slopes prohibited cultivation (fig. 2.3). By far the majority of the remarks describing land as "too steep for tillage" referred to the southern mountains or to rough, creek-dissected uplands in the

Table 2.1 Terrain assessments

Descriptive term	Number of observations by quality (%)						
	1	(%)	2	(%)	3	(%)	Total
Too steep (for tillage or cultivation)	42	(14)	109	(37)	147	(49)	298
Uneven, broken, rough, ridgy, irregular	2	(4)	41	(87)	4	(8)	47
Gently uneven, ascending, descending	65	(76)	20	(23)	0		85
Level, flat	43	(63)	25	(37)	0		68

central portion of the purchase (table 2.1). "Rough," "uneven," and "irregular" were also associated with excessively steep-sloped acreage.

Lands possessing little or no slope also received close scrutiny. Rolling, undulating areas were apparently preferred to those described as "level" or "flat," even though both types of land were frequently judged to be of first quality. The term "diversified" was often used to describe premium tracts characterized by small hillocky rises between twenty and fifty feet in height, gradually ascending and descending between alluvial lands and gently sloped hilltop tracts (fig. 2.4). Nearby land agent Charles Williamson believed that the superior farm included "a due proportion of high land and meadow" and that the ideal rural landscape would contain "a succession of gentle swellings of land."[33] Traveler John Melish concurred, describing portions of the central purchase as "in most places undulating and agreeably uneven."[34] Possibly the greater ambiguity that surrounded the quality of level land related to fears about low, wet, and swampy acreage. Ellicott, for example, described some of the northern townships as "badly watered, level flat Land," and Dutch company agent John Lincklaen linked "low and level" lands along sluggish creeks with a poor and unhealthy climate.[35] Conversely, "well watered" lands presaged successful farming and promoted good health. One early description of the region noted that "some parts . . . are very flatt and retain the water a long time; where the Country is not swampy, waters seem to run swift enough to carry it off as may be good for vegetation."[36] Complexity characterized such assessments, however. For some, "low lands" connoted rich bottomlands.[37] In addition, lands described as "level" or "flat" in generally mountainous areas were seen as desirable, while "level lands" in poorly drained regions were assessed negatively.

There was, however, universal agreement that swampy areas posed many

Figure 2.4 "Gentle Rises and Descents," Erie County

problems to potential settlement. Ellicott was well aware of the problems of such tracts, realizing that "people generally speaking are averse to settling near Swamps on account of Agues and Fevers that frequently prevail in such Situations."[38] Perceived connections between poorly drained lands and malarial fevers had long been a part of American and English traditions of land assessment. The belief that "mal-aria"—bad air—was related to swamp vapors helped deter settlement in portions of Essex and Kent, and such beliefs were also influential in the assessment of western New York lands.[39] Ellicott did believe, however, that swamps could "become by Clearing ditching and draining the best part of the Country."[40]

Soils and Vegetation

Other key elements of the wilderness landscape that the developer believed could be used to predict agricultural potential were soils and vegetation. Soil was assessed for its texture, color, and depth. Soil textures graded from fine clays to mixed loams to coarse sands and gravels (table 2.2). Clear preferences were evident. Clay soils were not associated with superior land because they may have been linked to areas too wet and heavy for easy tillage. "Marl" soils, higher in lime content and often more fertile, were rated superior to the clays.[41] The best lands had "loamy" soils, and surveyors described such acreage in a

Table 2.2 Soil assessments

Descriptive term	Number of observations by quality (%)						
	1	(%)	2	(%)	3	(%)	Total
Texture							
Clay	0		17	(100)	0		17
Marl	19	(58)	14	(42)	0		33
Loam	221	(81)	51	(19)	0		272
Sandy	3	(50)	3	(50)	0		6
Stony, rocky	2	(2)	66	(59)	43	(39)	111
Color							
Black	77	(95)	3	(5)	0		80
Brown or dark brown	25	(86)	4	(14)	0		29
Chocolate	85	(84)	16	(16)	0		101
Light brown	3	(11)	24	(89)	0		27
Red	46	(84)	9	(16)	0		55
Yellow	70	(64)	40	(36)	0		110
Depth							
Thin	0		27	(100)	0		27
Deep	14	(88)	2	(12)	0		16

variety of approving phrases such as "loam of an excellent quality" or "rich black loam."[42] Negative assessments classified "stony" or "rocky" lands as second- or third-quality acreage.

Darker soils tended to be assessed as more fertile than lighter soils, and surveyors recognized a relationship between the blackness of a soil and its organic content.[43] While black and dark soils were associated with superior lands, light brown soils were often rated "indifferent" and less fertile. Deep soils were also preferred over thin soils. Ellicott realized that a direct link existed between soil depth and land value, and he guessed that on flats "where the real vegetative Soil will average from 5 to 15 feet in depth," such acreage would bring prices ten times higher than on nearby uplands.[44]

Also imbedded in the common folk knowledge of the period was the clear relationship between the native vegetative cover and agricultural potential. Three questions connecting vegetation to land quality typically were raised. First, Ellicott and his contemporaries believed a link to exist between tree type and soil fertility. Second, they saw the quantity and diversity of vegetation as an indicator of potential fecundity. Third, they were uncertain of the value of plains and open meadowlands and gave varied estimates of the long-range agricultural productivity of such acreage.

Over 90 percent of the assessments contained information on dominant tree type (table 2.3). The diverse mixed northern hardwood forest, according to all authorities, indicated good and potentially bountiful lands. Surveyors did distinguish between types of mixed hardwood forest, however. Those dominated by sugar maple and basswood were frequently associated with first-quality lands. Particularly in the case of the sugar maple, some of this positive evaluation may have been related to the tree's potential as a commercial crop. Tapping for maple sugar was then being widely encouraged and tested in the region, and the Holland Land Company seemed especially interested in locating marketable stands.[45]

Beech trees indicated less favorable land and were often linked to acreage believed to be "ungenerous" or "clayey, wet, and cold."[46] Oak-dominated lands were also seen as less "luxuriant" than maple or basswood acreage, while such softwoods as hemlock and pine were associated with second-rate lands. As one potential settler noted, "if the Land is something uneaven if the timber is Beech

Table 2.3 Vegetation assessments

Tree type	Number of observations by quality (%)								
	1	(%)	2	(%)	3	(%)	Swamp	(%)	Total
Sugar maple	515	(68)	233	(31)	11	(1)	2		761
Beech	250	(44)	297	(52)	20	(4)	1		568
Hemlock	26	(6)	371	(81)	44	(9)	19	(4)	460
Black ash	6	(2)	40	(16)	0		197	(81)	243
Oak	37	(28)	85	(64)	10	(8)	1	(1)	133
Elm	48	(42)	58	(51)	1	(1)	6	(5)	113
Pine	22	(26)	54	(63)	9	(10)	1	(1)	86
Basswood	50	(63)	30	(37)	0		0		80
Ash	17	(42)	11	(28)	0		12	(30)	40
Chestnut	6	(16)	24	(65)	7	(19)	0		37
Butternut	22	(92)	2	(8)	0		0		24
Alder	0		4	(17)	0		20	(83)	24
Hickory	5	(45)	5	(45)	1	(10)	0		11
Tamarack	0		0		0		10	(100)	10
Birch	1	(11)	8	(89)	0		0		9
Walnut	6	(86)	1	(14)	0		0		7
Poplar	5	(83)	1	(17)	0		0		6
Sycamore	6	(100)	0		0		0		6
Cedar	0		0		0		5	(100)	5
Underbrush	187	(78)	34	(14)	5	(2)	14	(6)	240

maple Bass and Elm it will answer—but if Mountainous and covered with Hemlock Spruce and fir I Cannot go."[47] Pure stands of white pine, however, were widely recognized as excellent sources of building timber. Hemlock, on the other hand, emerged as one of the least desirable trees on the purchase.[48] Since hemlock often grew on slopes of steep, shallow-soiled, and virtually untillable hillsides, it was usually associated with second- and third-quality lands. Hemlock also dominated a number of low and swampy tracts, and this, too, contributed to the negative assessments.

Simply the amount and variety of vegetation were used to judge land quality because it was believed that the best soils for agriculture produced the densest stands of large trees and undergrowth.[49] "Thrifty" was defined during the period as "thriving, growing rapidly or vigorously, as a plant" and was used by surveyors to make a connection in their field notes between superior lands and a rich growth of natural timber. The diversity of species also indicated good lands: Holland Land Company explorer William Morris described parts of the region as being "cloathed with every Species of Timber, which indicate a rich and Kind Soil."[50] Simply the amount of undergrowth seemed to be connected to potential land quality (see table 2.3). In instructions to one of his surveyors, Ellicott noted that the most fertile bottoms were covered with "a Rich Growth of Herbage of Nettles."[51]

Much less certainty surrounded the question of the potential fertility of plains and meadows. The lack of trees in these areas led some to conclude that the acreage was barren and infertile, and, according to one observer, several such tracts on the purchase were believed to have a "hard, dry, and Stony soil."[52] Others, including Charles Williamson, reported that the fears surrounding plains sterility were nonsense and that such acreage was perfectly suited to agriculture.[53] Still others voiced more ambivalent opinions, noting simply that many of the open plains on the purchase appeared to have been burned off by Indians.[54]

Ellicott was optimistic with regard to the potential of the plains. Describing the open areas traversed in the northern purchase during the township surveys, he wrote of "Rich open plains or prairies requiring no other labor preparatory to putting Grain in the ground than just plowing and hoing and where plenty of good grass may be cut."[55] He did distinguish between rich and poor plains, however: portions of the open tracts might offer potential as good grain land, while hard and stony sections would limit agriculture in other areas.

A Regional Pattern Emerges

Ellicott refined his regional picture of western New York State with the completion of the township surveys. Carefully compiled and transcribed into the Range

Books, the field note assessments provided a comprehensive view of the purchase. Adding to this written record were the personal reports Ellicott received from returning surveyors and his own extensive travels in the region. These information sources became significant when Ellicott was placed in charge of developing the purchase after 1800. Ellicott approached the comprehensive locational questions facing him in the selling of lands, in the building of towns and mills, and in the opening of roads with a broad understanding of the varying potential of the purchase's acreage. The township survey notes offered Ellicott the foundation for that understanding.

The general division of each township perimeter into first-, second-, and third-quality lands can be used to describe in more precise terms the regional pattern of assessments that emerged from the township surveys. The mean rated quality of each of the 162 townships on the purchase (Iq) can be obtained by averaging the extent of first-, second-, and third-quality lands recorded for each township:

$$Iq = \frac{x + 2y + 3z}{n}$$

where x equals the number of chains of first-quality lands noted around a township perimeter, y equals the number of chains of second-quality lands, z equals the number of chains of third-quality lands, and n equals the total number of chains assessed around a township perimeter. If a township is bounded half by first-quality lands and half by second-quality lands, the index of quality is 1.5. Although such a measure simplifies the variety found in each township, it provides one way to summarize the regional picture available to Ellicott after the completion of the surveys.

Index of quality values varied considerably across the purchase (fig. 2.5). They ranged from 1.04 in Township 5 Range 3 to 2.35 in Township 2 Range 7. Townships that measured between 1 and 1.5 suggest that most of the acreage surveyed in these blocks was of high quality. Values above 1.8 were notable in townships dominated by second- or third-quality lands.

Much of the acreage in the southern purchase was rated poorly. These lands were rough, steep, and thin soiled. More detailed lot surveys subsequently confirmed to Ellicott that a number of these townships simply were "not fit for Settlement," and even as late as 1817, Ellicott referred to the region as the "great Wilderness of Cattaraugus County."[56] Another area of poorer lands was apparent in the northern purchase, extending from Township 14 Range 1 west along Tonawanda Creek to the Niagara River. Land in these towns was a mix of first-quality lowlands and third-quality swamp and marsh tracts. Acres to the north

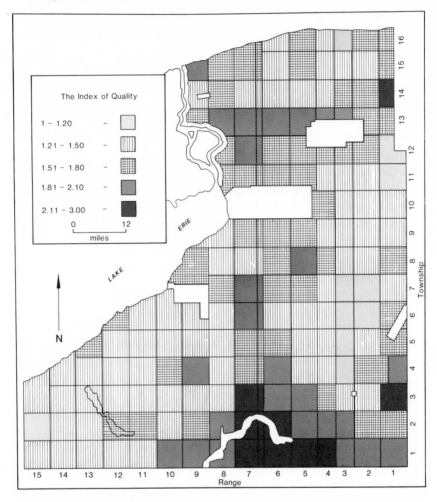

Figure 2.5 Overall Quality Assessments by Township

of the swamps were rated considerably higher, but this region near Lake Ontario suffered from widely held perceptions that it was unhealthy. Such beliefs were reinforced during the surveys when many of the hands working in these townships did become ill with fevers.[57]

Some of the best acreage on the purchase was located strategically in Township 11 Range 1 and Township 12 Range 1. Here the main east-to-west overland route through the region crossed into the Holland Land Company parcel. These towns had the dual advantages of possessing fertile lands and of having excellent accessibility to settled districts. The area was flat to gently rolling and was covered with a mixed hardwood forest. As one contemporary traveler reported, the region was "the Flanders of this part of America. . . . One continued flat country with no mountain and hardly a hill for 50 miles square, all excellent land."[58] Not surprisingly, when settlement commenced in 1800, these townships became an early focus of Ellicott's development plans.

Another area of above-average land was noted across a wide section of the southwestern purchase. These districts had fewer problems with steep terrain and rocky soils, and the gentle hills and fertile creek valleys near Chautauqua Lake were assessed as "very rich" acreage. In addition, excellent lands were discovered in the eastern section of the purchase just west of the Genesee River. Survey notes revealed that these townships were first-quality, rolling, "diversified lands" with rich soils. The distance separating this area from the main corridor of movement to the north, however, effectively removed it from early development.

Overall, the 1797–99 surveys revealed that the purchase contained large amounts of good land that the Dutch might develop and sell. It was equally clear that the company had purchased some rough and unattractive acreage, especially in the southern hills and in the northern swamps. Still, the long, straight vistas hacked from the forest by Ellicott and his surveyors were early, critical marks on the landscape and symbolized the imposition of a new cultural and economic order. They signaled the creation of a new image of the wilderness built around the hopes and plans of the frontier land developer. The information provided by the township surveys was a critical first step in domesticating that wilderness, and with the completion of the surveys, Ellicott had both enough information to open the company's lands and an orderly framework of townships to facilitate sales and guide development.

CHAPTER 3

Opening the Purchase

*In Conformity to a desire I have frequently
expressed . . . of having the direction of a
Settlement and retail of a Tract of Land in the
Massachusetts Genesee Pre-emption, I now
herewith . . . present you my proposals for
performing the services that will be required in
effecting the intended Settlements, together with
a System or plan that appears to me ought to
govern the agents in the sale of the land.*
—Joseph Ellicott

Development of the frontier necessitated careful planning. The Dutch recognized that settlers were not necessarily attracted to wild
lands and that initial investments to provide an
infrastructure of village centers, roads, and
frontier services had to be made. They were
also concerned, however, to limit such company expenditures. In other land-selling projects, the Dutch had become all too familiar
with the potentially enormous expenses involved in the development of wild lands. They
hoped to strike a balance between the scope of

their planned western New York investments and the constraints of an already depleted corporate pocketbook.

PLANNING FOR DEVELOPMENT

Sensitive to the needs for comprehensive planning and scrupulous budgeting, Theophile Cazenove sought advice from other land agents and company employees before opening the tract to settlement. These responses provide an enlightening view of decision making on the late eighteenth-century frontier. Everyone agreed that the success of the venture might well hinge on the amount and scope of initial investments. They disagreed, however, on how costly such efforts should be and on the kinds of investments that would be most necessary to spur settlement and regional economic growth.

Both William Morris and Joseph Ellicott suggested a modest and gradual approach to development.[1] Each advised against large initial expenditures; small sums wisely invested would encourage slow but steady growth. These notions of measured expansion contrasted with other plans, however. James Wadsworth, land agent at Geneseo, argued for the rapid development of the purchase, insisting that the Dutch make considerable capital investments in surveys, towns, and extensive frontier services.[2] In a similar vein, Charles Williamson, agent for the Pulteney Purchase, explained to Cazenove that it would take money to make money and that a substantial infrastructure of towns, roads, and services would be needed in such a development effort.[3] Thomas Morris, Canandaigua merchant and son of Robert Morris, also submitted his ideas to Cazenove and believed above all that success for the Dutch would depend on their ability to create and foster a commercial economy in the region.[4]

Two Dutch company agents who had served on other land-selling projects provided special insights for Cazenove. Gerritt Boon was employed as the company's chief agent on their Oldenbarneveld settlement in central New York near Utica.[5] Success there had proven elusive, however, and Boon was anxious for another opportunity to display his talents. Boon argued for wide roads, large mills, and moderately priced lands, but his already demonstrated tendency to overspend cast doubts on his planned expenditures. Another set of suggestions came from John Lincklaen, the company's agent on the Cazenovia tract, also located in central New York.[6] Impressed as Boon had been with the aggressive approach to development taken by Charles Williamson, Lincklaen advocated investments in a comprehensive economic infrastructure, a policy already carried out at considerable cost on Lincklaen's own agency in Cazenovia.

One of the more detailed and imaginative general discussions of land development during the period was written by the French statesman Talleyrand.[7] Talleyrand was a close acquaintance of Cazenove, and in the 1790s he became involved in a series of land speculation schemes. He was one of the many who were convinced that fortunes could be made by putting funds into well-situated wild lands in the North American backcountry. His "Observations on Speculation in Lands in the United States of America" presented detailed arguments on why such investments were sound and why the developer should feel compelled to make added improvements in the project.

Central to Talleyrand's reasoning was the notion that rapidly rising populations in the settled portions of the East would soon demand great amounts of wild land. Given such a scenario, Talleyrand predicted that 27 million acres of wild land would be put into cultivation in the next twenty years by a population that would increase steadily at an annual rate of 5 percent. He estimated that the resulting demand for land would insure a tidy 17 percent annual rise in land prices for the next eighty-five years and even higher returns in many mid-Atlantic states! Such profits could be increased further, Talleyrand argued, if an effort was made to develop the tracts and to assist the fledgling settlements. Well-placed investments would be returned many times over if they could attract larger numbers of desirable settlers into a newly opened frontier region.

Talleyrand stressed the advantages of connectivity over those of insularity. Navigable rivers and passable roads were of great value because they encouraged settlers to break new ground in remote regions and they allowed for the cheaper movement of goods to and from already settled districts. In terms of necessary improvements, Talleyrand believed that "a road running across good lands is equal to the discovery of buried treasure [as] it makes known situations that were not known [and] it renders accessible what was the same as lost in the immensity of the forests."[8]

He also recognized the importance of encouraging local service centers in the frontier economy and the need to "form a nucleus, a center of population."[9] Building sawmills and gristmills would provide necessary boards and flour to pioneer settlers. He cited stores, schools, and churches as other fundamental local institutions that might be assisted with appropriate investments. In the early stages of settlement, Talleyrand also reminded prospective developers that the financing of a regular system of lot surveys would lessen the problems of locating settlers and selling parcels. In addition, he recommended that special assistance be given to first settlers in a frontier area because it was particularly difficult "for an isolated settler, without neighbors and without aid, to commence a settlement, to build a first cabin, to cut down the first trees, to clear the

Table 3.1 Units of sales and settlement

| Name | Size of township | | Size of sales agency | | Size of retail lots |
	Miles square	Acres	Number of towns	Acres	
W. Morris	6¼	25,000	9	225,000	125
J. Wadsworth	6	23,040	25	576,000	125
C. Williamson	6	23,040	10	230,400	320
G. Boon	8	40,960	25	1,024,000	160
T. Morris	?	?	?	?	?
J. Ellicott	6	23,040	+20	+460,000	120

first acres."[10] Overall, Talleyrand estimated that these additional investments would total $20,000 to $25,000 for a settlement of 100,000 acres of land.

Many of Talleyrand's concerns were echoed by those responding to Cazenove's request for development plans. Several contributors focused on the role of lot surveys and sales policies. James Wadsworth and William Morris planned to survey much of the tract into 125-acre lots (table 3.1). Both men also suggested that some townships be held in reserve by the Holland Land Company for possible wholesale purchases of several thousand acres. The retail lots were to be priced reasonably, from $1.00 to $1.50 per acre, and sold on terms of credit ranging from six to ten years. Wadsworth cited the special need to encourage "birds of passage," those initial pioneers whose cheap labor was a valuable asset on the frontier. Wadsworth believed such "first adventurers" preparing the way for more permanent settlers should be granted lots at 25 to 50 percent discounts with no initial down payments required.

John Lincklaen and Gerritt Boon preferred 160 acres as the size of their retail lots. They also suggested offering larger units for sale, planning to leave some lots in 640-acre units and even to offer some quarter- or half-townships to wholesale purchasers. These larger sales would be encouraged by offering special low prices, but shorter terms of credit and higher down payments would be designed to discourage absentee speculators. Lincklaen, however, saw nothing wrong with resident farmers speculating in a small way by purchasing more land than they could farm themselves, holding it for a period of time, and then selling it at a profit. Ellicott's plan also favored a flexible lotting system, and he, too, advocated a retail parcel in which the acreage was designed to conform more or less to the size of a family farm. Ellicott limited the size of such a lot to 120 acres. The lots would sell at attractive prices and at liberal terms of credit to encourage small farmers. He did agree, however, that larger tracts of 1,440 acres might be reserved for future sale or offered at discounts of up to 30 percent to wholesale purchasers.

The sales policies advocated by Charles Williamson, the Pulteney agent, differed somewhat from the other suggestions received by Cazenove. Williamson wanted to see each township laid out in 320-acre lots to be sold to those who could afford to pay three to five dollars per acre—in short, to those who would contribute to Williamson's goal of forming "a genteel society." He saw no particular need to attract an initial class of poorer pioneers whose cheap labor some saw as an asset. To Williamson, such folk were "idle, disorderly people." In fact, Williamson's own agency at Bath repeatedly vied more for the attentions of monied land-seekers from Pennsylvania, Maryland, and Virginia than for the poorer Yankee "birds of passage" who might be emigrating from the rough hills of New England.

Cazenove was also urged to establish company towns. Without villages, pioneers could not be expected to single out the area for settlement simply on the supposed fecundity of its wild acreage. The chances for attracting to the region a class of industrious and prosperous settlers increased, however, if company-sponsored central places and services were established. The need for a regular, systematic village plan was recognized. The system of roads and the arrangement and orientation of lots concentrated activity at the village center. Suggested plats were sometimes divided into "in lots" and "out lots," clearly drawing on New England tradition.[11] With such a system, village residents would often own a central "in lot" for their business or house and an "out lot" just beyond the town on which they could "resort to for vegetables, the pasturage of some cattle, raising a little grain, etc."[12]

In terms of the number of such major centers, or "county towns," financial prudence seemed to suggest that, with the opening of the region to settlement, a single focus would suffice. Williamson, however, argued that a network of platted villages would be more desirable and that they should be carefully situated at the crossroads of his planned regional road network (fig. 3.1).[13] Others responding to Cazenove agreed on the principle of one initial center. The location of such a center was especially critical, however, since it would no doubt encourage the early and, it was hoped, vigorous development of the surrounding agricultural lands. It was important that the center be both in the midst of good lands and accessible to existing centers of settlement.

The consensus was that the focus of settlement be located somewhere in the higher-quality lands in the northern third of the purchase. Tonawanda Creek bisected the area and was favorably pinpointed as a potential site. If the

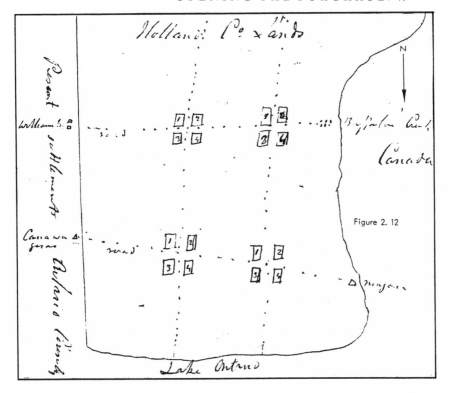

Figure 3.1 Williamson Plan

town was located on a navigable creek, it might offer accessibility to Lake Erie, and placing it on the main trail from the east would guarantee its connection with already settled districts. Its proximity to the Niagara River would place it in a forward position to watch over the British and, perhaps, to supply the American army on the east side of the river with necessary services and supplies.

Simply locating and surveying a county town might not guarantee its success, however. Further investments into its service and manufacturing economy were necessary, and, although the suggestions that Cazenove received agreed on the need for incentives, clear differences on the precise scope of such expenditures existed (table 3.2). The general schemes submitted to Cazenove can be displayed in schematic map form on a hypothetical landscape where only a stream pattern is assumed (fig. 3.2). Towns, mills, roads, and other features were placed by using sketch maps in the proposals and by the specific written descriptions that outlined desirable patterns of settlement.

Mills were a planned frontier service of primary importance. Both

Table 3.2 Planned frontier services

Name	Sawmills	Gristmills	Taverns	Stores	Mechanics	Churches and schools
W. Morris	2 or 3	1	1	1	1	5
J. Wadsworth	many	many	1	0	over 25	25
C. Williamson	10	10	4	1	4	0
G. Boon	4	4	4 or 5	1	0	5
T. Morris	1	1	1	1	0	?
J. Lincklaen	3	1	1	1	9	9
J. Ellicott	1	1	1	1	1	0

sawmills and gristmills were necessary elements of the frontier settlement system. Pioneers required good frame boards to build houses and barns, and they needed convenient centers to grind and process locally produced grain. Developers Wadsworth and Williamson planned the densest network of both saw- and gristmills, locating them in many townships (fig. 3.2b,c). Taverns and stores were other necessary economic services. Taverns quickened the flow of information by serving as meeting places for both travelers and locals. They could be built directly by the company or subsidized with special loans and land grants. Village centers served as one convenient location for taverns. Agent Boon also urged that they be "Regularly dispersed . . . Suppose every 8 or 10 miles along important routes."[14] Stores would be more limited in number, but, particularly in the first year of settlement, they were essential for many pioneers who would need to procure food, farm tools, and household goods.

The least centralized frontier services were provided by the local artisan or blacksmith shop and by the neighborhood meetinghouse. Every frontier community needed artisans to provide any number of services from nail making to ox cart construction. The developer could hire artisans directly, offer plots of free land in newly opened districts, or make available loans of money and tools. If the artisan was the most local expression of the planned frontier economy, the meetinghouse was the most local expression of dispersed social communities on the frontier. Cazenove was urged to donate between 200 and 360 acres in each surveyed township toward the support of schools and religion (table 3.2). Gerritt Boon's plan spaced meetinghouses in rural areas at almost equal distances from the county town (fig. 3.3). The plan expressed Boon's understanding that such outlying social centers were needed to serve populations that were

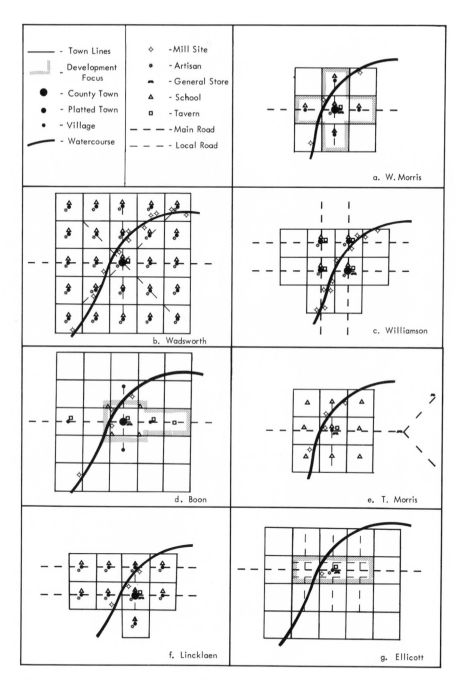

Figure 3.2 Regional Settlement Schemes

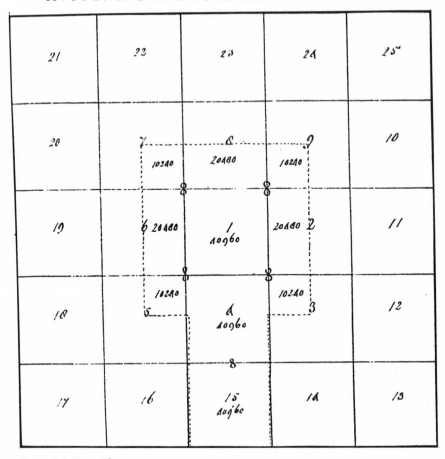

Figure 3.3 Boon Plan

located in townships at too great a distance from the central village to travel there conveniently.

Agents on the developer's frontier also believed that sustained growth could be assured only by integrating the frontier economy with the trading routes and commercial markets of the outside world. The importance placed on investing in roads and in developing and improving navigable waterways underscored this concern. Holland Land Company adviser William Morris saw Montreal's and New York City's markets as key commercial links that deserved both company and government financing. Agent Boon called for a major road cut "as straight as possible" to connect the county town with settled lands, and Thomas Morris argued that a similar "Very Wide" road he built eastward to the

Genesee River, where a store could be located to handle produce.[15] Ellicott also placed great emphasis on the planned construction of road networks and the creation of a commercial economy. In fact, Ellicott's suggested lotting system was originally designed so that every lot fronted on a road (fig. 3.4). In addition, he urged special company funding for a main thoroughfare to run through the northern purchase from east to west and connect with existing routes in central New York.

Cazenove and the Dutch were presented with a variety of alternatives as they reviewed the suggestions. William Morris envisioned the gradual development of stable, moral, New England communities if a sufficient number of Yankees could be induced to move out beyond the western edge of settlement.

Figure 3.4 Ellicott Lot and Road Plan

Agent Lincklaen agreed with Morris about the attractive qualities of Yankees but insisted on a more active role for the land agent and the company. Both Lincklaen and Boon had already demonstrated the dangers of overspending to the Dutch on other company projects in upstate New York.

The commercially oriented communities proposed by Thomas Morris and Charles Williamson also had their appeal. Visions of commercial empire would no doubt impress Dutch bankers; yet those pragmatic minds must certainly have questioned at least the short-term viability of such a scenario. Hopes for easy and early commercial success had already proven illusory at Oldenbarneveld, and the elaborate network of trading centers and shipping routes that both men advocated must have raised questions about what kinds of products could be raised economically in an area that was still the haunt of Indians, whiskey traders, and wolves.

Financial questions may have been raised by James Wadsworth's dense collection of proposed artisan shops, meetinghouses, and mills. How much sense did it make to give away so much free and valuable land to blacksmiths, preachers, and millers? If the settlement was destined to prosper, would not such individuals come to the area on their own, attracted by the same virtues that were so apparent to Wadsworth as he extolled the region's potential in his development plans? In contrast, Ellicott's ideas revealed a sober, economical approach to development that would offer only the most basic services. The relatively small investments needed for such an approach were surely attractive to the Dutch, but the correct placement of these ventures on the frontier landscape was made all the more critical by their limited number.

Cazenove and the Dutch undoubtedly saw many virtues in Ellicott's suggestions, however, and in early 1800 they selected him as resident land agent on the purchase.[16] Certainly one attractive feature of Ellicott's development scenario was that although he incorporated many of the ideas of the other contributors, he would attempt to limit spending wherever possible. His suggestions also revealed an attention to detail and an understanding of the land-developing business, reassuring since Ellicott had no previous experience as a land agent. Overall, Ellicott seemed to offer to the Dutch a proposal that was grand enough to appeal to their imagination but practical enough to fit their budget. His appointment culminated the nearly eight years of planning and assessment that preceded the opening of the purchase by the Dutch. For Ellicott, however, it was still only the beginning of a task that would see the landscape of the region transformed from a state of wilderness to a developed tract of farms, mills, and villages.

SETTING UP SHOP

In November 1800, Ellicott assumed his new role as the resident land agent for the Holland Purchase, charged with the considerable tasks of developing the region and producing profits for his Dutch superiors. His initial decisions would be especially critical since they would set the pattern for subsequent policies and, if successful, would promote the settlement and attract to the region a class of enterprising and industrious pioneers. The location of this sales agency was an early concern. Because of the great size of the 3.3-million-acre parcel, it was hardly possible or desirable for Ellicott to develop the entire region simultaneously. There was general agreement on the portion of the purchase that would receive the first attention: the northern corridor of lands lying along Tonawanda and Buffalo creeks was a historical focus of Indian settlement and overland travel in the region. It was clearly the district most accessible to existing roads and settlements, and its attraction had been increased further during the period of the township surveys when Ellicott established several survey supply storehouses and improved a number of supply routes in the corridor.

In May 1799, during the midst of the township surveys, Ellicott had suggested to his superiors that the "Buffalo Road," which crossed the northern Purchase to Buffalo Creek, be improved and that "part of three or more Townships Should be lotted immediately along the Road so laid out."[17] The following month he had submitted a more detailed plan that targeted three townships for initial lotting. The revised plan represented a slight shift from his exclusive focus along the road. Above all, Ellicott believed that the first townships should be located adjacent to already established settlements because this would permit the newly arrived pioneers to make use of the mills, stores, and conveniences of the existing centers. That all three townships selected by Ellicott bordered on the western, not the eastern, edge of the purchase demonstrated the perceived significance of nearby British Canada.[18] Ellicott saw the advantages of locating settlers near the small trading towns on the British side of the Niagara River.

Cazenove and Busti, the company's general agents in America, agreed with Ellicott on the desirability of a northern focus, but the western orientation of Ellicott's plan was unacceptable because the legal title of the land west of the sixth range of townships was still being disputed with representatives of Robert Morris. Until the matter could be cleared up, it would be foolish to concentrate company efforts and investments in these townships.

Instead, the Dutch suggested that Ellicott begin development along the eastern and central portions of the Buffalo Road. They foresaw a whole corridor of development focused on a number of local villages and taverns to be built along the road. Cazenove believed it would be wise to encourage "Some good Men to Settle themselves on this Road in Such a Manner that at about ten miles distance from each other, accommodations may be had for the traveler."[19] To encourage such a regional and linear focus, Cazenove gave Ellicott the right to sell 50- to 150-acre parcels to enterprising innkeepers at specially reduced prices.

The consensus reached between Ellicott and his superiors on commencing development in the northern corridor suggests the importance they placed on accessibility. They showed little apparent concern over land quality. In fact, of the townships bordering the Buffalo Road, only Township 12 Range 1 displayed any clearly superior lands in the initial township surveys. The other towns, including those designated by Ellicott, were of only average overall quality, a mixture of good and indifferent lands. This emphasis represented the governing attitude toward land quality and land settlement on the developer's frontier: unless acreage was clearly superior and of premium value or clearly inferior and of lesser value, accessibility to roads, villages, and commercial markets was most significant in determining the course and design of development.

The next issue to be resolved related to the size, number, and location of the sales districts to be established. This question was important to the company since it involved the number of land offices and land agents that would need initial funding. The geography of sales districts also played a part in establishing the structure and the nature of decision-making channels on key questions of development. Would one, two, or more local agents be planning settlements in different areas, and if several agents were involved, how would decisions on land prices, lotting procedures, road development, and other matters be coordinated?

Ellicott's ideas concerning sales districts were a part of his initial proposals to the Dutch. In characteristic fashion, he advocated land agencies of a moderate and manageable size:

> It must be evident that too small a body, would not answer, as the expense of the agent, clerks, surveyors, and other persons . . . might take all the profits arising from the sale of the lands . . . ; and on the other hand, too large a body of land could not be attended to, in such a manner as to make the best use of the District.[20]

Ellicott proceeded to suggest that an agency of between 500,000 and 1 million acres would be most appropriate. Although he offered no specifics on the number of initial agencies, he clearly conceived of more than one, suggesting that the "several Agents" meet every few months to coordinate their development activities.

Soon after Ellicott submitted his ideas, Cazenove suggested that Ellicott draw up a map that divided the purchase into six tracts of 500,000 acres and a seventh smaller tract.[21] Whether Cazenove believed that each district would contain its own agent is unclear. He did want to use the planned districts to make certain divisions among the various Dutch stockholders. Ellicott did as Cazenove had instructed, and in the north, where development was first planned, Ellicott in effect partitioned the Buffalo Road corridor into three north-south-oriented districts.

The following year, only minor changes were suggested by Paul Busti, Cazenove's successor as general agent. Busti also clarified that each northern district would function as a distinct sales agency. Initially, however, Busti wanted to limit the number of districts to two in order to save money.[22] Both areas targeted for opening were in the north: Ranges 1, 2, and 3 to the east became District P, and to its west, District O was established in Ranges 4, 5, and 6. Although additional western and southern districts were designated and would someday be opened to settlement, the company was to hold these lands in reserve for several years. Another feature of Busti's plan was to run the two land agencies, O and P, under the direction of one local agent, Joseph Ellicott.[23] He planned to open approximately half of each district to settlement: about 150,000 acres in each tract would be open and 125,000 acres reserved for later sale, making the two agencies combined about 550,000 acres. Furthermore, only 50,000 acres in O and 50,000 acres in P would be lotted initially in small retail parcels.

Although the limited sizes of Ellicott's initial land agencies were certainly manageable, the planned division of the acreage into two sales districts made the job more complex, because each district was to be treated as a distinct sales entity. Ellicott originally suggested that such an economic division of district duties was appropriate, but it is doubtful that he conceived of a single agent keeping the books on the expenses and profits of both sales units. Complicating Ellicott's duties further was Busti's request that Ellicott "divide . . . Exertions in such Manner that the Settlement might proceed on an almost even footing on both tracts."[24] To facilitate such a balanced approach, Busti suggested that Ellicott locate his land office central to both Districts O and P, but Busti approved of Ellicott finding a location wherever "easy and convenient . . . so as to induce the Emigrants to visit you."[25]

With general district boundaries established and the guidelines for development set, Ellicott was free to begin lot surveys. In late 1800 he arrived on the purchase as its new resident agent. He spent his first several weeks at the small trading post at Buffalo Creek, the site of his township survey headquarters in the previous year. Soon, however, he realized the virtues of selecting a more central spot and moved his land office to a newly constructed log tavern along the Buffalo Road about twenty miles east of Buffalo Creek. Owned by Asa Ransom and financed with company assistance, the tavern served as Ellicott's land office during 1801.

Even before he had settled on the purchase late in 1800, Ellicott had approved the partial lotting of several townships.[26] Portions of five townships were surveyed and divided into retail lots before the end of the year. Four of the towns were focused around Ransom's tavern in sales District O, with only one town lotted in District P (Township 12 Range 2). Although the surveys undertaken did not reflect the balance requested by Busti, the pattern did display Ellicott's own continuing preference for development in the western purchase. The following year, however, the three newly opened townships were all located in the more eastern District P and were centered on a new, planned village being laid out in the same season. Another incentive for opening the more eastern townships was the increasing pressure from potential settlers desiring to occupy the district.[27] During this same period, Ellicott also pressed vigorously to open some of the townships that bordered Lake Erie and the Niagara River completely west of District O. Specifically, he noted to his superiors the special value of Township 11 Range 8 as an area of potential trade and development because it bordered the east end of Lake Erie. Company officials, however, because of the persistent land disputes with Morris, continued to restrict development west of District O for another two years until the matter could be resolved clearly in the courts.

Ellicott and his superiors adopted a restrained policy of company assistance to frontier services that paralleled the limited and decentralized approach Ellicott had originally suggested. Departing from the proposals submitted by most of the agents and advisers to the Dutch, Ellicott did not direct his preliminary attention to the initial platting of one or several formal villages. The village of Batavia was the first formally platted center established by Ellicott, but surveys did not even begin on the spot until two years after the first arrangements had been made to place several taverners along the Buffalo Road. Ellicott and his superiors agreed in 1799 that taverns would act as way stations for travelers and would serve as important but informal nuclei of activity on the purchase.

two roads leading out of Batavia, one northwest toward the Niagara River country and the other due north toward Lake Ontario.[36]

PROMOTING THE LAND

The successful land developer also needed to be a skillful land promoter. Ellicott spread the word about the purchase in a number of ways. He understood that settlers would come to the region only if they knew something about its resources and its promise. Once they arrived, prospective buyers needed more detailed information about the location of available parcels, their assessed land quality, and their retail price. Coordinating such information became a key part of Ellicott's job in managing the growth of the developer's frontier.

Beyond the bounds of the purchase, Ellicott adopted several advertising strategies to bring attention to the region. Especially in the early years of his sales agency, Ellicott invested company funds in newspaper ads, handbills, and maps. Each form of advertisement had its advantages. Newspaper ads might attract urban dwellers in eastern cities. Handbills could be displayed easily in taverns and meetinghouses or mailed to post offices. Maps provided a particularly graphic picture of the size, variety, and special features of the land agency.

Production of these published materials was concentrated in the first five years of settlement. Announcements appeared in Albany, Baltimore, and New Haven. A vigorous campaign in 1803 and 1804 included a set of published advertisements directed especially toward the Pennsylvanian population.[37] Pennsylvania received attention for several reasons. Ellicott still had many personal and professional connections to his home state. The Holland Land Company's American headquarters were in Philadelphia. Ellicott also expressed a clear preference for Pennsylvania settlers, especially Germans. He preferred "monied" Germans from Lancaster County and "their Industry and Economy" because he believed the cash raised from the sale of their sizable farms would allow them to make substantial down payments on their New York lands.[38] Ellicott's most ambitious single advertising effort occurred in the fall of 1803. In September, Ellicott employed a Canandaigua printer to produce six hundred handbills. The resident agent then mailed the advertisements to different locations throughout the United States and instructed local officials to display them in prominent places.[39]

The ads described the location of the purchase in New York State, typically associating it with the rich acreage of the nearby and well-known Genesee Valley. Further commentary on the wealth of the soil reassured the skeptical. Details on the company's liberal credit policies appealed to those with great industry but little cash. Special provisions for group settlement provided incentives for whole neighborhoods to relocate. In addition, descriptions of village centers and road networks suggested the accessibility of the purchase to already settled lands. Maps of the region offered added up-to-date details on newly constructed routes and settlements.

It is difficult to assess the impact of these long-distance advertising efforts. No doubt much information was spread simply by individuals exchanging news with friends, relatives, and neighbors when they traversed, visited, or settled in the region. In several instances, however, settlers wrote to Ellicott for information, noting they were responding to specific advertisements that had appeared in local newspapers.[40] Still, one of Ellicott's associates may have been right when he cautioned Ellicott not to be too sanguine about the impact of the ads, "as but few persons who buy land read newspaper advertisements."[41]

On the purchase itself, Ellicott needed to supply settlers who had already arrived in the region with the necessary details that might encourage them to purchase land. Prospective buyers had to know where parcels for sale were located, the assessed land quality of a parcel, its retail price, and any terms of credit that might be available. In the earliest years of the land agency, Ellicott coordinated all of this critical information through the central land office at Batavia. All of the early townships opened on the purchase either bordered directly on Batavia or were accessible in nearby areas along the Buffalo Road. Numerous clerks at the land office or Ellicott himself provided maps, survey notes, and other background material to potential settlers. The site served as the official focus of information in the region.

The company's information management problems multiplied, however, after the first few years. As lands further and further from Batavia were opened to settlement, it became more difficult for potential buyers to check in with the central land office in the northern purchase. In fact, by 1803, many townships in the south were fifty or more miles distant from Ellicott's central office and unconnected by any convenient roads to the northern settlements. Rather than creating a series of formal subagencies in these isolated areas, Ellicott chose to enter into a series of more informal arrangements with knowledgeable and influential settlers already living there.[42] If a willing settler in an isolated district agreed to assist prospective buyers, Ellicott supplied the surrogate agent with the necessary maps, survey notes, and land price information. In some cases, Ellicott also gave these agents the right to enter into land contracts if the agents agreed to travel periodically to Batavia to register the sales. In return, the agents received a small commission in cash or land. The boundaries of these surrogate agent "districts" were loosely defined, but they were typically limited to the few townships in which the agents had the greatest local familiarity. Most agents were at least forty to sixty miles from Batavia, thus saving several days' travel to the settler who made use of their services and information. Ellicott entered into at least eleven working relationships with surrogate agents.

Where possible, Ellicott selected important local social and political figures to serve as surrogate agents in their particular neighborhoods. For example, Ellicott encouraged Jacob Taylor, an influential member of a small Quaker settlement near the Pennsylvania line, to assist in land applications in the area, and when a new Quaker group settlement was established nearby, Taylor also helped in locating their lands.[43]

The geography of sales administration and the task of providing official information was simplified in subsequent years. Better roads lessened the isolation of the southern and western tracts. After 1810, Ellicott began to establish formal subagencies that reduced the importance of Batavia as the sole land office on the purchase. Soon, three formal subagencies replaced the more numerous surrogate agents scattered across the region. One subagency, established in 1810, was located in the far southwestern purchase at Mayville on Chautauqua Lake. Another was formed in 1817 at Ellicottville in the south central purchase, and a third was created in 1825 at Buffalo on the eastern end of Lake Erie.[44]

In a much more subtle fashion, Ellicott also understood that the landscape itself was a powerful source of information for prospective settlers. On the developer's frontier, what better advertisement of the quality of the purchase's lands than acres of cleared farms and thriving crops? What better testimony to the civility and progress of the area's towns and villages than their wide, straight streets and imposing buildings? Ellicott managed the landscape in order to promote development; he hoped to communicate a clear message to potential new settlers by using the accomplishments of the old.

The "company farm" was one method of modifying the landscape and of demonstrating the excellence of the region's acreage. The idea did not originate with Ellicott. Charles Williamson suggested to the Dutch as early as 1796 that large, prospering farms should be worked by each sales agent on the tract. According to Williamson, who used the technique on his own land agency, such a farm would "at once procure plenty, an appearance of business and show what the Country will do."[45] It was an advertisement on the landscape. Ellicott saw such enterprises in similar terms, and he offered grain samples from Frederick Walther's company-assisted farm, located at the strategic and highly visible east end of the purchase, as evidence "that strongly proves the uncommon strength and fertility of the soil."[46] On his own village land in Batavia, Ellicott kept a large garden planted in corn, potatoes, and other vegetables, probably less because he needed to grow his own food than to use the plot as a handy tool in his land sales pitch.[47]

Cleared and fenced land symbolized progress on the developer's frontier. Densely forested lands might have indicated potential fecundity, but they also suggested the time and labor needed to bring to fruition the bounty of the first hard-won harvest. Ellicott was keenly aware of both the monetary and the symbolic value of cleared land because each felled tree added value to a parcel and each small clearing made the purchase appear less a wilderness and more a settled landscape. Through his sales policies, Ellicott encouraged the rapid clearing and fencing of parcels by requiring that settlers who bought land on credit agree to clear, fence, and plant portions of their acreage within a specified time. If they succeeded in meeting the deadline, they would receive discounts in their initial interest payments, but if they failed to improve their parcels, they risked losing their claim to the land. In lieu of cash payments, therefore, the cleared land acted as a demonstration of good faith by the settlers to Ellicott, a kind of visible contract expressed on the landscape that promised eventual payment.

Cleared, fenced, and developed lands were of special importance in the planned villages. Village centers were to be more than collections of buildings and frontier services. They were symbolic centers, and their landscapes communicated messages about the state of the company's improvements. In Batavia, Ellicott refused to grant deeds for village lots until land clearing was underway.[48] Ellicott also recognized the need to provide wide "vistas" that would improve the visual character of the village of Buffalo. For example, Ellicott suggested clearing a number of lots bordering on Lake Erie because they were "so situated lying in a State of Nature, the Timber standing on them, as to shut the Village out of a full view of the Lake."[49]

Substantial, permanent structures were also advertisements on the village scene, and Ellicott also played a role in their construction. In some cases on key lots Ellicott would not sell the parcel unless the buyer promised to build on the spot a structure of certain minimum dimensions. In other cases Ellicott agreed to sell a lot to a settler only if the buyer had the intention of "gracing" it with "a handsome Building, which will add Respectability to the Village, and the Price of it (the lot) will in a Measure depend upon the Size of the Building you may erect."[50] In addition, since the land company paid for the construction of county courthouses in the region, Ellicott exerted special control over the appearance of these important structures. The presence of substantial, multistory public buildings on large, landscaped lots added further to the image of the purchase as a viable, permanent community quickly removing itself from the grasp of primitive frontier isolation.

Route landscapes were another critical focus of information management and land promotion. Ellicott believed that "the more Intercourse we can continue to pass through our Country, the more value will be attached to the Property, and the more likely to increase the sale of it."[51] For this reason, Ellicott was especially anxious to sell lots that bordered on the region's main thoroughfares. Even though initial sales were less than overwhelming in 1800 and 1801, Ellicott was pleased that, along the Buffalo Road near Batavia, sixteen settlers had begun improvements "in view of the Traveler, as well as some others forward out of the view of the Road."[52] Always the perceptive land developer, Ellicott was clearly concerned about making the purchase appear as a settled land, even though only a few sales had then been made.

Ellicott's road construction crews carefully managed the landscape as well. Ellicott instructed them to widen portions of some secondary roads that led into villages or that intersected main thoroughfares, apparently so that the roads would appear to be better traveled than they were. In one case, Ellicott instructed his laborers to open up a new side route off the main Buffalo Road in Township 12 Range 4. The road was to be cleared only fourteen feet wide, but Ellicott promised a cash bonus if the last half-mile before its junction with the Buffalo Road "should be cut handsomely 25 feet wide."[53] Always sensitive to appearances, promoter Ellicott knew that broad thoroughfares, even if they led nowhere, were better than no thoroughfares at all. In fact, however, his initial attempts to produce settlement did lead somewhere; slowly, but with increasing certainty, the pace of sales and of landscape change accelerated after 1800.

CHAPTER 4

Settlement Policy on
the Developer's Frontier

*Such are the varieties of situations in this part
of the Geneseo country, every where almost
covered with a rich soil, that it is presumed that
all purchasers who may be inclined to
participate in the advantages of those lands,
may select lots . . . that would fully please and
satisfy their choice.*

—*Joseph Ellicott*

After 1800, Ellicott was confronted with several significant and interrelated geographical
problems that dealt with shaping the spread of
settlement across the purchase. Four issues demanded his continued attention. The tract's
considerable size suggested that it would be
costly and foolish to open all the townships for
immediate retail sale. The location and timing
of newly opened townships thus became a policy issue of considerable import for both
Ellicott and potential settlers. Second, the resi-

dent agent was responsible for affixing prices to land parcels once they were made available for sale. A third issue focused on the placement of company-financed village centers. Their geographical situation relative to settling townships and to distant centers of population and trade could spell the difference between their success or failure as frontier communities. Finally, roads were needed to provide accessibility to isolated areas, and investment in the network had to be coordinated with the pace of settlement and the platting of village centers. Clearly, as Ellicott demonstrated in 1800 and 1801, each of these settlement issues involved related approaches to problems of location. The continued effectiveness of Ellicott's evolving development policy after 1801 would be measured by his ability to integrate each component into a comprehensive effort, a strategy that successfully balanced the resident agent's own settlement initiatives with the demands made by the settlers themselves.

GUIDING THE SPREAD OF SETTLEMENT

Beginning with a limited sales domain of several lotted townships in 1800 and 1801, Ellicott guided the opening and spread of lotted towns by both responding to and anticipating the needs of retail settlers. Between 1801 and 1811 virtually every township was partially or completely opened to settlement, and the pattern of expansion that characterized the intervening decade is an invaluable record of early nineteenth-century developer-inspired regional planning (fig. 4.1).

In the first two years of Ellicott's agency (1800–1801), official company policy restricted sales across much of the purchase. One nucleus of development focused on Ransoms in the west, while a second area of lotting centered on the new village of Batavia in the eastern purchase. Overall, sales were permitted in only about 60 percent of the initially designated lands in Districts O and P.[1]

Beginning in 1801, however, Ellicott lobbied hard to expand his land agency and thereby include some of the more western townships along Lake Erie and near the Niagara River. Ellicott's efforts to change company policy intensified in 1802 as settlers inquired about lands in the western tracts and increasingly grumbled that the company was reserving all of the good acreage so that it might reap excessive profits in subsequent years.[2] Ellicott was particularly concerned that the valuable strip of land owned by the state of New York along the eastern end of Lake Erie and the Niagara River would be auctioned off to independent investors and developed before the Dutch lands in that vicinity were even opened. The Dutch, however, were reluctant to alter their policies, even after the dispute with Morris was settled, because they believed all of the

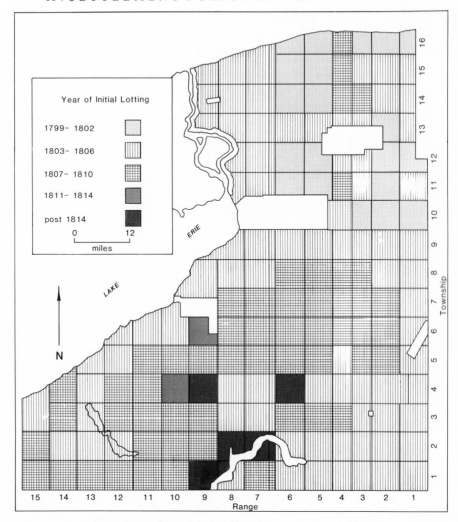

Figure 4.1 Year of Initial Lotting by Township

best acreage would immediately be bought at the low initial prices, leaving the company with only the poor lands for subsequent sales. On the other hand, Ellicott saw the lackluster demand for lands in 1800 and 1801 and felt the need to offer more choice to settlers, especially in areas of the western purchase that were already receiving attention from potential buyers.

By 1802 Ellicott's call for expanding his sales agency began to meet with greater Dutch company acceptance. Busti agreed with Ellicott's request to open

oper to incorporate two components into a strategy of settlement expansion. On the one hand, as resident agent he had his own notions of where to guide settlement and did his best to open those areas to development as swiftly as possible. On the other hand, Ellicott also responded to settler demands for parcels not intended for immediate development by successfully pressuring his superiors to open areas in the west and southwest. The result was a geography of settlement expansion that reflected the actions of both developer and pioneer and that within the short span of a decade propelled the settlement frontier across a region heretofore beyond the pale of civilization.

PRICING THE LAND

Every parcel that Ellicott opened to settlement he also priced, and the resulting geography of land prices provides intriguing documentation of how frontier Americans in the early nineteenth century valued land and how developers hoped that spatial variations in pricing policies would shape the course of settlement. Valuing wilderness landscapes required a special talent because prices needed to be high enough to secure a profit but low enough to attract ready buyers. Many variables affected the price of land. Demand was a significant factor: if Ellicott believed that certain lands were in considerable demand, he could raise prices; if other lands attracted little or no interest, he might lower prices to encourage prospective buyers. Other financial considerations that affected price varied with time and with changing sales policies. They included the quantity of land bought, the percentage paid in cash, and the length of the term of credit extended. Two other factors, geographical in nature in that they varied over space, were also significant. Price was related to the quality of the land in terms of its terrain, soils, and vegetation and also varied with respect to its proximity to roads, navigable streams, villages, and other valuable situations.[10]

Before sales commenced, Ellicott and the Dutch decided on a number of initial pricing policies. In his early development proposals to the Dutch, Ellicott stressed the need for a sizable cash down payment of 25 percent before allowing settlers to take possession of a land parcel. Ellicott believed that this policy would attract real settlers but discourage absentee speculators. The nearby Pulteney Purchase offered further lessons for the Dutch: many believed that agent Williamson, who allowed new settlers to occupy lands with little or no down payment, had in the process attracted too many undesirables to the new settlement.[11] By 1800 and the opening of the Holland Purchase, Ellicott and the company agreed to relax the policy somewhat, but they still insisted on a 15 percent cash down payment.[12]

Ellicott wavered in his recommendations concerning the terms of credit to be offered. Initially in 1799 he proposed a five-year term, comparable in length to the six years being offered by the Connecticut Land Company in northeastern Ohio and to the four years offered in the Federal Land Act of 1800 in public sales in the Northwest Territory.[13] Ellicott changed his mind the following year, deciding that a six-year term of credit was more suited to give settlers enough time to pay off their loans.

Though some discounts for cash sales and for large purchases were to be allowed, the initial base price of lands was not cheap by the standard of the period. Busti informed Ellicott that Ellicott could set prices as he saw fit but to target most of the acreage at between $2.00 and $2.50 per acre.[14] When Ellicott completed his comprehensive land sales planning early in 1801, he settled on $2.75 per acre for acreage purchased on credit, while the same lot would sell for $2.20 per acre if purchased with cash.[15] For wholesale buyers interested in an entire township, lands might be sold for as little as $1.54 per acre. Above all, Ellicott recommended a simple, stable, and equitable pricing system on which settlers could depend.

Ellicott's established prices compared with a low $1.00 per acre on lands in New Connecticut in nearby Ohio.[16] Elsewhere, acreage in parts of the federally administered Northwest Territory went for $2.00 per acre.[17] Extremely liberal policies adopted by the British in Upper Canada offered settlers acreage at such low fees that Ellicott noted such sales arrangements could "more properly be considered as Gratuities."[18] Other acreage surrounding developed upstate New York villages, however, did command a premium: rural lands in the vicinity of Canandaigua, for example, typically sold during the period at between $5.00 and $6.00 per acre.[19]

In 1801 the flow of settlers into Canada and into the Ohio Country, as well as the notable lack of cash arriving with most of those settling on the purchase, convinced Ellicott to push for a rapid liberalization of company pricing policies. Ellicott was also determined to attract enough settlers onto the purchase to create a new county in the area conforming more or less to the lands of the Dutch company. These concerns resulted in new pricing initiatives. In February 1801 Ellicott reduced the 15 percent minimum cash down payment to 10 percent, and just a month later he began allowing settlers to take possession of their lots with no cash down payments whatsoever. Desperate to encourage sales, he initiated the policy without company approval, even using his own capital to meet the official minimum requirements established by the company.[20] Though admitting to Busti that such "provisional sales" were not "strictly conformable" to his original instructions, Ellicott believed that the new policy was needed to attract settlers. Further, he argued that simply the clearing of lands and the associated improvements would add value to a parcel even if a settler stayed a year or two and then left without making a single cash payment. The company eventually approved of the policy, although settlers who paid cash were still offered a 20 percent discount.

In 1803 pricing policies shifted in other ways that made it easier to acquire land. The company lengthened terms of credit extended to new settlers from six to ten years. When initial land prices failed to spark much enthusiasm, Ellicott lowered them: he offered some wholesale acreage for as little as $.75 to $1.00 per acre and sold retail parcels originally priced at $2.75 per acre for $1.50 per acre.[21] Wisely, Ellicott showed some reluctance in dropping prices too much, however, as "it creates great uneasiness among Purchasers who have given higher Prices."[22] In general, therefore, Ellicott lowered prices only in isolated areas while maintaining price stability in other, already settled townships. Still, by 1804, of the thirty-nine towns in which lands had been sold, the median price per acre was under $2.25 per acre in over half the towns, significantly below the original planned rates (fig. 4.2).[23]

After 1808, the company again altered sales policies, and land prices rose across the region. By 1811, the median land price of many of the northern townships rose to $3.50 and $4.50 per acre (fig. 4.3).[24] Only in the central and southwestern purchase could land be purchased at less than $3.00 per acre. This shift to higher prices accompanied what Ellicott saw as a more mature stage of settlement, especially in the northern purchase. The price boosts also corresponded with brisker sales throughout the purchase. Busti approved of the increases as long as Ellicott exercised care, but he urged caution lest "the sudden increase in prices should operate as a check in the Sales, like a Sudden jolt occasions a stop to the Wheels of a carriage."[25] Busti did agree with Ellicott that all provisional sales be ended, insisting only that they be continued in the remaining frontier areas. Ellicott also suggested that the terms of credit be reduced from ten to six years in more settled areas and to eight years in the less-developed districts of the south.[26]

Overall, between 1800 and 1811, Ellicott coordinated various shifts in his pricing policies with his strategies for guiding the spread of settlement. Initial periods of restrictive policies (high prices, tight credit, limited land choices) were quickly replaced by periods of more liberal policies (moderating prices, loose credit, greatly expanded land choices). Finally, as Ellicott saw that the purchase had reached a certain stage of development, a retightening occurred (higher prices, shorter terms of credit, an end to new lot surveys).

Varying land quality and the relative "situation" of a land parcel also

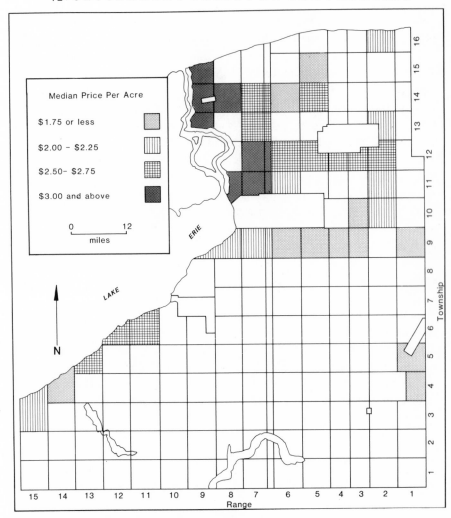

Figure 4.2 Median Price Per Acre by Township, 1804

shaped a varying geography of price levels across the purchase. Ellicott raised prices on lots that included premium bottomlands. The detailed lot survey field notes made the precise location of these well-endowed parcels possible. Rich bottoms were valued especially in the southern purchase because so much of the remaining acreage was too steep or rocky for farming. Ellicott's lots along the Genesee and Allegheny rivers sold at $3.00 per acre, while surrounding upland tracts went for half that price.[27] In the southwestern purchase, Ellicott

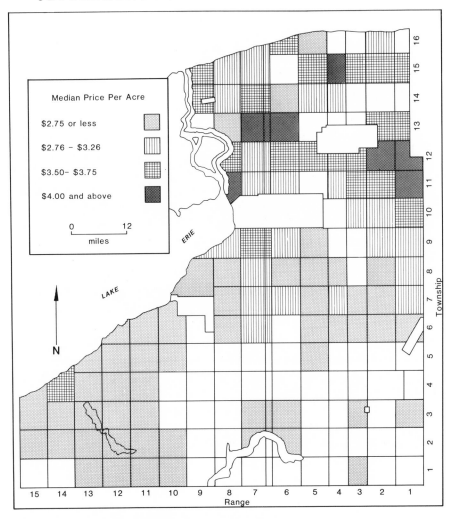

Figure 4.3 Median Price Per Acre by Township, 1811

instructed his subagent to price fertile bottomland lots 10 to 30 percent higher than the upland lots, depending on their precise qualities.[28] Higher initial cash down payments were also required on some stream-fronting lots.

Inferior lands prompted downward price adjustments. Steep, hilly acreage was sold at a discount, and Ellicott dropped prices on rough lands in the southeastern purchase.[29] Prices were also reduced on swampy, poorly drained lands. Townships near Lake Ontario acquired a negative image because of their proximity to low-lying land, which was believed to encourage disease. By 1806 Ellicott reported that the entire region in the vicinity of the lake, opened with such high hopes just a few years before, seemed to have slipped into steady decline. Lots originally priced at between $2.50 and $3.00 per acre sold for $2.00 per acre or less to attract buyers. In a candid statement to his superiors, Ellicott admitted that some of the swamp tracts in the north were worth less than $.50 an acre.[30]

A parcel's relative proximity to navigable streams, roads, and settlements could also both enhance or detract from its value. Premiums attached to stream-fronting lots reflected their dual advantages: frequently the land was of good quality, and its situation offered at least seasonal access to important navigable waterways. Such was the case on the company lots located near the Niagara River: when the towns were opened in 1803, Ellicott priced many of the lots at record levels that ranged from $3.50 to $10.00 per acre "proportioning the price according to the distance from the Niagara River."[31] In fact, prices for lots across the entire northwestern purchase were relatively high because of their proximity to the navigable waters of Lake Erie and to the river and its string of British settlements.

Roads added value to other parcels. Lots bordering on the busy Buffalo Road consistently brought prices 10 to 20 percent above parcels that were one or more lots distant from the road. Elsewhere, the pattern was the same. Along the Erie Road in the western purchase, Ellicott priced lots $.50 to $1.00 per acre higher than on surrounding lands. In areas of slow sales, Ellicott often dropped the price of lands distant from roads while maintaining existing price levels along the road.[32] Such a relationship between roads and price levels clearly encouraged the construction of new routes by the company, and Ellicott often argued that the cost of marking and clearing a road would soon be paid for as adjacent acreage gained value and was subsequently sold.[33]

Ellicott's price discounts for initial settlers in a newly opened township provide another example of the relationship between land price and accessibility. Typically, the first five or ten settlers in a township were sold land at price discounts to attract pioneers into the more isolated, inaccessible sections of the purchase. This policy began in 1802, and Ellicott noted its immediate success.[34] Lands normally selling for $2.00 to $2.75 per acre were offered to the first few settlers in a town at prices of $1.50 to $1.75 per acre.

Valuing the land was a complicated part of Ellicott's settlement policy. His approach, geared toward attracting retail purchasers, was flexible—he altered the price of land through time and in different areas of the purchase. By adjusting prices along routes and in isolated districts, he encouraged dispersed sales and development throughout the purchase. The understandable predilections of settlers to select lands and to live along a road and near village centers were met by the higher prices set by Ellicott in such areas and ideally offset by the special discounts he offered for pioneering in more marginal and isolated districts.

PRINCIPLES OF VILLAGE LOCATION

For the developer's frontier to flourish, Ellicott believed that it had to be an urban frontier, its economic infrastructure focused on established service centers that answered the needs of local settlers and that offered an opportunity to make enduring connections with commercial markets far beyond the borders of the purchase. Frontier central places were thus essential components of Ellicott's western New York settlement policy. The seven villages that he located between 1801 and 1811 reflected varied notions of regional economic planning in the early nineteenth century (fig. 4.4). The placement of each village fit into broader frameworks of settlement and development. Every center was therefore an expression of Ellicott's own development philosophy and a display of how such strategies shaped the course of settlement on the developer's frontier.

Ellicott chose the village of Batavia as his land-selling headquarters. The spot, originally dubbed The Bend during initial surveys, had an obviously strategic location: it lay near the eastern boundary of the company's lands at a point where the main pathways forked, one leading to Buffalo Creek and the Ohio Country and the other to the Niagara River and Upper Canada. Its eastern position enhanced its potential as a new gateway trading entrepôt for the purchase.[35] Contrary to initial advice he received, Ellicott chose not to locate the village in the middle of the purchase, opting instead to maximize the center's accessibility to the external trading network. An added attraction was "the Tonnewonta Creek, a stream of water 80 feet in Breadth," which met local water demands and offered mill sites for possible development.[36]

New Amsterdam, soon renamed Buffalo, was undoubtedly the most carefully located of all Ellicott's platted centers. He saved the still little-developed spot from being included in the Buffalo Creek Indian Reserve during the initial township surveys and subsequently used the site as an important survey supply center. By the time he opened the purchase for development in 1800, there were "present Several families residing Consisting principally of Mechanicks Tavern Keepers and Merchants."[37] The site was also near a mill works and other small settlements in adjacent Upper Canada. Ellicott recognized the inherent advantages of investing time and company funds in already existing centers: the site

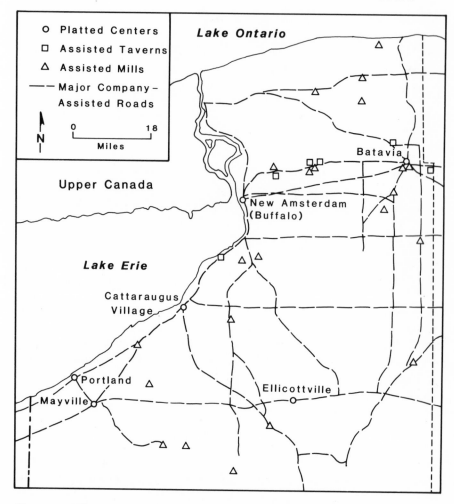

Figure 4.4 Village Nuclei and Major Company Roads, 1801–1811

would attract further development because settlement there had commenced already and showed every indication of continuing.[38]

Ellicott's ebullience was fueled further by New Amsterdam's key placement in the region's evolving transportation network. Before the village was formally laid out in 1803 and 1804, Ellicott described its strategic qualities to the Dutch:

> When it is considered that vessels from seventy to ninety tons . . . may navigate from hence [to] all the great lakes to the West and Northwest . . . through an

immense extent of adjoining country that is rapidly settling . . . ; that almost every article of trade will either be imported through or near this place; and that the road of communication from all the Eastern states to Upper Canada, Presque Isle, New Connecticut, and Detroit passes over ground projected for this Town . . . ; it will appear evident that this situation must naturally become a place of great consequence, and of considerable advantage to the Company's Land.[39]

Obviously, from the village's inception, Ellicott saw its great potential as an interregional trading entrepôt.

The shores of Lake Ontario, on a site almost due north of Batavia, provided the setting for Ellicott's third platted village in the northern purchase. Coincident with the opening of townships near the lake, Ellicott established a village in Township 16 Range 2 "as the Farmers in this Purchase will require a Place to convey their Pot Ash to deposit on the Lake in order to be sent to Montreal or New York . . . and also for a place to receive their salt."[40] Surveyed in 1803, the village of Manilla was also to act as a convenient shipping point for travelers and settlers arriving by way of the lake to inspect newly opened townships in the northern purchase. Unfortunately, painfully slow sales paralyzed the area's development before 1809, and the village never gained an enduring place in the region's urban hierarchy. Soon the village lot lines became overgrown with brush and disappeared from the landscape.

Four additional village centers were located in the southern purchase. A valued ferrying point at the mouth of Cattaraugus Creek was the site of one center platted in 1804. Ellicott had ambitious plans for the place, believing that Cattaraugus Village could serve as another key transshipment point in a developing commercial infrastructure. Only a short twelve- or thirteen-mile portage separated the village from upper Connewongo Creek, a tributary flowing into the Allegheny and Ohio river systems in western Pennsylvania.[41] Ellicott guessed that the portage might play a major role in the flow of trade between the Great Lakes and the interior river systems. The portage route also became part of a much longer and valuable road connecting the purchase with Philadelphia.

Similar commercially inspired planning strategies guided Ellicott's platting of the villages of Mayville and Portland southwest of Cattaraugus Village. The centers were located at either end of another portage route connecting Lake Erie to the Ohio drainage system. Originally an Indian path, the portage was first recognized by Ellicott as a strategic crossing in 1787, when he served on the state boundary survey expedition led by his brother Andrew.[42] Salt was to be the main ingredient in the commercial success of these centers. Ellicott thought that the Portland-Mayville trading alignment would challenge the role of Erie in northwestern Pennsylvania as a transshipment point for the rapidly growing salt trade between Lake Onondaga in central New York and new settlements on the Ohio River.[43] Of the two new villages, Mayville was also to serve as a stimulus to local agricultural development. The platting of Mayville was coordinated with the opening of surveyed lots throughout the southwestern purchase since the center was designed especially to attract the attention of potential settlers in nearby Pennsylvania.[44]

Ellicott did not formally survey the last of his platted centers until after the War of 1812, but he pinpointed its precise site in 1808.[45] He selected the location, and a committee appointed by the state legislature approved his choice. Three criteria guided Ellicott in his decision: first, in the rough hills of the southern purchase, it was essential to place the center in an open valley bottom with access to a mill stream; second, it made sense to place the platted center along an east-to-west road being constructed across New York's southern tier region; finally, Ellicott thought it would be desirable for the site to be "sufficiently central" in the area incorporated by the new county.[46] Ideally, then, all settlers would have optimal access to local political and economic services and thereby add to the commercial success of the village, eventually named Ellicottville.

Several location principles guided Ellicott's decisions as new urban centers were planned. Where possible, Ellicott saw the virtues of investing in places that had already seen earlier development. He also believed that the company's urban framework should encourage the growth of commercial trade in the region. Portage routes, transshipment points, and road junctions thus became potential urban sites. The dispersed nature of the planned urban system suggested Ellicott's evolving commitment to developing the entire purchase and his recognition of the need, given the size of the tract, to orient different sections of the purchase and different urban centers toward different commercial markets. In addition, Ellicott realized that his planned nuclei were wedded to the local needs of settlers because, as he told General Agent Busti, ultimately, "Towns and Villages can only increase with the population of the surrounding Country."[47]

PRINCIPLES OF ROUTE LOCATION

Between 1800 and 1812 Ellicott contributed to the construction of over one thousand miles of frontier roads in the western New York wilderness (see fig. 4.4). The routes made a fundamental imprint on the area and shaped the circulation and orientation of settlement in the region. Good roads served a variety of functions on the developer's frontier.[48] Routes that simply attracted through traffic were desirable because some travelers might decide to remain in the area while others passing on would help to spread the word about new possibilities for settlement. Ellicott believed that through roads would raise the visibility of the entire land sales venture.[49] Good roads were a visual advertisement on the landscape, informing all who passed their way that the region was favored by a forward state of development and by prospering citizens who could afford the costs of building superior routeways.

Ellicott also used roads for the purpose of inducing settlers into previously isolated areas of the purchase. Often he coordinated the opening of new townships with the opening of new roads and thereby offered a convenient avenue along which settlers could inspect the unsold acreage. Roads also guaranteed that pioneers would have some degree of access to needed supplies, mills, and mail and stage services. Ellicott stressed to his superiors that "A Tract of Country, although good as to the Quality of the Land, could scarcely be settled unless facilitated by the opening of Roads of Communication."[50]

Ideally, roads also lowered the costs of transporting locally produced goods for commercial sale. In western New York, roads were deemed particularly essential in tying the region to commercial markets because the area's interior location placed it far beyond the convenient reach of rivers emptying into the Atlantic. Miserably slow, rutted, and muddy routeways, however, were endemic in the America of 1800.[51] Overland transport costs remained high even after roads were constructed, and they inhibited the outward movement of grain, lumber, and other products. Undoubtedly, even with the problems of poor road conditions, Ellicott believed that such investments made economic sense in the long run and that even if commercial links were not immediately forthcoming, the increased price of acreage received for land adjacent to routeways would substantially defray initial construction costs.

The company financed its road network in several ways. Cash was a rare article on the frontier, especially in times of slow sales, and Ellicott preferred to pay his construction crews in land.[52] Often, one-third of the costs were paid in cash with the rest being paid in land. Even with this method of payment, Ellicott occasionally ran out of company cash and was forced to finance the roads out of his own pocket.[53] The initial marking of a road cost the company only about $2.50 per mile. The main expenses came with the actual clearing of the route, which involved the time-consuming tasks of chopping trees and clearing underbrush.[54] Clearing costs varied with the width of the road. A major thoroughfare cleared forty feet wide cost $40.00 per mile to clear while narrower "one rod" roads that were less than twenty feet wide averaged only $10.00 per mile.[55]

Road costs also varied with the terrain, the density of the stream network, and the amount of low-lying land along the route.[56] Rough and hilly land demanded longer routes, more digging and filling, and more ditching to ensure a passable roadway. Many streams meant many bridges, an expensive investment on the frontier: even small wooden bridges could cost $50.00 to $300.00 or more to build. Low-lying lands turned many roads to mudholes, and the only solution was causewaying, in which logs were chopped and laid on the pathway to provide a better surface for travel. Causeways were costly, however, averaging $1.00 to $1.50 per rod (16½ feet). Their tendency to decay rapidly also demanded frequent repair.

Town governments played an important role in road construction. Local control and maintenance of roads was an American tradition. In western New York, local town and county governments aided Ellicott in laying out and improving many roads. Many short, local routes, often less than one mile in length, were marked and opened completely independent of direct company assistance, though company taxes paid to local authorities indirectly funded much of the work.[57] Close coordination also existed between the actions of the resident agent and those of the town highway commissioners. Often a new road was marked by funding from local government authorities and then opened and cleared with the help of company financing. In some cases Ellicott coordinated the marking of a road between commissioners of adjacent towns and then financed its actual construction with company funds.[58] Important local settlers also shared with the company some of the costs of road construction. In several instances purchasers of large wholesale tracts felt that it was in their interest to invest in local road-building projects.[59] After all, realistically their acreage could be peddled only if roads made the tract accessible to potential settlers.

Even with this assistance, Ellicott and the Dutch controlled the construction and improvement of the region's road network. Company investments shaped the overall structure of the transportation system, and company influence guided the decisions made by local politicians and other area landowners. On the developer's frontier, roadbuilding was coordinated with such other planning activities as lot surveying, land pricing, and village platting. Each route had its purpose, its role to play in the movement of pioneers, products, and information, and each road became a significant and logical segment in Ellicott's larger regional design.

In many ways Ellicott's road network mirrored elements of the earlier Indian trail network. Fully one-half of Ellicott's twenty major roads followed or closely paralleled important sections of Indian trails. Such was the case across much of eastern North America, where the frequent use of Indian trail networks facilitated the initial penetration and settlement of a new frontier.[60] Ellicott and his surveyors recognized that laying roads along the course of Indian trails could save weeks of exploration in the dense forests of the region. Some improved company roads were directly on the course of older paths, but most were cleared "along or near" the paths, following the tract in some areas, departing from it where a better, often straighter, route could be found.[61]

Undoubtedly, the most important early route was the Buffalo Road, which cut an east-to-west course across the northern third of the region between Batavia and New Amsterdam. Originally an Indian path, the route was improved and substantially modified by the Company. Much of its central portion was resurveyed south of its earlier course in 1801, and seven years later an alternate and more direct route was opened by cutting several miles off the older road between the eastern purchase and Lake Erie.[62] This corridor of movement was of great importance because it served the most densely populated district in the region and because, for many travelers, the landscapes along the road shaped their perceptions of the entire purchase. The condition of the road itself, typically horrific, probably added little to positive assessments.[63] Contrary to Ellicott's hopes, the road did little to suggest a forward state of settlement in the region; rather, the route enhanced the perceptions of early travelers who believed they had left civilization and had entered a frontier district barely removed from a state of wilderness.

Other important company-sponsored east-west routes also funneled people and goods into and through the region. Southwest of New Amsterdam, the Erie Road, which paralleled the lakeshore, offered an avenue into the Chautauqua region of the purchase and into Pennsylvania and the Ohio Country further west. North of the Buffalo Road, Ellicott built the Ridge Road, which was the western extension of a longer route originating at the Onondaga saltworks in the central part of the state.[64] To the south, the Middle Road, the Cattaraugus Road, and the Southern Road each offered access to the ninth, seventh, and fourth tiers of townships, respectively (see fig. 4.4). The construction of these routes coordinated with the surveying of lots and with the opening of settlements along their lengths.

Several major north-south routes connected the less-developed southern purchase with the northern axis of settlement. Some were designed to serve as important links to commercial trading opportunities beyond the purchase. The Allegany and Big Tree roads, aimed in different ways at encouraging Pennsylvanian connections, the former by way of Olean and the Allegheny River and the latter via Bath and the Susquehanna River. Also fostering connections to the south was the Pennsylvania Road, which terminated at Cattaraugus Village and extended through the company's lands, not only in western New York but also into Pennsylvania. Other roads constructed in the southern purchase were geared more to opening up areas to new settlement than they were to offering interregional transport links to new commercial markets.[65]

These decisions continually linked road construction with settlement policy on the western New York frontier. Throughout his tenure as resident agent, Ellicott viewed the task of settlement across the region with a careful and flexible eye toward the logical interrelationships between such things as roads, newly opened townships, land prices, and urban centers. As the years passed, his own growing knowledge and experience combined with the demands and suggestions of arriving pioneers to encourage policy change where it was needed. The result was a planned framework for a geography of settlement that by 1811 stretched from Lake Ontario to the Pennsylvania line and expressed in its considerable extent and varied structure the carefully articulated locational strategies forged by Ellicott on the developer's frontier.

CHAPTER 5

Commercial Policy on the Developer's Frontier

Whatever be the fertility of the soil, its value is very low, whenever the exportation of the productions is made impracticable by distances or other causes.

—Paul Busti

Assistance on the developer's frontier often entailed more than simply guiding the direction of settlement. Ellicott and his superiors realized that sustained economic growth was likely only through the successful fostering of commercial markets for goods produced on the tract. A commercially oriented economy brought needed cash to a developing region, helped justify rises in land prices, and made the area even more attractive to new settlers. Its benefits also spread broadly—helping the merchants and artisans of the village in addition to the farmers and herdsmen of the rural areas.

83

Therefore, another fundamental component of the land agent's policies on the developer's frontier involved investments that spurred commercial economic activity. Not only was Ellicott compelled to shape the direction of settlement; he was also obliged to see it prosper and thereby secure the continued growth of company profits. Such strategies aimed at two different but often interrelated areas of economic activity. Ellicott directed his attention toward greasing the wheels of the local economy through a variety of economic and political initiatives. In addition, he actively experimented with long-distance trading connections by exploring the possibilities of opening markets for western New York goods in Pennsylvania, British Canada, and elsewhere. Just as with his general settlement directives, the results of these specifically commercial policies shaped the spatial structure and the functioning of the frontier economy.

ASSISTANCE TO THE URBAN CENTERS

Ellicott's views on assisting the growth of his planned urban centers were consistent with actions taken by many other land agents in the region during the period. In fact, their well-known predilections for overspending were continuing concerns for Ellicott and his superiors. Still, from the outset, Ellicott suggested that the company assist in the financing of selected elements of the infant frontier economy. Especially singled out for aid were saw and grist millers and, to a lesser extent, taverners, storekeepers, and other local providers of services. Such assistance was even expected by would-be settlers. Numerous artisans, doctors, printers, and others regularly wrote to the resident agent assuring him of their commitment to the venture "if sufficient encouragement could be given."[1] Ellicott proved to be a responsible handler of the company's purse strings. With the exception of Batavia, Ellicott preferred not to encourage new local economic activity in his urban centers with direct gratuities of cash or land. In this regard, he was more sober minded than most of his colleagues on the developer's frontier.

In Batavia, however, Ellicott took direct action to spur the growth of the local economy. Perhaps Batavia received more assistance because it was Ellicott's first village and the seat of the land office. The site also became the region's initial county seat, and it was usually the first village encountered by travelers and potential settlers from the east. More than any other nucleus, Batavia required a boost to make it the unrivaled local trading and administrative center of the region. Ellicott supervised construction of a sawmill and a gristmill, which remained in company hands during the first decade of settlement. The sawmill came first, beginning operations in 1802; though initial costs were high, the project proved profitable to the company in subsequent years.[2] The gristmill was constructed two years later on the same site in the village—a mill seat that, according to Ellicott, "was as central to the Settlements and as commodious as any in the surrounding Country."[3]

The impact of these early investments multiplied through the village economy in different ways. Obviously, the community reaped the immediate benefits of a convenient sawmill to cut boards for building and a gristmill to grind the grain grown in nearby fields. Ellicott purchased mill parts and equipment through the newly established merchants in the village. Many laborers were hired to construct the mill race, mill dam, and associated buildings. Workers were paid both in cash and in land. Land payments to the workers encouraged them to remain as permanent settlers once a project was completed. Ellicott also compensated local inns and taverns at a rate of two dollars per week per man to feed and house the mill workers, thereby aiding this sector of the local service economy as well.[4]

Craftsmen and professionals were attracted to the village through other similar incentives. A blacksmith was sorely needed, but Ellicott knew that "in the Infancy of Settlements where there are not prospects of constant employment few mechanics of this class will come forward unless we hold out an adequate inducement."[5] William Wood, deemed qualified for the job, was attracted to the village in 1801. Ellicott gave him free village land and loaned him $380 to assist in setting up his shop.[6] James Brisbane, an old acquaintance of Ellicott's from their days in Philadelphia, was induced to remain on the purchase as the prime storekeeper. In Brisbane's case, his decision was made easier with a hefty $3,000 loan from the company for which Ellicott took partial personal financial responsibility.[7] In 1807 a druggist named David McCracken relocated in the village with the help of a $600 loan and Ellicott's assistance in the purchase of needed supplies.[8] Some grubstakes came especially cheaply. Ellicott aided leatherworker Simeon Cummings with a loan of only $150, enough to expand his saddler's shop in 1811.[9]

Other general sales policies benefited village economies in more indirect ways. The net effect, however, was to provide a positive climate for economic growth by assuring the sale of reasonably priced village lands to actual settlers who would spur additional investments in the local economy. Pricing policies illustrate the impact of such company actions. In every village prices were kept at very reasonable levels. Village centers would not be the focus of huge company profits. Rather, moderate terms enabled and encouraged small, industrious buyers to purchase and develop parcels. In Batavia, Ellicott offered "liberal Terms" for lots: prices averaged only five dollars per acre in the village.[10] Inner lots in New Amsterdam were more costly, but a small lot just north of the center of town could be purchased for fifteen or twenty dollars.[11]

Obviously, the chief danger in promoting such a policy was that speculators would move in and buy up large amounts of village acreage at low prices. This could defeat the whole purpose of such initiatives. Ellicott was aware of the problem and guarded against it. In New Amsterdam, for example, the more lots a buyer purchased, the higher the per-acre price charged. It was the opposite of the price discount policy given to large wholesale purchasers of rural acreage. Ellicott was even more restrictive in Batavia, where lots were to be sold only to actual settlers and where each buyer was allowed a limited number of parcels. Ellicott explained, "My intention in laying out this Town was for the purpose of forming a compact Settlement, and should I dispose of four or five Lots to one Man my object would be defeated."[12]

Improvements clauses in village land contracts also limited wholesale speculation. All buyers of village land agreed to clear and improve a portion of their parcels as part of the sales agreement. In New Amsterdam settlers typically agreed either to build a structure of certain minimum dimensions if they purchased an inner lot or to clear and fence a small area if they bought an outer lot.[13] Potentially damaging wholesale speculation was also contained through Ellicott's policy of reserving selected village lands for future sale. This gave Ellicott considerable control on when and where development occurred, and it also acted eventually to increase company profits by delaying the sale of some village lots until they might bring higher prices. Ellicott's approach was flexible and pragmatic: while liberalizing the company's restrictive policy of reserving whole regions of the purchase, he approved of additional company reservations of the valuable village lots.

SHAPING THE LOCAL POLITICAL ECONOMY

Ellicott also became adept at manipulating the local political bureaucracy to encourage economic growth in his planned villages. He quickly recognized the advantages of combining the political and commercial functions of his platted centers because it would add to their economic and social centrality. First, Ellicott lobbied for the creation of new county and town units that would be focused on his planned villages and that would give more representation to settlers on company land. Second, he encouraged the election and appointment of officials who were apt to support Holland Land Company interests. Finally, Ellicott pushed for other federal measures that would provide additional governmental services in the platted villages.

The creation of a new Genesee County that would focus on the company lands was an early priority. When settlement commenced, all of western New York was a part of Ontario County. This created a number of problems for Ellicott. He felt that Ontario County levied inordinately high taxes on the Dutch lands.[14] Because the county seat was in Canandaigua, residents on the purchase were forced to make a long, inconvenient trip in order to conduct any county business. Even before the first surveys in Batavia, Ellicott envisioned that his village would serve as an ideal replacement for Canandaigua as a new county seat.[15] The new county would give settlers on the purchase increased control over local revenues and would add to the prestige and convenience of Batavia as an important village. He believed that a county town added to the value of adjacent lands and helped to speed the settlement of the entire region.[16] Ellicott used company attorneys to draw up the official petition that presented the proposal to the New York State legislature in Albany, and he traveled to the capital in 1802 when the proposal came before the legislature, lobbying intensely for its passage.[17] To quicken the pace of decision making, Ellicott presented cash gifts totaling two hundred dollars to the appropriate influential parties, and he also pledged, as part of the agreement, to finance through company funds the expenses of erecting a county courthouse and jail in Batavia.[18] He succeeded in influencing the composition of the state-appointed commission to oversee the fulfillment of that promise: two of the three commission members were surveyors Ellicott had hired in the township survey project of 1797–99.[19] The efforts proved successful, and in 1802 a new Genesee County was created, most of which contained only Holland Land Company lands. Batavia was selected as the new county seat and received the benefits of serving the entire region in local political matters.

A second task was to divide up the new county into a set of civil townships that would allow the company to control the county board of supervisors and would further add to the political role of such places as Batavia and New Amsterdam. Even before settlement began in the latter village, Ellicott wanted the site to become the center of a new western township.[20] When Genesee County was created in 1802, all of the purchase lands were included in the town of Batavia. Unfortunately, three other small townships within the county just east of the purchase were therefore able to retain control of county affairs. In 1804, however, Ellicott successfully lobbied for an act that divided the old town of Batavia into four new towns, giving settlers on the company lands effective control over the entire county.[21] The new law divided the purchase into four north-south-oriented strips, still an impractical size and shape for a township but better than the earlier single town of Batavia. The new town of Batavia was limited to the eastern purchase, while the town of Erie gave a new and desirable political role to New Amsterdam. The two other towns—Willinks, in the central purchase, and Chautauqua, in the far southwest—also added to the representative role these areas played in local political affairs.

A third major reshuffling was necessary several years later. In 1807 Ellicott, with the encouragement of area settlers, began a new lobbying effort to divide Genesee County into four counties. The area of the original county had already been reduced slightly in 1806 with the creation of Allegany County, which included a portion of the southeastern purchase.[22] In his new proposal, Ellicott envisioned a smaller Genesee County still focused on Batavia, a new Niagara County with a county seat at New Amsterdam, a Chautauqua County in the southwestern purchase centered on Mayville, and a Cattaraugus County in the isolated southern interior with its county seat to be determined later.[23] If passed, the plan would fix the site of every western New York county seat in a village platted or to be platted by Ellicott.

Ellicott lobbied hard for the new county bill. When the issue came before the legislature in 1808, Ellicott was fortunate to have friends in both legislative houses to guide the bill through any opposition. Alexander Rea led the company fight in the senate, while William Rumsey managed the bill in the assembly.[24] Both men had served as surveyors for Ellicott, and he had backed their elections as state representatives. In addition, Ellicott hired a lobbyist to guard against changes in the bill that were being advocated by other land agents in the region who were interested in forming counties that coincided with their own interests. As before, Ellicott volunteered company funds in the construction of the new courthouse and jail at New Amsterdam.[25] When the measure was finally approved, his suggestions to the governor also aided in influencing the composition of a state committee organized to fix formally the site of each new county town.[26] The men chosen, all friends or employees of Ellicott's, agreed to establish new county towns at New Amsterdam, Mayville, and a site Ellicott chose near the center of Cattaraugus County, later platted as Ellicottville.

Ellicott contributed so much of his time and energies to shaping the local political geography of the purchase because town and county governments wielded considerable power. Each county elected a board of supervisors that levied taxes, and a landowner as substantial as the Holland Land Company needed all of the tax breaks it could receive to reduce the yearly costs of retaining its unsold acreage. Furthermore, a major portion of county revenues was allocated to road surveys, road construction, road maintenance, and bridge building. All of these activities were important to Ellicott because the decisions of the board affected patterns of circulation and accessibility on the purchase. Ellicott also wanted to coordinate his own Dutch-financed program of road building with that supported by public funds. Much of the county road revenues were allocated to the individual towns for their own use, but a general fund was also maintained by the county to finance particular projects each year. The county treasurer, appointed by the board, was in charge of managing the funds. A county clerk, named directly by the state council of appointments, had the important job of recording all land transactions. Sheriffs and judges, also appointed by the state council, maintained law and order in each county unit.[27]

Many decisions were also made at the town level. Specific disbursements for road surveys and maintenance were allocated by the towns. Several commissioners of highways directed these projects, delegating further authority to local "path masters" who were each responsible for seeing that a several-mile stretch of road was adequately maintained and the lands bordering it properly fenced. Town officers also had the job of actually assessing and collecting taxes. Other officials regulated local and state elections. Towns were responsible for encouraging moral order by issuing local inn and tavern licenses and by aiding the poor. Town governments also posted bounties on wolves and regulated the wanderings of local livestock.[28]

To increase his control at the town and county levels, Ellicott influenced the composition of local elected and appointed governments. Political and company divisions blurred: with Ellicott's help, public and private interests intertwined intricately.[29] For example, with the creation of Genesee County, Ellicott succeeded in getting his office clerk, James Stevens, appointed as the new county clerk. The post of county sheriff was filled by Robert Stoddard, Ellicott's surveying associate in earlier years. Ellicott's brother Benjamin was appointed county judge after Ellicott himself turned down the job. Ellicott did accept, however, the position of county treasurer, which enabled him to participate directly in the decisions of the county board of supervisors.

At the first town of Batavia meeting in 1803, many town officials were selected from the ranks of Ellicott's employees and associates.[30] Town supervisor was Peter Vandeventer, owner of a tavern that Ellicott assisted in financing in 1801. Of the four town assessors, two were surveyors for the company, and a third, Asa Ransom, owed the company considerable sums of money. Two of the three commissioners of highways had been employed recently in company survey and construction projects. Others in the town government had additional business and personal relationships with Ellicott. This pattern repeated as new towns and counties were created. Local officials and opinion leaders were beholden to Ellicott for part of their success and desired his support in taxing, road construction, and regulatory decisions. When Niagara County was created, Ellicott succeeded in having his friend and surrogate agent in New Amsterdam appointed as county clerk.[31] When Chautauqua County was organized formally in 1811, Ellicott gained direct influence with the appointment of William Peacock, his new subagent in the area, to the post of county treasurer.[32]

Lobbying efforts at the federal level paralleled these links to positions of local influence. In May 1802 Ellicott lobbied for a new post office at Batavia. He wrote to the postmaster general to acquaint him with the necessity of creating a new office in the village, and he also corresponded with another surveying associate, Seth Pease, who had useful ties with the postmaster general. The office opened in 1802, and another Ellicott surveyor, Ebenezar Cary, became postmaster.[33] Ellicott was also intent on attracting a new Indian agent onto the purchase to settle in one of the platted villages. In 1802 he wrote to the agent of Indian affairs asking him to consider Batavia as a future post. Ellicott noted its centrality in terms of the Seneca tribes but also confided that the village would be far enough away from other tribes to avoid being perpetually "bothered" by them.[34] He offered the agent a village lot "on such Terms that you will have no Reason to be dissatisfied with the Price."[35] Eventually, the Indian agent decided not to locate in Batavia, but he did choose New Amsterdam, which pleased Ellicott because he believed the choice was sure to benefit the village.[36] In sum, all of these actions uniting company policy with political institutions were designed to strengthen the dominance of Ellicott's planned urban centers and thereby contribute to the region's growing commercial economy.

SPECIAL ASSISTANCE TO MILLERS AND TAVERNERS

Beyond the bounds of the company's platted villages and county towns, additional commercial aid was limited to a selected number of taverners and millers deemed worthy of assistance (see fig. 4.4). In the first decade of development, after initial subsidies to both mills and taverns, Ellicott's policies for these two key commercial activities diverged. The reason no doubt related to the differing start-up costs of these two operations. Taverns played an important role in the community, but anyone with a crude log cabin and a stock of cheap whiskey could fancy himself a taverner.[37] A commercial-scale miller, on the other hand, needed to expend considerable capital to begin a sawmill or a gristmill. Ellicott realized that the company's financial resources were best directed to the latter enterprises, judging that without company assistance significant portions of the purchase might go unserviced by saw- or gristmills. It was a proper decision; as a result, fewer than 10 percent of the more than five dozen taverns opened on the purchase before 1812 received any company assistance, while 30 percent of the seventy-two mills constructed during the same era profited directly from Ellicott's aid policies.[38]

The average pioneer often possessed neither the capital nor the technical expertise to commence milling operations. Not surprisingly, the company was considerably more active in assisting commercial milling ventures than it was in assisting taverns. Sawmills provided boards for building walls, roofs, and floors. Gristmills allowed settlers to grind their corn and wheat, either for personal use or for commercial sale or barter. Ellicott believed that sawmills and their "Supplies of Boards for Building are indispensably requisite in the first Instance."[39] He added that gristmills were "equally necessary" but that they were needed only after "Settlers have raised Crops to furnish them with Employment."[40] In addition to their economic role on the frontier, mills, akin to taverns, also served as meetingplaces in areas where most settlers lived on isolated farmsteads. The miller was a link to the larger world, and the mill was often the center of a local information network.[41] Visits to a nearby mill thus yielded more than good pine boards and ground flour; settlers also met friends and neighbors and exchanged news and gossip.

Initially Ellicott urged assistance in the construction of only one gristmill and one sawmill at a cost of four thousand dollars. In addition, he advised his survey teams to pinpoint superior natural mill seats that might attract future settlers. The Dutch owners saw no problems with identifying potential sites, but they did want to limit actual development expenditures if possible to only "a Small gratification in Money."[42] Ellicott agreed with the policy, but he noted "where the Necessity of the Settlement of a Country requires, it is an evil that must be submitted to, in order to produce an Advantage that will more than Counter-balance the Evil."[43]

Before 1812, Ellicott contributed to the construction of twenty-two milling projects. Company aid proved particularly significant between 1800 and 1806. During this period, 74 percent of the mills constructed received some form of land company assistance. Thereafter, less than 20 percent of mill building involved Ellicott's encouragement. Clearly, he pinpointed the early years as a critical period in which private initiative had to be supplemented with land company incentives. The geography of assisted mills suggests that company aid spread to all portions of the purchase (fig. 5.1). Not surprisingly, some clustering of both company-assisted and independent mills is evident in a band of relatively dense settlement across the north-central and southwestern purchase.

Company aid to milling activities took several forms. Only rarely did the Dutch totally finance mill construction. In the case of Batavia's sawmills and gristmills, however, such investments were deemed necessary. They provided key commercial services in a rapidly settling portion of the purchase at an early date. A third mill also built by the company operated briefly in Township 15 Range 3, north of Batavia.[44] Ellicott and members of his family became person-

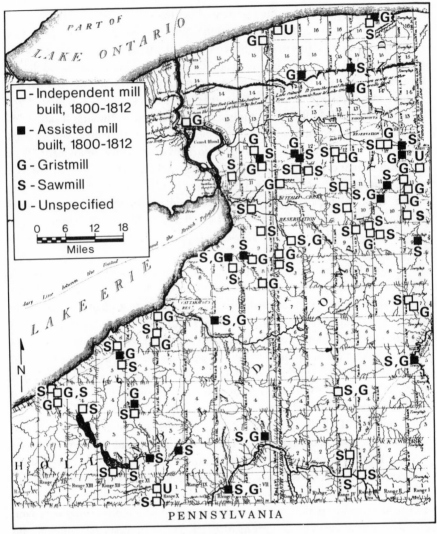

Figure 5.1 Mills Established, 1799–1812

ally involved in several other milling projects before 1812. His brother Benjamin contributed to a sawmill in the western purchase.[45] His nephew Thomas
Kennedy from Meadville in western Pennsylvania was encouraged to venture
further north into New York. Kennedy established sawmills along the Connewongo, a tributary creek of the southward-draining Allegheny.[46] Finally,
Ellicott and another nephew, Andrew, invested in commercial flour mills along
Oak Orchard Creek south of Lake Ontario.[47]

In most cases, however, independent settlers approached Ellicott concerning the possibilities of company assistance. Mill construction sometimes came about as part of more general land discounts to groups of settlers. In 1803 Ellicott struck a deal with a number of Quakers from Pennsylvania to settle in the far southern reaches of the purchase along and near the Allegheny River. The group received substantial discounts, purchasing their tract for one dollar per acre and were thus able to finance a sawmill and a gristmill in the isolated area within two years.[48] In a similar effort, Ellicott offered general land discounts to Rev. Ephraim Sanford and his small group of Baptist settlers in the southeastern corner of the purchase.[49] Soon after purchasing the tract, the group was able to build a set of mills to serve their isolated colony.

Other deals focused even more specifically on agreements to begin milling in particular areas. Edward Work, a friend of Thomas Kennedy's from Meadville, was induced by favorable land prices to migrate north and begin his own set of mills near his associate from Pennsylvania, but Ellicott required provisions on Work's contract that stipulated the bargain prices only if the mills were built and put into operation.[50] Direct cash loans were the most straightforward forms of assistance. Typically, a pioneer newly settled in an area who wished to supplement his ongoing commercial or agricultural enterprises with a saw- or gristmill operation came to Ellicott, described the setting and situation, and stated that he hoped the resident agent recognized the potential value of such facilities in a particular neighborhood. Ellicott responded with loans generally ranging from as little as one hundred dollars to over eight hundred dollars, depending on the size of the planned mill and the amount of assistance necessary.[51] Both of Asa Ransom's early mills west of Batavia were financed in this fashion. In fact, Ellicott, with his family background in milling, was able to supervise personally the precise location of Ransom's mills along a branch of Tonawanda Creek. In some cases, loans of as little as one hundred dollars made possible the purchase of necessary parts and equipment. That modest amount enabled Samuel Sinclear to commence operations in the south-central purchase. His gristmill was not large, but by 1811 it supplied ground grain to a frontier township that had only been opened to settlement for two years.

Through such efforts, Ellicott managed to shape the growth of small but crucial parts of the local commercial economy. The millers were aided in their immediate financial endeavors, surrounding settlers benefited from the proximity of basic services, and the company profited from the upward pressure such incentives put on land prices and the pace of sales. The mills thereby served as local frontier growth centers in the economy beyond the bounds of the formally platted villages. Ellicott saw the role of the land developer, with minor exceptions, not as the principal locator and initiator of such activities but rather as the institutional agent who could and would respond to demands for such facilities where they were needed and recognized by the settlers themselves. In such a way, the purpose of his commercial policy was clear: he was less interested in controlling the frontier economy for its own sake than in simply encouraging growth where it had already commenced. The desire for profits rather than power shaped his actions.

FOSTERING LONG-DISTANCE TRADE

Vigorous economic growth would be helped by prospering villages, a local political system sensitized to the needs of the developer, and a willingness to aid critically important frontier services, such as mills. But Ellicott and the Dutch from the beginning realized that such incentives for local commercial development alone would not guarantee success. Sustained commercial prosperity hinged on the region's ability to establish economic links with long-distance markets. Geography suggested a variety of potential outlets (fig. 5.2). Far to the southwest was Philadelphia, one of the nation's great cities and home to the American representatives of the Holland Land Company. Down the Allegheny River, Pittsburgh was a rapidly growing settlement in 1800; beyond, the entire Ohio and Mississippi valleys lay as potential markets for western New York goods. To the immediate west was the British possession of Upper Canada, already well settled by the time western New York was opened. Further north, Montreal was a significant urban link to both settlements in the Saint Lawrence Valley and profitable European markets. Finally, Albany and New York City to the east offered other outlets for local products.

The importance of commercial links during the early years of settlement in western New York can be debated. What is certain, however, and what seemed to characterize the developer's frontier, is that, even before settlement began, the Dutch owners and agent Ellicott envisaged a frontier that would be well connected commercially to the outside world. Ellicott's development policies steered in this direction from the outset, and this strategy became an enduring part of the western New York landscape in the form of roads, villages, assisted mills, and strategically opened land parcels. The successes of Ellicott's efforts were often elusive, but their impact on the landscape long outlived the commercial links first envisioned.

There was a flexibility and a sense of experimentation in the policies Ellicott advocated to spur commercial links. It was an early and important stage of regional development, a period of fluid and often unknown opportunities in which different products were tested and different potential markets tapped.

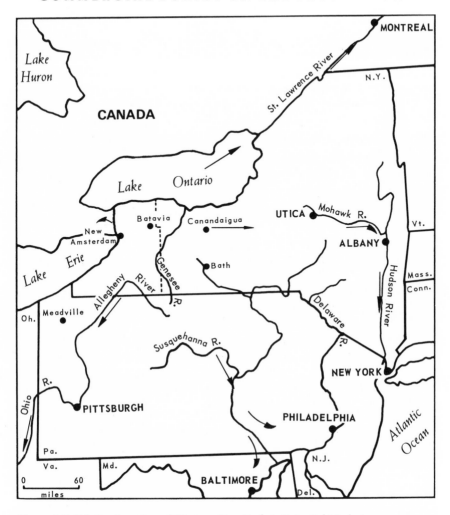

Figure 5.2 Relative Location of Western New York to Potential Market

The region was still a part of what Edward Muller has termed the Pioneer Periphery, in which settlers were "searching for viable crops, and experimenting with export commodities in a context of remoteness from external markets."[52] In western New York this era spanned the first ten years of settlement, and it was a decade in which the region's relative proximity to a number of commercial centers and its relatively unfocused transportation system allowed for and encouraged experimentation. Much of Ellicott's development strategy and the frontier landscape owed their character to Ellicott's perceived need to tinker with the early frontier economy, testing the market for lumber in one place, shipping cattle to another, and exploring the overall relative commercial potential of different regional centers for different locally produced products.

Clearly, such an era is not a part of every frontier's development. The purchases's relative proximity to a number of potential markets was important. If the region had been quite close to a single, large, well-established center, its commercial orientation would perhaps have been decided from the start; if, however, the region had been far beyond the economically feasible reach of all centers, commercial links of any sort would have been minimal. Only where a frontier—like the Holland Purchase—fell spatially beyond the inner limits of a single captive market's orientation but within the outer limits of all economically feasible trade could such a period of experimentation be expected to occur.

Experimentation was also encouraged by the spatial structure and the technological sophistication of the transport system that connected the purchase to potential markets. In 1800 possible routes of travel included several natural waterways oriented in every direction and a slowly increasing number of narrow, often muddy, and sometimes impassable roads. The multiplicity of early routes contributed to the range of potential commercial links. Clearly, this would not be the case on a frontier opened by a single canal or rail line. That type of spatial design encouraged the early capture of a frontier's commercial potential by the single center serving as the focus of the regional network. In western New York, such a pattern developed after the Erie Canal was completed in 1825. The strong east-west orientation of the canal cemented the connection between western New York and points east and west. In the early years of development, however, no such strikingly east-to-west corridor of movement and trade existed. The map was not, as it is today, an orderly alignment of roads, rails, and settlements that stretch from Albany westward to Buffalo and Lake Erie; rather, Ellicott's plans envisioned quite a different map, one that opened the way as much to opportunities north and south as it did to possibilities east and west.

Little significant commercial trade was carried on across the purchase before 1800. Some bartering for pelts and furs was carried on at Buffalo Creek between local Indians and itinerant white traders. The exception to this pattern of limited activity was the trade that passed through the Niagara Corridor from the Upper Lakes into the settled districts of Canada. Portage trails around Niagara Falls were crowded with the fur traffic, and adjacent military posts provided a local market for garden crops and livestock.[53] Beginning in the 1790s, a new commercial product gained in importance: agreements between salt producers at Onondaga Lake in central New York and merchants at Pittsburgh directed an increasing flow of the frontier staple via the Niagara portage. A new fleet of boats was constructed on Lake Erie to handle the salt, which passed southwest from the Niagara to the new village of Erie, Pennsylvania, where it was portaged on its way to Pittsburgh.[54]

Before 1800, in areas just east of the purchase, merchants and settlers established various commercial ties on the Pulteney Purchase. In 1793 Thomas Cooper believed that all of southern New York near the Susquehanna and Delaware rivers would "of course find vent for its produce at Philadelphia."[55] Agent Charles Williamson saw the region's commercial markets even further south at Baltimore. He described that city as "the natural seaport for this part of the country."[56] He encouraged the shipment of cattle, corn, and other frontier produce southward along the Susquehanna. Pulteney agents also developed facilities on Lake Ontario at Sodus Bay to encourage commercial connections northward to Canada via Montreal and eastward to Albany and the Hudson via Oswego.

With such an orientation on the Pulteney Purchase and Ellicott's own familiarity with Pennsylvania, it is hardly surprising that when Ellicott opened the western New York lands in 1800 he envisioned a growing network of commercial connections from the southern and southwestern sections of the purchase to markets in the Keystone State. To develop such links, company capital was invested in roads, villages, mills, and special commercial projects. Philadelphia was to be one focus of the Pennsylvanian trade. Ellicott and his Dutch superiors had numerous connections with Philadelphia merchants and businessmen. In 1805 Ellicott opened the Pennsylvania Road, which connected the purchase to other company-constructed routes in Pennsylvania. Several years later Ellicott also financed McClure's Road with the view that it shortened the distance between New Amsterdam and Philadelphia. The Southern Road, which crossed the fourth tier of townships, was also seen as binding the region to Pennsylvania since it connected the southern purchase with the Susquehanna River basin at Bath, New York.[57]

Cattle was the only local product, however, that found an important early market in Philadelphia.[58] Beginning late in the summer of 1802, annual cattle drives moved herds from the purchase southeastward to Philadelphia. When the trade began, cattle owned by both the company and local settlers were gathered at Batavia and then moved south to a farm just outside Philadelphia. By 1810 Ellicott believed that the trade had so much potential that he suggested a series of company-financed "grazing farms" be established at each county seat to take livestock as payment in kind for land and to serve as roundup points for larger shipments to the south. A drop in beef prices during that year discouraged such plans, however, and they were abandoned entirely as war approached early in 1812.

Ellicott believed that even greater potential markets for company produce existed to the southwest. Pittsburgh tripled in size between 1800 and 1810.[59] Ellicott became convinced that the Allegheny River system would "one Day be much used for the transportation of Articles from the waters of the Mississippi to the [purchase], and Vice Versa."[60] Other settlers also sparked Ellicott's imagination: Adam Hoops was convinced that the Allegheny River was the region's commercial avenue to all of the "Western Waters" of the Ohio and Mississippi rivers, and many settlers as far north as New Amsterdam believed that New Orleans would one day become the dominant commercial market for western New York goods.[61]

Ellicott spurred settlement and commercial ventures that strengthened connections to southwestern Pennsylvania. He fostered special early sales in the southern purchase to individuals from Pennsylvania who might direct trade to the south and southwest. Ellicott also fostered group settlements of Pennsylvania Quakers in several locations across the southern purchase. Company-financed roads also made the Quaker settlements more accessible to one another and to other settlements. He encouraged the development of a commercial lumber trade that had its market in Pittsburgh and that used the Allegheny and its tributaries in the southern purchase to transport the logs downstream. The white pine forests that clothed the southern purchase were so attractive for commercial development, in fact, that Ellicott had real problems with "timber rustlers" who ventured into areas near the Allegheny River, cleared off the prime pine acreage, and then floated the lumber to Pittsburgh.[62] By 1809, especially with the completion of the company-encouraged Kennedy and Work mills in Township 2 Range 10 and Township 2 Range 11, more and more pine boards floated south. With Ellicott's encouragement, attempts were even made to penetrate the lumber market far beyond Pittsburgh. New Orleans offered long-distance possibilities, and in 1808 and 1809 several boat loads of lumber made the lengthy journey from southwestern New York to Louisiana.[63] By 1811, however, declining lumber prices in New Orleans did what falling cattle prices accomplished in the Philadelphia market: it simply became uneconomical for settlers in western New York to ship these products to such distant destinations.

Ellicott's greatest contributions to a Pennsylvania-oriented development strategy centered on the salt trade. Ellicott was anxious to produce salt locally or to see Onondaga Lake salt pass through the purchase on its way to Pittsburgh. Demand for salt was rising rapidly in the West, and Ellicott jealously eyed the explosion in commercial activity. Between 1801 and 1809, the annual number of salt barrels passing through the port of Erie rose from 398 to 14,000.[64] Ellicott wanted a portion of that increasingly lucrative trade. Unfortunately for the Dutch, the independently controlled Porter, Barton and Company all but monopolized the salt trade, directing it through their facilities on the Niagara River and then transporting the barrels to Erie and on to Pittsburgh.[65]

One way to join the salt trade was to encourage the local manufacture of the frontier staple. Ellicott discovered a salt spring near Batavia in 1802, and within a year he eagerly began work on a salt production facility that would challenge the Onondaga trade in western Pennsylvania.[66] Ellicott erected boiling houses and furnaces, constructed a new sawmill, shipped in salt kettles, and built roads to connect the site with nearby settlements. By 1805, however, Ellicott's great plans for the region's salt works began to fade: the local deposits were simply too weak and proved too costly to refine.[67] Although a limited amount of salt was produced at the site and shipped to Pittsburgh, the operation never reached a scale large enough to become significant.

Another approach toward increasing the company's participation in the salt trade was more successful. Beginning in 1803, the company developed two new portage routes on the purchase that competed with the established route through Erie in Pennsylvania. One portage crossed the divide between Lake Erie and the Allegheny system just south of Cattaraugus Village.[68] Even more successful was the link via the Portage Road, which led from Lake Erie at Portland Village to Chautauqua Lake and the village of Mayville. The village centers and the road improvements tied directly to Ellicott's Pennsylvania strategy, and indeed the route did capture significant salt traffic after 1809.[69]

Just as the southern purchase seemed destined to be tied to Pennsylvanian markets, the northern and western sections of the region were in close proximity to British settlements on the Niagara peninsula and, via Lake Ontario, to other Canadian centers farther to the northeast. Especially in the first years of settlement, villages on the British side of the Niagara supplied western New York pioneers with glass, paper, flour, hay, and other products.[70] Ellicott was eager to increase these Canadian connections, hoping that the British settlements would act as potential markets for goods produced on the purchase. His early lobbying for the opening of townships in the western purchase was part of this push for development. The timely construction of roads leading to and along the Niagara River also enhanced the links between the settlements on the British and American sides of the corridor.

Ellicott also hoped to encourage commercial links between the northern purchase and Montreal. For many years these efforts failed miserably, but, when events entirely beyond Ellicott's control radically changed patterns of trade, commerce suddenly flourished between the two areas. After years of languishing in the backwater of Ellicott's development program, the Lake Ontario region boomed after 1808. The catalyst for the turnaround in the area's fortunes was the American embargo against trade with Britain and her possessions.[71] Because there were so many opportunities for violating the embargo on the lightly patrolled upstate New York frontier, potash, pearl ash, flour, beef, and other goods began flowing northward in an increasing volume during 1808. When trading restrictions were relaxed in 1810, the well-established flow of goods increased further.

By the summer of 1808, Ellicott noted that new settlers were arriving in the northern purchase to make potash and pearl ash and to ship it to Montreal, where it received $190 per ton.[72] The villages of Black Rock and Lewistown served as prime smuggling centers to Queenstown and Montreal, and other smaller shipping points were located along Lake Ontario east of the Niagara River. By the close of 1808, thirty thousand barrels of American potash were received in Montreal, perhaps double the amount imported a year earlier. Western New York is estimated to have supplied half of that.[73] Less significant quantities of timber, beef, and lard were other commercially exported products traded during the embargo.

When the trade ban was lifted in 1810, the demand for western New York products was stronger than ever, and Ellicott became convinced that "Montreal affords a better Market than New York" for potash and other products.[74] Ellicott made fresh investments to expand the area's roadways, and he financed harbor improvements at the mouth of Quottehonyaiga Creek on Lake Ontario.[75] He also began building, with the help of his own funds, a large commercial flour mill on Oak Orchard Creek, and plans for enlarging the Batavia gristmills were also discussed.[76] Ellicott further demonstrated his own conviction about the area's potential by purchasing, along with his brother Benjamin, over six thousand acres of land near the lake in 1811, no doubt hoping to cash in on the excitement of the Montreal trade.[77]

The Canadian trade crashed in 1812, however, a victim of the direct hostilities that broke out between the United States and Great Britain. The trading corridor through and across the Niagara River became a war zone. Montreal became an enemy headquarters rather than a commercial entrepôt. Even so, between 1800 and 1811, important sections of the western New York frontier were shaped by Ellicott's Canadian development strategy. Land sales, platted centers, mills, and roads on the landscape expressed Ellicott's belief that

Canada would play a central role in the region's evolving commercial trading network.

Even with the commercial opportunities to the north and south, Ellicott persistently encouraged an east-to-west corridor of development into and out of the purchase. The Buffalo Road across the northern interior was a principal highway into the region that funneled in both settlers and supplies.[78] Soon after 1800 it became an avenue for eastbound grain and potash. Ellicott's construction of the Ridge Road and the Southern Road were also tied to their wider function as connecting routes to points east.[79]

Canandaigua played an especially important role in the development of the purchase. It was a major supply point during the township surveys, and it later became a source of tools, farm machinery, food, paper, and other frontier provisions. Many local Canandaigua professionals, merchants, and businessmen, in turn, frequently had close connections with associates or suppliers in Albany or New York City.[80] Further east, a special financial link was forged with Utica. Ellicott reached an agreement with the Utica branch of the Manhattan Bank that enabled the company to send the bank all the variety of bank notes it regularly received as payment for land.[81] This arrangement provided a convenient collection point for redeeming bank notes issued throughout the East. Ellicott's choice of Utica may have been influenced by the many pioneers arriving on the purchase from the upper Mohawk Valley and, undoubtedly, making down payments with notes obtained in the Utica area.

As early as 1800, Albany became a market for surplus wheat grown in western New York.[82] Even with Ellicott's encouragement, however, there was never a flood of frontier products moving eastward before 1812. Repeatedly he complained that such trade was uneconomical because of the high transport costs involved in shipping goods to the Atlantic markets.[83] Of greater significance was the flow of manufactured goods into the purchase from Albany.

The linear arrangement of trading centers that stretched from Buffalo and Batavia to Albany and New York City via Canandaigua and Utica was the precursor of the "lakes alignment" urban pattern that took shape after the completion of the Erie Canal in 1825 and that included the newer centers of Syracuse and Rochester.[84] The earlier Batavia-Canandaigua-Utica-Albany corridor focused on the turnpike network, but, akin to the later canal-oriented pattern, it displayed the characteristics of a gradually unfolding, linearly organized trading entrepôt alignment. As new and more westerly settlement frontiers were opened, each focused along the turnpike network and each encouraged the extension of an urban system based on supplying the area with needed manufacturing goods and collecting from its hinterlands the raw staples of farm and forest.

An added stimulus to the east-west pattern may have been Ellicott's promotion of the Erie Canal project. Such a canal, according to Ellicott, would enable settlers "to transport Produce, Pot Ash, etc. to Market at less than half the Price than it can be done at Present."[85] Ellicott also estimated that the canal would raise the price of company lands adjacent to it from three dollars per acre to over twenty dollars per acre. Ellicott advised state officials on the prospects of a canal through the northern purchase, but no clear agreement was reached. In fact, by 1811, talk of a western New York canal had diminished significantly, buried in the barrage of excitement over the blossoming Montreal market. John Melish reported that Batavia residents believed that "the principal market is on the Lake [Ontario], and it is believed by the people here that it will always continue to be so; they seem, so far as I have yet collected their sentiments, to consider the projected canal as of no importance to them."[86] Even General Agent Busti assured Ellicott, "You'll do well to turn your thoughts toward the Ontario for if transportation through that lake to Montreal can be obtained at a reasonable rate Canada must be the market for the Genesee."[87]

Busti's geographical logic was overturned by the war, which reaffirmed the importance of east-west connections in New York State as men and arms were shipped toward the border on the Niagara River. Following the war, lobbying for a canal again increased within the state as the apparent viability of connections to the north and south lessened. Ellicott continued to assist in the canal project, finishing important feasibility surveys in 1816. The canal's completion in 1825 cemented the east-west trading corridor in the region. In 1811, however, such a commercial orientation in Ellicott's strategy for regional growth was only one component of a flexible and dynamic development plan. As land developer and agent, Ellicott was willing, even eager to explore all of the commercial possibilities of the region, and the complexity of his development schemes and road networks are a vivid testimony to that experimental and fluid era on the western New York frontier.

CHAPTER 6

Settlers on the
Developer's Frontier

People are very much governed by Whim and
Caprice in selecting Lands.

—*Joseph Ellicott*

Settlers as well as land agents shaped the developer's frontier. The pace of settlement and the
predilections of the pioneers themselves did
not always parallel the policies adopted by the
Holland Land Company. In addition, the
source area, socioeconomic status, and desired
destination of incoming settlers varied considerably and molded the cultural geography and
evolving human landscape of the region in
ways well beyond the control of land agents
and land company policies. Overall, the settlers' experiences in western New York, although influenced by the special character of
the developer's frontier, mirrored the common
challenges and opportunities of pioneers
everywhere in the early nineteenth-century

North American backcountry. Life was hard and frontier communities quickly changed in character; the landscapes that reflected these dramatic social and economic transformations were a product both of large-scale developer-formulated settlement policies and of the individual, sometimes unpredictable, decisions made by pioneers on the purchase. Ellicott was repeatedly frustrated by the unpredictability of settler decisions regarding land selection.[1] This and the general volatility of the land-selling business made his task as developer incalculably more complex and created a continuing need to balance company demands with those of the varied immigrants.

SETTLER ORIGINS

In June 1804 James Cochrane, a New Haven journalist, wrote to Ellicott, reporting "In this thickly settled Country they are highly in the spirit of moving to the westward."[2] Cochrane's comment was appropriate, not only for westward-bound New Englanders of the period but also for the young nation as a whole. In the over 150 years of European occupancy of North America before the Revolution, the population showed a stubborn reluctance to flood into the trans-Appalachian interior. With the exception of movements into southwestern Pennsylvania and scattered outposts in Tennessee and Kentucky, colonial politics, Indian threats, and more accessible opportunities elsewhere discouraged pioneers from venturing across the mountains. With the Revolution, old imperial constraints on inland migration were replaced by a genuine and increasingly well-articulated national policy of allowing and even encouraging a rapidly expanding western frontier. In the thirty years between 1790 and 1820, more land was freshly occupied than in the previous 180 years of North American settlement.

Migration data, though fragmentary for the early national period, argue that the era was one of increasing geographical mobility in the country.[3] People moved frequently, and even those that did not talked incessantly of the latest news from this or that frontier settlement. Rumors flew concerning fertile lands and boomtowns, and many common folk in postrevolutionary America not only listened but gave up jobs, farms, and familiar surroundings for something potentially better. Indeed, for many people, the most tangible way to participate in the fruits of the American Revolution was to create a new life geared to promises of heightened social mobility in a frontier community.

People moved for many reasons. One of the most powerful attractions to western New York and to other frontiers was the hope for a better economic future, both for oneself and for one's children. Like many uprisings, America's revolution was one of heightened expectations, and perhaps with such new possibilities came a greater willingness and capability to experiment and to take risks previously untenable.

Another consideration was simply the availability of land complete with the public and private institutions necessary to effect sales and confirm titles. After 1800, such mechanisms were in place on the purchase, but the Holland Land Company's domain was only one of many settlement options for the potential migrant. In fact, a continuing source of frustration for Ellicott was the steady march of settlers through the purchase as they continued westward to Upper Canada or to the Ohio Country. This era saw vast acreages of the South, old Northwest, and interior Northeast opened to settlement. No doubt a significant problem for the migrant of the period was sifting through the bewildering assortment of possibilities and arriving at a suitable destination for resettlement. The Prendergasts illustrate the dilemma well. In 1805 this family, along with a half-dozen other families, left Rensselaer County in eastern New York and traveled caravan-style first to Tennessee and Kentucky and then to the Ohio Country looking for suitable acreage. After weeks of perusing alternatives, the group split up. Some headed for cheap lands in Upper Canada, while the remainder established themselves, to Ellicott's satisfaction, in the southwestern purchase near Chautauqua Lake.[4]

The relative accessibility of a frontier area influenced the pattern of migration. By any account, the nation's transportation system in 1800 was abysmal, even in many long-settled districts, and once one left civilization behind, even narrow, rough roads often deteriorated to mere traces in the forest. Any move into the interior was a challenge that called for planning and forethought. In upstate New York, most settlers kept to a few main east-west thoroughfares. Some routes were turnpiked and thus improved by private investors, while others received occasional local and state funds or, simply through frequent travel, assumed a considerable, albeit well-rutted, importance. The Mohawk River provided a corridor into central New York, and some settlers made use of Lake Ontario for westward movement, but most migrants bound for the western extremity of the state and the acreage of the Holland Purchase usually arrived overland. Incoming settlers usually saw their first glimpse of the region from the famed Genesee Road. It passed through the frontier towns of Geneva and Canandaigua, crossed the Genesee River, and then continued onto the purchase and to the villages of Batavia and New Amsterdam.

Perhaps most important, people were more likely to move to a place if they knew something about it. Information was vital. Published advertisements provide interesting insights into the company's promotional strategies, but they were only one, probably secondary, source of information on the region. Undoubtedly of greater significance was that the tract bordered the widely publicized Genesee Valley. The rich alluvial soils lay immediately east of the purchase, and the Holland Land Company lands continually basked in the glow of the famed region. In traveler's accounts and in settlers' perceptions, the Holland Purchase gradually became a part of a larger "Genesee Country" that encompassed much of western New York State.

The reknowned nature of the area originally spread with the accounts of returning soldiers from the Revolution's Clinton-Sullivan Campaign.[5] The mostly New England-born patriots reported extraordinarily rich soils and luxuriant Indian farmlands in the Genesee Valley that surely compared favorably with the limited agricultural resources of their native region. Thereafter, "Genesee," an Indian word meaning "shining-clear-opening" or "pleasant-open-valley," was splashed broadly across standard maps of the state: both John Adlum's 1791 map of the mid-Atlantic region and Samuel Lewis's widely used 1795 map of New York State included the purchase in a larger "Genesee Country."[6] Thus, as settlement of the actual Genesee Valley accelerated in the 1790s, its fame paved the way for migration to the Dutch company's acreage immediately to the west. The company's early reports on their "Genesee lands" reinforced the connection: explorer-employee William Morris happily proclaimed the soils of the purchase "exactly Similar" to the soils of the famed valley.[7]

Even with the positive assessments of the region that came through advertisements and the general fame of the "Genesee," it often took more personal forms of persuasion to convince people to make the actual move. Glowing reports assumed special meaning when they came from a friend, neighbor, or family member who had settled in the region and returned on a visit or had mailed letters describing the promise of the new tract. This information diffusion often resulted in a process of chain migration in which a neighborhood, once an initial migrant ventured forth, continued to send additional pioneers westward as positive reports returned from the frontier.

Numerous examples of the phenomenon in western New York may be mentioned. Two members of the Clark family left Brookfield, Massachusetts, in 1807 and took up lands south of Batavia in Township 11 Range 2. Within a year they had encouraged two additional siblings to migrate to the region.[8] In 1810 a friend convinced Stoughton Morr of Pompey, New York, that superior acreage was available in the vicinity of Chautauqua Lake. Morr was intrigued enough to write to Ellicott for more information on the rapidly settling region.[9]

Local opinion leaders played particularly important roles in transferring several settlers from selected old neighborhoods to new. Lawton Richmond moved to the southwestern purchase from Herkimer in central New York. He bought a lot, cleared some land, and put ten acres in grain. His role in encouraging migration to the area from his old neighborhood is clear from a letter he wrote to Joseph Ellicott:

> I have had a number of gentlemen this Spring out to see me and view the Country from the same Town that I come from and I still expect more. I have written letters to several gentlemen of my acquaintance in the Town of Fairfield and the adjacent towns advising them to sell their farms . . . and set out for Chautauque.[10]

Further north, in the Eighteenmile Creek settlement in Erie County, Vermonter David Eddy performed a similar function. Eddy was a pioneer settler in the district and an enthusiastic promoter of its potential. He encouraged Thomas Ragen and Clandieus Britton from his old Vermont neighborhood to come and visit the western New York frontier. They were so impressed that they decided to relocate.[11] Eddy promised Ellicott "to use what influence I possibly can to encourage Settlers and Invite those of my acquaintance in Different parts and Different States to Come and See."[12]

More formal information networks also operated to encourage settlement on the large wholesale parcels purchased from Ellicott by entrepreneurs and small speculators. When Oliver Phelps and Samuel Chipman purchased large portions of two company townships in 1804, they returned to their home region of New England and aroused settler interest in migrating to the purchase.[13] Similar arrangements with wholesale buyer John McMahon in the southwestern purchase prompted the Pennsylvanian to return to his native Susquehanna valley to recruit interested buyers for his western New York lands.[14] Other wholesale purchasers also functioned as important middlemen in the geography of information that linked company lands and potential migrants.

In addition to incentives that pulled settlers toward the frontier, other factors encouraged emigration from their home regions. Developed districts in the East were filling up rapidly during the period. The percentage growth rate of the continent's European population, by natural increase and with new overseas arrivals, was the highest in history, averaging 4 percent per year between 1750 and 1800.[15] Fertility rates were high: women in 1800 averaged seven childbirths.[16] Such demographic trends, when contrasted with the rapidly diminishing quantity of productive agricultural acreage in New England, the Hudson-Mohawk Valley, and Pennsylvania, meant that considerable pressure often existed to leave one's farm and expand to larger holdings on the frontier. Undoubtedly the incentives to leave were especially apparent to children in large families whose prospective per capita farmholdings were small. Buying additional developed acreage in the neighborhood often meant purchasing expensive and overworked land. Employment opportunities in the manufacturing sector were also limited: large-scale industrial employment in southern New England and in East coast cities did not blossom until after 1820. Marginal lands in northern New England or upcountry Pennsylvania might be closer to one's home, but could they hold a candle to the fabled Genesee Country? Many migrants preferred to believe that they could not, and, spurred both by the limited opportunities at home and by better possibilities elsewhere, they decided to move on.

The typical migrant arriving in western New York came as part of a single nuclear family or, quite commonly, in a small, loosely organized group of several families. In 1808 John Williams and Robert Andrews traveled together to the region to help one another choose lands and begin settlement.[17] Two years later, Robert Dodge and Matthew Nealy came with a group of their Vermont acquaintances to join "our Selves in neighborhood together" in Township 3 Range 13.[18] Often a young male made the initial foray into the region, selected the acreage, and then made a second trip to bring the entire family. Ellicott reported arrivals in all seasons. Summer, however, was often relatively quiet because most potential migrants were busy on their existing farms.[19] Fall and winter, by contrast, were frequently bustling with new arrivals, many finding that traveling on the snowpack was easier than fighting the mud of springtime roads. In fact, Ellicott reported that midwinter arrivals were often so numerous that acute housing shortages developed, forcing several families into a single house until new homes could be built the following spring and summer.[20]

The socioeconomic status of the incoming migrants was not the ideal mix Ellicott desired. The character of the influx resembled a pyramid: small numbers of skilled professionals and craftsmen at the top, a considerable quantity of lower middle-class farmers and semiskilled artisans in the middle, and a large majority of rather poor, though generally hard-working, settlers with little money at the bottom. Members of the first group were often able to pay cash for lands, while those of the second were capable of a modest down payment, but most came hoping that the company would bank on their pioneer optimism rather than on their pocketbook. For this last group, after the costs of the journey, often not even one dollar was available to make a down payment.

The source areas of these arriving settlers are not easy to reconstruct precisely. No census of the period recorded data on place of origin. Three dominant and several less important source areas can be identified, however, from information in Ellicott's correspondence, contemporary travelers' accounts, and published county histories and settler biographies. Primary source areas were New England and elsewhere in upstate New York, while Pennsylvanians also dominated selected portions of the region. Of lesser significance were migration streams from New Jersey, the Chesapeake region, Upper Canada, and Europe. Within the region itself, neighborhoods sometimes tended to cluster on the basis of source region because of the geography of incoming transportation routes and the processes of chain migration already described.

Considerable evidence suggests New England's importance in contributing migrants to the region. By the 1790s, most of the good and even average farmlands of that region had been occupied. At the aggregate level, according to data on probable emigration reconstructed for the period, the New England states of Massachusetts, Connecticut, Rhode Island, and New Hampshire probably recorded net losses of migrating population between 1800 and 1810, and thereafter Vermont saw rapid increases in its levels of emigration.[21] Historians and historical geographers agree that the majority of the emigrating Yankees moved in a generally westward direction, thus creating an "extended" New England culture area that stretched across upstate New York and eventually westward into the Great Lakes region.[22]

On the purchase, New Englanders were on the scene from the beginning, although some evidence suggests that both their dominance and certainly the pace of their arrivals increased after 1805.[23] Travel narratives between 1805 and 1810 by Joseph Avery, J. U. Niemciwicz, and John Melish all dwell on the dominance of Yankees in the region.[24] Ellicott's own correspondence pinpoints the potentially special role Vermonters played in this New England stream. By 1805, he stated, "the greater part of our Settlers" came from Vermont, and two years later he noted Vermonters as the "greater Portion of the People that have settled on the Holland Purchase."[25] Ellicott suggested that they came both because of the familiar limitations of the New England environment and because the migrants desired "Settling in a Country where the Winters are less severe than they are in the State of Vermont."[26] In later years, Vermonters emerged prominently in several neighborhoods, especially in regions rapidly settled between 1808 and 1811. They were notable in the Eighteenmile Creek settlement in southern Erie County, in portions of Wyoming County near Warsaw, and in townships of Chautauqua and Cattaraugus counties that were opened to settlement during the period.[27]

Although "Yankees" and "New Englanders" are everywhere mentioned in contemporary descriptions of the region, other evidence suggests that a second and in many ways related source area was of equal if not greater importance. Settled portions of New York State contributed large numbers of migrants.

Indeed, these were often second- or third-generation New Englanders who were continuing their westward drift. By virtue of proximity, accessibility, and the continuing flow of information about the purchase that passed eastward, it is logical that central New York south of Lake Ontario, the Mohawk Valley, especially around Utica, and the banks of the Hudson itself supplied significant numbers of migrants. Some of these districts, especially in the east, were settled before the Revolution, although most of the areas from the Upper Mohawk westward had been settled since 1785.[28] Still, evidence suggests there was a great deal of interest, even on the newly settled tracts, in moving to the company's lands west of the famed Genesee River.

The best source of information arguing for the importance of adjacent source regions of upstate New York are the postmarked letters of incoming inquiries to Ellicott's land office. Between 1800 and 1811 Ellicott received over two hundred inquiries from individuals, families, and groups requesting information on the price, location, and quality of available lands.[29] Although not directly indicating source areas of actual migrants, the letters do measure the interest generated about the purchase in different communities. The geography of settler inquiries suggests that other upstate New Yorkers were very interested in migrating westward. Changes in the pattern also reveal how information concerning the purchase diffused to more distant areas.

In the first few years of sales, most inquiries came from neighboring settled districts just east of company lands (fig. 6.1). Knowledge of the purchase, akin to a process of contagious diffusion, spread most quickly and directly to these adjacent areas. Many of the field laborers for the initial township surveys on the purchase lived in these nearby districts.[30] Returning workers' descriptions of the newly opened acreage may have prompted friends and neighbors to write Ellicott. Curiosity was also probably sparked in travelers who entered or left the purchase via the Genesee Road, which passed through the heart of settlement districts in which inquiries clustered. Beyond this focus, fewer inquiries came from New England and scattered areas of Pennsylvania.

Between 1804 and 1807, the well-developed clustering of settler inquiries was apparent in an elongated region east of the purchase that was aligned along turnpikes passing through the Finger Lakes region (fig. 6.2). Considerable letters arrived from the New Military Tract and adjacent acreage in central New York State, an area opened to settlement for only about ten or fifteen years but apparently already a potential source region of settlers anxious to move west. Inquiries were often clustered from particular communities, such as the central New York townships of Ovid and Marcellus, suggesting once again a process of chain migration.

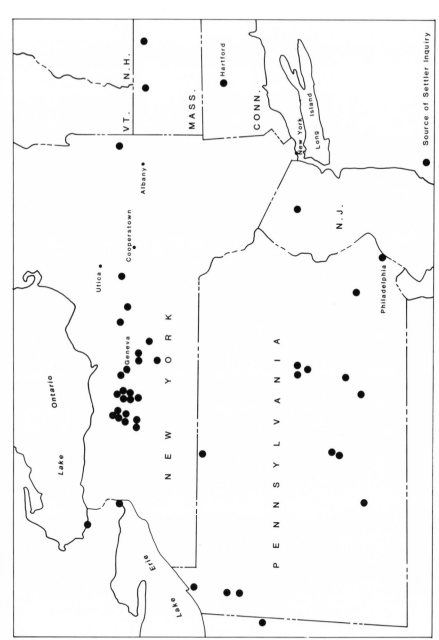

Figure 6.1 Source Areas of Settler Inquiry, 1800–1803

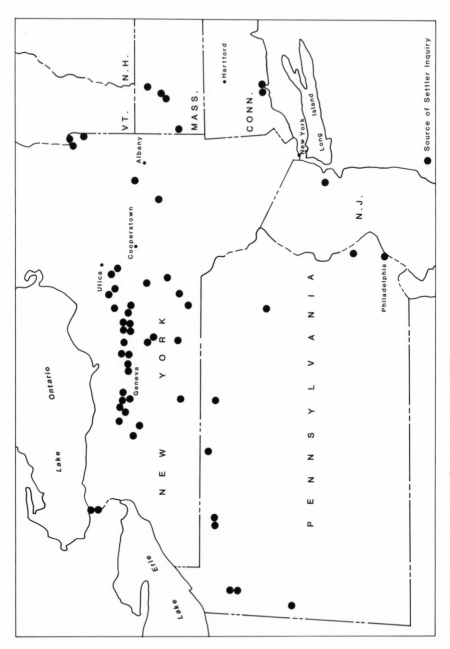

Figure 6.2 Source Areas of Settler Inquiry, 1804–1807

After 1807 the concentration of inquiries from central New York continued, although more interest from the Hudson Valley and New England was evident (fig. 6.3). Relatively fewer inquiries came from districts directly adjacent to the purchase. The bulk of interest shifted east to the New Military Tract and to the upper Mohawk Valley near Utica. The continued spatial elongation of this pattern of expanding inquiries was shaped mainly by the density of population to the east and by the sustained importance of turnpikes as information corridors. Nearly half of the letters recorded as received by Ellicott between 1808 and 1811 came from settlers who lived within ten miles of the turnpikes connecting the upper Mohawk Valley with the village of Batavia.

The third source region of considerable importance during the frontier era was Pennsylvania. Almost one-third of the letters received by Ellicott between 1800 and 1803 arrived from widely separated areas of that state. Part of this pattern might be accounted for by tracing the origins of the skilled surveyors and technical personnel on the township surveys. Many of these men came from Pennsylvania, and several of their home counties generated letters of settler inquiry. The Holland Land Company was headquartered in Philadelphia and already held similar large land tracts in Pennsylvania, which no doubt contributed further to this initial interest. In addition, Pennsylvania itself possessed relatively little good additional farmland for expansion, and so nearby Genesee Country beckoned even more brightly.

Migrants from Pennsylvania settled on the purchase in considerable numbers, especially in southwestern and south-central portions of the region.[31] In Chautauqua County, John McMahon recruited settlers from the Susquehanna Valley.[32] Several Quaker group settlements from Pennsylvania also acquired acreage in Cattaraugus and southern Erie counties.[33] Aside from a probable sprinkling of Pennsylvanians elsewhere across the purchase, the only other significant concentration was east of Buffalo in a neighborhood settled by Pennsylvanian Germans from Lancaster and Dauphin counties in 1809.[34]

Both Ellicott and Busti wanted to encourage these Pennsylvanian migrants, especially the Germans. Busti in particular recognized the potential for the southwestern purchase to generate interest among Pennsylvanians. In 1804 he urged Ellicott to speed lot surveys around Chautauqua Lake because it would surely "attract the attention of the pennsylvanians."[35] Ellicott also wanted more settlers from Pennsylvania, noting that "monied Germans from Lancaster County" were highly desirable settlers because they possessed down payment capital "as well . . . as . . . Industry and Economy."[36] Ellicott believed their greater financial resources to be a function of the larger, more profitable farms they left behind. He noted that the average New England Yankee was selling a

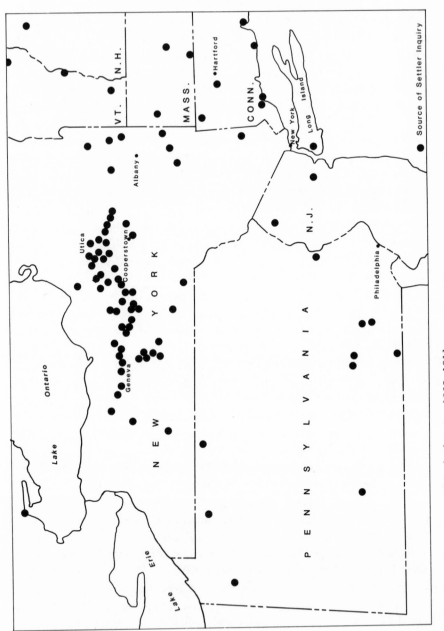

Figure 6.3 Source Areas of Settler Inquiry, 1808–1811

small fifty- or one-hundred-acre farm, while the Pennsylvanian might have three or four times that acreage.[37] Ellicott did differentiate sharply between German and Scotch-Irish Pennsylvanians, however. Clearly, he ran into some rough customers: in 1808 he was provoked to note that "a set of Pennsylvania Irishmen" visited the land office and that "it is Characteristic of those People to possess the largest share of downright Effrontery and blunt Impudence of any other, at least ever since I have had any Acquaintance with the Manners and Customs of Mankind."[38]

In addition to Yankees, New Yorkers, and Pennsylvanians, smaller numbers of settlers came from other regions. The only source area of any significance in the South was the Chesapeake Bay area of Maryland and Virginia. Ellicott received occasional visitors and new settlers from that region, although probably not as many as ventured to the land agencies just east of the Holland Land Company's acreage.[39] That district attracted interest because it was directly accessible from the Chesapeake through upper branches of the Susquehanna River and because agents on the Pulteney Purchase, especially Charles Williamson, continually attempted to sell lands to the monied planter class in the southern region.

Some migrants came from adjacent portions of Upper Canada, especially along the Lake Ontario shoreline and inland through portions of Niagara County.[40] Some were British subjects, while many others were Americans returning to native soil after trying their hand at settling west of the Niagara River. Foreign immigrants, aside from the British Canadians, were few. The western New York frontier opened several decades before the great mid-nineteenth-century rush of European immigrants. As a result, its rural cultural geography, unlike that of the ethnically diverse Midwest and Great Plains, was rather homogeneous and was dominated overwhelmingly by native-born Americans rather than by newly arrived immigrants. The initial migration flows into the region generally reflected internal transformations and forces within the new nation rather than massive inputs from overseas.

The mix of settlers arriving on the purchase during the frontier era was a logical expression of the generally westward-moving bias of North American migration that characterized a good deal of the nation's late eighteenth and early nineteenth centuries. In all likelihood, the fact that the Holland Purchase was a private rather than a public land-selling venture did not alter in any fundamental way the magnitude of this flow. Ellicott's advertisements, letters to potential settlers, and his general predilections for particularly desirable pioneers no doubt had their effect, but his liberal sales policies permitted a wide variety of frontier folk into the region.

THE PIONEER IN 1800

Those who settled in the wilds of western New York State in 1800 and soon thereafter reflected the broader personalities of migrating pioneers on the American frontier and the larger character of the nation as a whole. From the perspective of the late twentieth century, the individuals on the western New York frontier surely belonged to a generation of experimenters. These people were willing to take risks that in modern America would seem extraordinary, even foolhardy. The social and economic environment of the age encouraged the geographical mobility and occupational flexibility so typical of this group of pioneers. This was an era of experimentation in science, in government, and in the lives of common citizens. It was this creative, often unpredictable, sometimes shiftless, but always dynamic surge of settlement that peopled the Holland Purchase in its first dozen years. Every settler shaped in small and large ways the surrounding landscape and community. The experiences and contributions of these individuals, though not always matching the powerfully formative influences of such leaders as Joseph Ellicott, still compose a central chapter in our account and understanding of the developer's frontier. Without settlers, Ellicott's surveys and plans would have been to no avail.

One such pioneer was William Rumsey.[41] Rumsey was born in 1774 in Fairfield, Connecticut. Leaving that state for the New England frontier, he relocated as a young man to Hubbardtown in western Vermont and was living there in 1800 when he heard of land opportunities in the Genesee Country. He left his farm and family and, venturing west, hired on as a lot surveyor for the Holland Land Company. He found a 150-acre roadside lot to his liking just east of Batavia. By 1802 he had relocated his family from Vermont to his new acreage on the purchase and had built a small house along the Genesee Road. He also convinced a first cousin and his family to join them, and the group settled on an adjacent parcel. By the time of Rumsey's death in 1820 he had fathered ten children, a large family even for that era, and, in addition to farming, had served as a local justice of the peace, as an assessor, and as a state assemblyman. His estate holdings reveal a typical picture of the frontier farmer. Rumsey kept fourteen cattle, over a dozen hogs, three dozen sheep, an ox, and the usual assortment of farmyard fowl. His forty acres of cultivated land reflected a diverse but grain-dominated agricultural complex. He planted fifteen acres in wheat, eight in corn, seven in rye, and six in oats. In smaller plots he raised peas, buckwheat, beans, and flax.

West of Rumsey, David Eddy was an early settler in southern Erie County in the Eighteenmile Creek settlement. Eddy, also a native New Englander, came to the region from Vermont. In 1804 he traveled west with his brother Aaron, sister May, and brother-in-law Nathan. The small band built a log house, which sufficed until they had constructed a sawmill two years later. Eddy noted that locals depended considerably on the Indian economy. Settlers baked their first cornbread from grain purchased from the Indians, and early chores of black-smithing were performed by a local Indian artisan who had picked up the trade somewhere. According to Eddy, the native inhabitants "were always friendly, good neighbors. . . . they seemed pleased to have white neighbors, and there used to be much traffick between them and the new Settlers."[42] Eddy also noted his own role and the importance of other initial settlers in feeding freshly arrived pioneers. Although interregional commercial trade was not feasible, the local commercial demand for foodstuffs in such growing communities as Eddy's was often considerable and was spurred by the demand created by the stream of new migrants.[43] By 1810 Eddy had emerged as an important neighborhood leader and had served in various positions of local government. He remained in the district until his death past the age of seventy.

Reuben Wilson arrived in western New York a few years later than Rumsey or Eddy, but his prior experience and his choice of isolated acreage in the northwestern purchase certainly acquainted him with frontier life.[44] Leaving Massachusetts in 1805, Wilson first settled in Otsego County near Cooperstown before moving to Coburg in Upper Canada two years later. This was not unusual. Many Americans ventured across the border, not out of the fears that had motivated Loyalists in the 1780s but simply because land there was cheap and easily available to settlers from the United States. In fact, by the War of 1812, about 80 percent of the region's population were of American origin.[45] Wilson, however, did not remain in Upper Canada. In April 1810 he decided to cross western Lake Ontario with his wife and five children and the family of John Eastman to establish a residence near the mouth of Twelve Mile Creek in the northwestern purchase. Wilson drove his two cows around the western end of the lake to join the family on the new farm. He bought 170 acres of land with no money down and with only the promise to Ellicott that he would erect a house and begin immediately to clear his parcel. In the first year, he procured food from the nearest settlements, which were in Canada. By the second year, he had raised a small grain crop, although he was still compelled to take it across the international border for grinding. A small settlement began growing in Wilson's vicinity, thanks in no small part to his own fathering of fourteen children. The usual assortment of mills, taverns, and pioneer schools gradually ushered in the conveniences of development by 1820.

Women on the western New York frontier were a minority, especially in the years of initial settlement. Many did come, however, either as single women, usually with parents or siblings, or as wives of pioneers. The wife of John Forsyth came with her family to the Genesee River in 1790 or 1791.[46] Her father, Capt. John Ganson, had served on the Clinton-Sullivan Campaign during the Revolution and had viewed the rich possibilities of the Genesee Country. His family initially located four miles east of Avon, but in 1798 they pushed westward to open a tavern near LeRoy, just east of the Holland Purchase. She married John Forsyth in 1802 and moved onto the Dutch company tract, about five miles west of Batavia. Finally, she relocated a fourth time to Cambria Township in the northern purchase. Her mobility, even after arriving on the purchase, was representative of the era. Many settlers made initial improvements on their Dutch company acreage, sold out, and applied for new undeveloped lots.

John Young's wife accompanied her husband from Virginia in the fall of 1804.[47] They approached the purchase via Pennsylvania, facing a long and arduous journey through the rugged and "painter"-filled Allegheny Mountains. Having survived the mountain lions, they arrived at Pine Hill just north of Batavia and found that the Clark family, who had preceded them in the area, was willing to give them shelter for a few days until they could construct a temporary shanty. Their first house was windowless, only ten feet square, and roofed with a rough covering of split ash shingles. The Youngs fashioned chairs from cut logs, created a bed by stuffing a cotton bag with cattails, and procured initial cookware and crockery from Brisbane's general store at Batavia. Typical of many pioneers in the northern purchase, Young's wife contracted and recovered from a case of malaria in her first year of residence as her husband struggled to clear an initial four acres of land.

One thing is clear from these experiences. Even though the developer's frontier offered an important institutional framework that allocated land and located villages and roads, initial living conditions for many pioneers were primitive. The daily lives of these people were filled with the same chores that occupied any pioneer family. They raised children, cleared land, built houses and barns, planted and harvested crops, and tended livestock. The land company influenced these activities in important if indirect ways, but it did not fundamentally reshape the character and the drudgery of frontier life itself. That was a long-term evolutionary process accompanying changing technologies, improving accessibility, and rising standards of living. Ellicott's investments in roads, towns, and services contributed to that evolutionary process, no doubt accelerating it, but they did not eliminate or circumvent it. The initial years of struggle, typical of many North American frontier settings, were also experienced on the developer's frontier.

THE SPREAD OF SETTLEMENT

As settlers arrived on the purchase, their initial location decisions were shaped by their knowledge of the region as well as by the settlement and commercial policies of the Holland Land Company. With the planned opening of lotted townships, Ellicott hoped to guide the expansion of settlement across the purchase. The settlers, however, did not necessarily cooperate with Ellicott's plans. He found it extraordinarily difficult to anticipate their preferences and even to gauge the number of new settlers from one land-selling season to the next. One way to measure the success of Ellicott's development plan is to examine where and when pioneers settled and compare those patterns with the managed spread of the lotted townships. Ellicott's relative lack of success can be identified in those areas where lands that were lotted remained unsettled for many years.

Delimiting the extent of settled lands is a complex matter.[48] In western New York the date of the first articled sale in each town can be used to map the general spread of settlement (fig. 6.4).[49] This measure is limited—it provides no insight into the volume of initial settlement—but it does offer one way to compare Ellicott's development strategy with the decisions made by the settlers themselves.

In the northern half of the purchase, settlement came early; over a half-dozen townships surrounding Batavia were opened by 1802. Westward, selected lands along the important Buffalo-Genesee road also received attention. The expanded opportunities that came after the liberalized sales policies of 1803 are broadly reflected in numerous settled townships in the northwestern purchase and in the ninth tier of towns. Less attractive acreage in the poorly drained lands along Tonawanda Creek (the thirteenth tier of towns) and in the northeastern purchase were not settled until after 1807.

Overall, settlement was even slower in the southern purchase. More favorable lands in the southeast and southwest were occupied first. Early independent promoters in the southeast, such as Adam Hoops, Ephraim Sanford, and Joseph McClure, encouraged early sales near their parcels, while, except for John McMahon's wholesaling efforts, the southwestern district was settled simply by individual families migrating to the region. After 1810, the only major areas yet to be settled were in the south-central purchase south of Cattaraugus Creek and a few isolated districts in the far southwest. Most of these acres

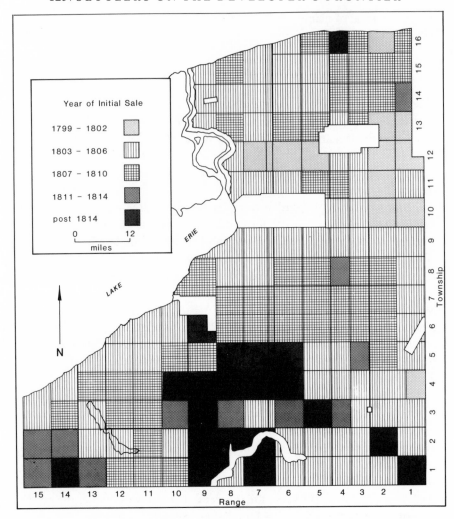

Figure 6.4 Year of Initial Sale by Township

offered so little potentially cultivable land to settlers that whole townships remained uninhabited for many years.

Mapping the lag time between initial lotting and initial settlement for each town reveals the degree to which settlers were attracted into newly lotted townships (fig. 6.5). In only a few scattered instances did settlement appear to precede formal lotting by more than one year. Settlement took place within a year of initial lotting in about 40 percent of the townships. The majority of

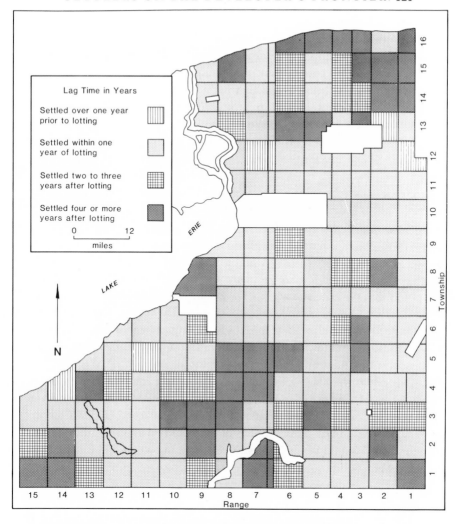

Figure 6.5 Lag Time in Years between Initial Lotting and Initial Sales

townships, however, went unsettled for two or more years following their opening by Ellicott, a broad indication of the slow pace of sales in many years and of the reluctance of pioneers, Ellicott's price initiatives notwithstanding, to select lands in unsettled areas.

Ellicott's expansion policies and the decisions of settlers to purchase land did align closely in important districts. Lands across much of the central and north-central purchase were surveyed and settled in the same season. Ellicott's persistent claims to his superiors that settlers were demanding lands in the northwestern purchase were also borne out by the quick settlement of the townships near Buffalo Creek and along parts of the Niagara River. Strong demand for lots near Lakes Erie and Chautauqua was also revealed. Patterns of settlement in the southeast were somewhat misleading, however; many townships in which lands were sold to such investors as Adam Hoops were not actually settled for a number of years.

Ellicott's lack of success was obvious in several important districts. One perennial problem area for the resident agent was the north-central and northeastern purchase between Tonawanda Creek and Lake Ontario. Some of these towns, especially those along the creek itself, had broad expanses of poorly drained land, a fact that had emerged clearly in Ellicott's initial township surveys of the region in 1798 and 1799. To the northeast, however, the initial township reconnaissance was quite favorable, and Ellicott had high hopes that acreage along and south of Lake Ontario would settle rapidly. He opened the district early but found few takers. Many were convinced that "lake fever" was associated with the area, and why increase one's risks in an already challenging frontier setting? Ellicott's strategy to open isolated townships along the Pennsylvania Road in 1805 also failed. In fact, even though Ellicott wisely delayed the survey of many of the townships in the south-central purchase, once the lotting was initiated, little demand for the acreage was apparent.

One critical variable over which Ellicott had little control was the number of new settlers. Demand for land fluctuated widely from one year to the next and was a source of constant consternation for the resident agent. Ellicott's success in managing the growth of the settlement depended on a steady influx of new pioneers. Although, in general, sales increased from 1800 to 1811, settlement grew in three rather distinctive surges, each separated by times of slowed activity. Ellicott's development plans were continually complicated by these fluctuations.

The first real surge of buying did not come until the summer of 1803.[50] It continued into the fall, and Ellicott related the pickup in activity directly to the rapid expansion of lotted townships on the purchase. By February of the following year, Ellicott hired another clerk to help with the now hectic pace of the land office. With the arrival of summer, however, the general level of activity had again slowed, with the exception of brisk sales along Lake Erie. Another wave of new settlers arrived in 1805, and the influx continued throughout the following year. In November 1805 sales were "middling brisk," and by the following spring Ellicott noted that the number of interested settlers in the region was twice that of any previous year.[51] Ellicott sold a record 60,000 acres in 1805, compared with a meager 4,500 acres in 1801.

A second slowdown hit the region suddenly in mid-1807 and persisted through much of 1808. Much of the decline was related, no doubt, to rising tension between the United States and Britain. With a potential enemy just across the Niagara River, settlers understandably were reluctant to locate in the region. Indian troubles in the vicinity of Detroit may have been an added concern. Sales reached their nadir in the spring of 1808 and then began to rebound slowly as war fears eased. The initial focus of renewed activity was in the southwest, but soon Ellicott reported brisk sales across the entire region. By 1809 the pace increased further, and both 1810 and 1811 were considered boom years.[52]

In March of 1811, "the office [was] thronged each day and week from morning till night with land purchasers, land jobbers, and land speculators," and in that single month, Ellicott reported as many sales as in all of 1808.[53] Much of the increased activity was in the previously shunned northern townships, where a new illegal trade thrived between local settlers and Montreal- and Niagara-based Canadian buyers of officially embargoed produce, lumber, and potash. The large volume of trade continued after it was again legalized in May 1810.[54] The crash came a year later; the War of 1812 marked a sudden and decisive end to the early spread of settlement on the purchase. By early 1812 not only were new sales few and far between but panicked settlers were evacuating from much of the purchase, especially in the west. On June 12, 1812, Congress declared a state of war to exist between the United States and Great Britain. Military clashes along the Niagara River commenced in July and culminated in the burning of the village of Buffalo in December 1813.

By the eve of the war, much of the purchase had seen at least a thin veneer of settlement. The Census of 1810 reported over fifteen thousand persons on the purchase. Approximately 25 percent of the settlers resided in the southern half of the purchase, while the remaining 75 percent lived in the northern half. A general idea of the districts that received the focus of settler interest just before the war can be reconstructed from mapping sales for 1811. Ten or more articled sales were made in 39 of the 162 townships.[55] Using this figure as a guide to the townships of most rapid settlement, five distinct growth areas of the purchase that included established areas of population as well as emerging regions of new importance can be suggested (fig. 6.6).

In the northern purchase, a broad, east-to-west corridor of settlement continued to be the central focus of development (fig. 6.6.A). From Ellicott's

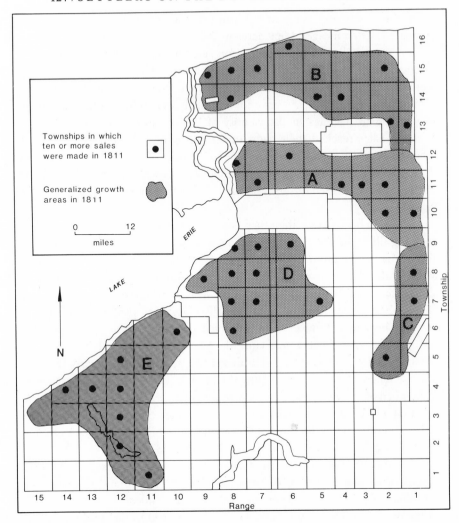

Figure 6.6 Growth Areas, 1811

earliest development plans, the corridor from Batavia to Buffalo was of great importance. Townships southwest of Batavia and north and east of Buffalo also saw considerable new activity. Small villages, such as Attica in Township 10 Range 2, grew rapidly and acted as local frontier service centers.[56] A growth area emerged in the northern purchase in response to greatly increased trade with Canadian markets (fig. 6.6.B).[57] Suddenly, lots Ellicott might not have been able to give away in earlier years became strategically important because of their proximity to Lake Ontario. The worst of the swampy tracts adjacent to Ton-awanda Creek, however, continued to see little buying activity.[58]

Several districts of rapid settlement were noted south of the tenth tier of townships. One focus of interest was located near the north-south road in the eastern purchase that opened in 1805 (fig. 6.6.C). The village of Warsaw in Township 8 Range 1 acted both as a key local service center in this area and as the meeting place for a newly created political town unit. In the western purchase interest continued between Buffalo and Cattaraugus creeks, and Eighteenmile Creek, south of the Buffalo Creek Reservation, became the destination for many new residents (fig. 6.6.D).[59] Most settlers here were from Vermont or other sections of New England. Several groups of Vermont and New Hampshire Quakers settled between 1807 and 1811 in Township 9 Ranges 7 and 8.[60] Another group of Quakers from Philadelphia settled just east of the Cattaraugus Reserve.[61] Finally, in the southwest, land in townships along Lake Erie and in the interior continued to be sought actively during 1811 (fig. 6.6.E). In 1810 this region contained over two thousand inhabitants.[62] Two villages served as focal points of development: Mayville, the company village, grew steadily, and Fredonia village, on Canadaway Creek in Township 5 Range 12, was a second center of activity.[63]

These patterns suggest that Ellicott's success in shaping the spread of settlement was a function of decisions made by the settlers themselves. The development of the tract did not always mirror Ellicott's expectations or desires in either its intensity or its direction. Sometimes with impressive foresight and sometimes with unfounded optimism, Ellicott with varying good fortune did, at least, provide a rational blueprint for settlement across the region, and his ongoing penchant for comprehensive management continued to reflect the key role of the land agent and of his retail land policy in making the developer's frontier. It remained for settlers to take possession of the land and to create communities on the western New York wilderness.

LIFE IN AN UPSTATE VILLAGE

Frontier communities in the early nineteenth-century North American back-country offered the rudiments of civilization, but early residents could also attest to the rough-edged character of settlements. Western New York villages were no exception. They provided basic services and supporting social institutions, although many luxuries of the time were conspicuously absent. Such was the case both in villages platted and assisted by Ellicott and in those that evolved independently and without direct company assistance. Although the developer played a part in the growth of every village, company sponsored or independent, by lotting and selling land, building roads, and perhaps offering nearby services, even in such major company settlements as Batavia and Buffalo, the developer's impact on the routine chores and challenges of daily life was minimal, and settlers succeeded or failed from their own efforts and fortunes. The developer provided the infrastructure for settlement in broad and fundamental ways, but he could not control every element of frontier village life or eliminate its uncertainties.

To a pioneer riding into Batavia in late 1801, the initial, albeit untidy, impress of both developer and settler was everywhere in evidence. The village, recently surveyed by company employees, still lay in the midst of a wilderness. Major streets were being cleared of trees and shrubs.[64] Piles of logs and underbrush gave the scene an unkempt and certainly unfinished look. The ten or twelve structures in the village were generally one-story log buildings: a company-sponsored sawmill was still under construction near the center of town.[65] Many village lots were undeveloped and uncleared, indistinguishable from the forest. Only the dozen or so lots near the center of town had been sold, and the amount of cleared land on those was probably minimal. As November snows began to fall around the hamlet in late 1801, it was still a small, isolated frontier outpost.

By 1805 settlers arriving from the east saw a considerably more impressive scene. Most lots in the village had been sold, and a good number had seen some improvements. After a year or two, typically four to eight acres had been cleared on a forty-acre village lot.[66] Many of the thirty houses were wood-frame buildings, although some log dwellings still stood. White paint ornamented several frame homes, stores, and other businesses.[67] Small gardens of corn, beans, potatoes, and other fruits and vegetables grew behind many houses. Wandering livestock added life and no small nuisance to the village scene—a lack of fences made the animals difficult to control. The large number of roads that converged near the village center had been much improved from their overgrown state in 1801. More brush had been removed, and village residents were in charge of maintaining portions of the roads that bordered their improved parcels. The village was now a county town, and a large attractive frame courthouse sat at the center of the settlement.[68]

During the next five years, the village and the entire purchase experienced considerable, although uneven, growth. By 1810 most newly arrived residents would have reached the community through a now densely settled rural district that bordered the Genesee Road. Over fifty mostly wood-frame houses, interspersed by a few finer brick buildings, accommodated several hundred residents.[69] More lots had been improved, and some houses were surrounded by decorative gardens that began to soften the severe, chopped frontier landscape. Ellicott noted that many houses "stand in railed Enclosures handsomely covered with a Sward of English Grass, Clover etc. with Trees of various Descriptions such as the Lombardy Poplar, Sugar tree, Elm, Tamerack, Spruce, etc., planted with some Taste in and about those Enclosures, which are beginning to form shades from the Heat of the Sun in Summer."[70] Although Ellicott's allusions to the widespread art of ornamental planting may be overstated, the decade of 1800–10 saw considerable change for those arriving and living in the settlement.

After securing a lot, a villager's first order of business was to build a structure to house a family and perhaps a business. In the first two years of the center's existence logs were procured from a nearby pinery, and, probably with the help of friends and neighbors, a settler would erect a rough-hewn one-story log dwelling in a small clearing near the front of his lot.[71] By 1802 frame boards from the company sawmill offered settlers an alternative to the one-room log cabins of the first years. Chopping and clearing a portion of the lot was another early and important task. There were straightforward financial incentives to clearing land in company-developed villages such as Batavia: Ellicott granted only provisional sales contracts to purchasers until they had begun improvements.[72] In all centers, however, land clearing was a necessary, slow, and exhausting process.[73] In the case of Batavia, it was a rare settler indeed who was able to chop and clear even half of his granted lot within five years of purchase. Enough land for a house and a small garden sufficed for many.

Daily life was filled with the household chores of premodern existence. Furniture and clothing were still widely homemade in 1800.[74] Table fare was ample but simple, and meal preparation was time-consuming.[75] Corn was ground into meal for cornbread or prepared as hominy. Wheat and potatoes were also consumed in considerable quantities. Settlers prepared beef, bacon, salt pork, and mutton, although venison and bear occasionally offered important alternatives and geese provided a dependable source of poultry. Beans, squash, peas, and fruit, especially apples, supplemented settler diets. Tea and coffee were not inexpensive, and cheaper cider was often a preferred alternative. Many settlers consumed beer and liquor in generous quantities. In fact, by 1810, Genesee County alone was home to eight distilleries and one brewery.[76]

Five economic services operating in Batavia and in every village its size helped to make life easier. The general store was a critical repository of frontier necessaries. Everything from groceries and dry goods to liquor, lard, and leghorn bonnets was sold.[77] The store was the frontier consumer's connection to the outside world. James Brisbane, a native of Philadelphia and Batavia's first storekeeper, stocked his shelves with goods from faraway Albany and New York.[78] Brisbane acted as a key middleman in the neighborhood, trading his store goods for locally produced crops and products in the cash-poor frontier economy.[79] Brisbane's business was supplemented by a second store opened in 1803 by Timothy Burt of Canandaigua and Richard Stoddard of LeRoy.[80] The pair built a small frame building and provided some competition for Brisbane's operation. By 1810, Ellicott reported that there were "four large Stores of Merchandise, who now afford many articles at the New-York prices."[81]

A second service present in every frontier village of any size was a milling facility to provide frame boards and ground grain. Newly arrived settlers took immediate advantage of a sawmill to procure boards for house and business, preferring frame construction over log. If they raised corn or wheat on their plot they also used the local gristmill. In Batavia, somewhat unusually, both the sawmill and the gristmill were completely funded by the land company. In other villages, either Ellicott provided some assistance to private millers or entrepreneurs developed such facilities independently. Regardless of the source of capital, these services became a standard feature of the frontier village's economic landscape, often within two or three years of initial settlement.[82] In Batavia, the sawmill was completed by late 1801, while because of construction problems the gristmill was not finished until 1804.

Blacksmiths and carpenters were everpresent in the frontier village. Settlers needed their services for many tasks that demanded more materials or skills than they might have had themselves. With his anvil and forge the blacksmith created the nails, household tools, iron tires, and horseshoes that held together and transported the pioneer community. Just as important were the carpenters, joiners, and coopers who, in the wooden age, crafted cider barrels, butter tubs, wagons, and house frames for village folk. William Wood from nearby Avon was Batavia's first smithy, locating in the village in 1802.[83] By that year at least five carpenters were in the town busily erecting buildings and providing necessary household goods. One was Isaac Sutherland, who left his Dutchess County, New York, home in 1800, bound for Upper Canada.[84] He never got there, choosing instead to remain in western New York and, in 1801, to settle in Batavia.

A fifth economic function of undeniable import was performed by local taverners. These essential folk were sprinkled along every main road of the village. They provided beer and liquor to quench the often considerable thirsts of the pioneer population. Often they accommodated overnight travelers. Taverns were meeting places in the village for permanent settlers and interlopers to exchange important information, to say nothing of braggadocios, tall tales, and whiskey-inspired speculations.[85] Incoming news was liberally distilled and dispersed from the tavern's eating and drinking tables, where strangers fresh from the Hudson Valley or the Ohio Country parlayed with the local folk, filling them with the latest rumors from east and west. Often the tavern served as a formal place of local assembly: town and county meetings convened amid the bottles of grog and rum, and religious services were even conducted there if an itinerant missionary happened through.[86] Abel Rowe built Batavia's first log tavern in 1801.[87] The place quickly became a community focal point, and Ellicott used the site to house early company workers.[88] By 1810, four taverns served local Batavia residents and passersby.[89]

In addition to these five services, other amenities made life in Batavia more tolerable. Within the first decade of settlement, David McCraken served as the community's physician and druggist. McCracken was "a Physician of the old school . . . affable and familiar in his manners . . . with a ready wit, ingenuity, and peculiar tact of inspiring in his patients courage and confidence."[90] Originally from Washington County in eastern New York, McCracken ventured west in 1801 and thereafter consoled if not cured Batavia's pioneer stock. An especially debilitating and deadly malady was malaria, whose cause and treatment was beyond McCracken's ken. Known as "ague," "fever," or "Genesee fever," it killed many in the fledgling community. In 1805 and 1806 malaria was so widespread that McCracken ran out of medicine and had to appeal to Ellicott for assistance.[91]

Migrating from nearby Bloomfield, Stephen Russell was another key person in early village life. Russell doubled as taverner and tailor and was one of the first pioneers to apply for land in the new settlement.[92] Down the street, Simeon Cummings operated a harness shop and saddlery, performing the community's leatherworking tasks in its early years.[93] Cummings also served as a local judge in the village before moving south to Wyoming County after the War of 1812.[94] Other urban services included local brewers and distillers who supplied taverns and stores with suitable libations. Boot- and shoemakers, brickmakers and bricklayers, printers, hatters, and weavers also ornamented the local service economy by 1810 and gradually freed the village from its early bonds of isolation.[95] Occasional Yankee peddlers who wandered through the settlement loudly hawking their tinware and wooden clocks added periodic variety to the everyday supplies available at the general store.

The social dimension of village life focused around several institutions. At the center was the nuclear family and links to other nearby relatives and friends. Beyond that, informal social gatherings were probably of greater importance than the formal institutions of church and school in the frontier era. Concerning the role of religion in western New York, one early historian of the Presbyterian church noted, "Mr. Ellicott disregarded the Sabbath, and was hostile to religious institutions. . . . it was a common observation, that Sabbath-day did not extend westward beyond the Genesee River."[96] When Joseph Avery, a member of the Berkshire Missionary Society, arrived in 1805 to preach, he notified settlers of his planned evening lecture, "but nobody came."[97] A year later, Rev. Roswell Burrows called the entire region a "Wilderness land that is devoid of much of any kind of religion."[98] General Agent Busti was concerned about the lack of permanent churches in the town, arguing that "the casual service of some transient preachers" added little to the community.[99] Finally, in 1811 the Hampshire Missionary Society of Massachusetts formally incorporated a Congregational church in the village, and others followed later in the decade.[100] The evidence suggests, however, that before the War of 1812 formal church institutions did not perform important social functions in the frontier community.

Early schools did provide some social focus, especially for village youth. By 1802 Ellicott reported that "a School has been opened, and on the first Day of Meeting 25 Scholars were found to compose the School."[101] It is likely that the first school for local children was a one-story log house, cold, poorly lighted, and filled with rough, splinter-prone benches for seats. The fundamentals of reading, writing, and mathematics were stressed in the four- or six-month sessions, and the teachers, often sincere if naive graduates of similar institutions, had "no appliances, except the rod," to smooth the surely rough path to knowledge.[102] Still, these frontier schools provided important educational and social functions in the pioneer community.

The most important social institutions in the village were probably of a less formal nature. Many tasks such as building homes, erecting barns, and harvesting crops were performed by community "bees," loose assemblages of neighbors who helped one another when work was required.[103] Such gatherings often evolved into dancing, eating, and drinking affairs where neighbors could catch up on the latest news and youngsters could court their sweethearts. Daily or weekly gatherings of men at taverns and mills or women at quilting and sewing parties provided additional, usually sex-segregated, social outlets in the frontier community. The result was a life made slightly less tedious and a chance, if only briefly, to share the burdens and fruits of pioneer existence.

The land company's role in shaping many of these settler institutions was peripheral. The developer's frontier offered a setting for communities that then evolved as expressions of its pioneers. The result was a frontier society made possible by the original designs of land agents and their key institutional investments but then textured and elaborated by the efforts and predilections of the settlers themselves. The landscape mirrored this development; its broad, sweeping lineaments and structure were an articulation of land company policies, while its detailed look and personality were a function of how individual settlers cleared land, arranged farmsteads, and built their houses and barns.

CHAPTER 7

The Changing Frontier Landscape

Our human landscape is our unwitting
autobiography, reflecting our tastes, our values,
our aspirations, and even our fears, in tangible,
visible form.

—*Pierce F. Lewis*

Developer, traveler, and settler witnessed the
changing frontier scene from varied perspectives. Their perceptions form a picture of a
rapidly evolving frontier cultural landscape.
The developer's view reflected a need to shape
and control the advance of settlement, to give it
an order and simplicity that maximized company profits and minimized its costs. The cadastral landscape of property lines best symbolized this attachment to design, and its
expression across the face of the region was
exclusively the developer's doing. The traveler
held a second view of the landscape. The words
of the interloper, from the early recorded tra-

verses of French fur traders to the more mundane narratives of early nineteenth-century travelers, translate into a view of landscape that, although often experienced for only a few days, at its best, captured the look of a roadside scene or the feel of a village tavern in insightful, enriching ways. The settler viewed landscape in a third way. In innumerable localities, western New York pioneers both created and experienced landscape change. Their perceptions of the visual scene, woven into biographies, were best articulated in the daily chores of frontier existence, in acres slowly cleared, in houses and barns raised and improved, in crops planted, tended, and harvested. That most pioneers wrote little of such experiences in such self-conscious ways does not mean that they lacked a close relationship to the land and to the recognized need to reshape its wild abundance into a domesticated landscape of farms and villages. This experience with landscape, although affected everywhere by the developer's hand, was crafted ultimately by the settler.

FASHIONING THE CADASTRAL LANDSCAPE: THE DEVELOPER'S VIEW

From the developer's perspective, the most self-conscious and direct contribution to the shaping of the frontier landscape was undoubtedly the lot survey geometry that marked every township, no matter how isolated its situation or indifferent its lands. By 1811, Ellicott had commenced such surveys in all but seven township units. In general, his approach reflected a mix of regularity and flexibility, a fusion of varying surveying traditions that would minimize expenditures and confusion and maximize company sales and profits. Almost all of his lot units were rectangular, and almost all displayed a bias toward cardinal alignment. As resident agent, he was given the freedom by his superiors to use his own judgment regarding the size and shape of the lots surveyed: Busti instructed Ellicott that towns were "to be laid out and put up for sale in forms of such dimensions as you may think most convenient."[1]

The Rural Lot Landscape

Ellicott did have his own ideas for an initial lotting system, and his preliminary framework resembled, to a remarkable degree, the federal township survey plan of thirty-six lots per town unit (fig. 7.1).[2] As early as 1798, Chief Surveyor Ellicott had envisaged thirty-six 640-acre lots per township in a manner almost identical to the well-known "sections" of the federal system. Only his proposed lot numbering system departed slightly from the national plan. The pattern was brought one step closer to reality in late 1798 or early 1799 when, after many of

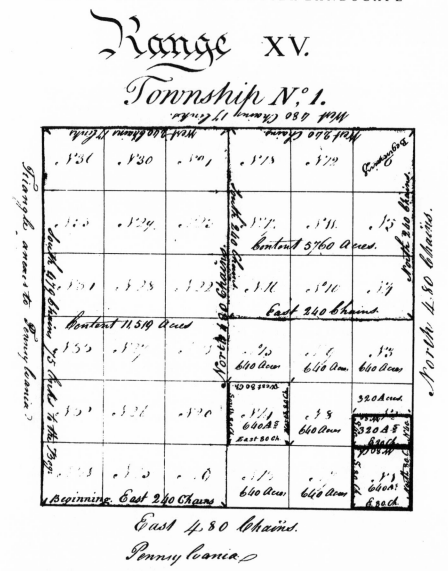

Figure 7.1 Hypothetical Thirty-Six-Lot Township

the township perimeters had been established, Ellicott submitted preliminary maps of their boundaries, along with his planned, but still hypothetical, lot lines already sketched in.[3]

During the spring of 1799, however, Ellicott discarded the thirty-six-lot pattern in favor of a new system designed to give all farms access to at least one road. The size of the standard lot unit was also reduced from 640 to 120 acres. Both shifts clearly demonstrated Ellicott's increased concern for attracting the small retail buyer onto the purchase. The plan resembled the lotting systems used across much of nearby Upper Canada, where planned roads were incorporated into the initial lot landscape and each lot fronted on a road.[4] Ellicott believed that the roads would be a positive selling point and would enhance the value of every lot. Each town was to be divided into sixteen "sections," or "tracts," and each section into twelve rectangular 120-acre lots, one-quarter of a mile wide and three-quarters of a mile long (fig. 7.2). Planned roads would run east to west along every section line and north to south along alternate section lines.

The system was put to use in township lotting projects between 1800 and 1803 (fig. 7.3). Several problems, however, were soon apparent. The dense network of roads that had served as part of the original inspiration for the plan

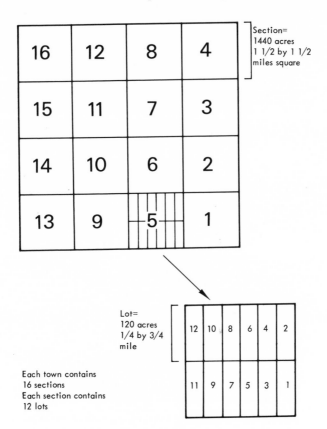

Figure 7.2 Ellicott Lotting System

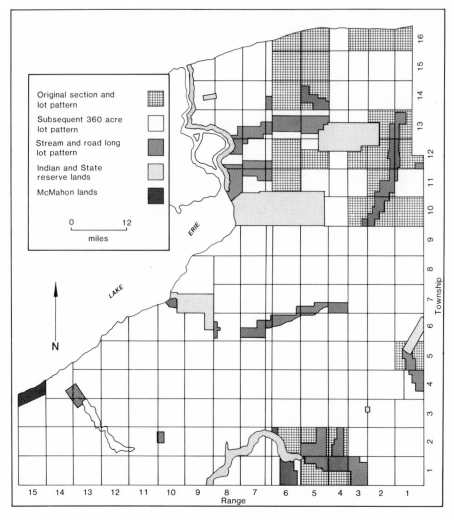

Figure 7.3 Lot Survey Types

evidently proved too costly because that aspect of the plan was eliminated. The system of small 120-acre lots also caused problems. Some surveyors simply made repeated and gross errors as they attempted to lay out the lots on the wilderness landscape. The system was costly, too, especially after the lackluster sales of 1800 and 1801. There was also the confusing problem of lot numbering for both settler and developer. Bookkeeping and land selection were made more complicated by giving lots in different sections of a township the same numbers.

As Ellicott later lamented, "the Addition of Sections adds much to Complexity as well as Perplexity."[5]

As early as the summer of 1802, a new unit of lot survey began to appear in Ellicott's descriptions of the initial system. He offered price reductions to settlers if they purchased three lots (a quarter-section) instead of a single lot. He described to a settler the procedure of "laying the Township out into Sections Quarters and Lots, and that a Section would contain as near as may be, 1440 acres, then consequently the quarter of a Section would contain 360 acres or thereabouts."[6] The reference to a quarter-section of 360 acres came at a time when there was still no formal recognition of this survey unit on the landscape. A quarter-section was simply three adjacent 120-acre lots.

The following year, however, Busti suggested that Ellicott's 360-acre quarter-section become the standard unit of a new, simpler, and less expensive lotting system.[7] Ellicott agreed, and townships surveyed that year began to reflect the new pattern. Under the new lotting geometry, each township contained sixty-four 360-acre lots, without any reference to sections. Each lot was a square parcel, each side three-fourths of a mile long (fig. 7.4). With some

64	56	48	40	32	24	16	8
63	55	47	39	31	23	15	7
62	54	46	38	30	22	14	6
61	53	45	37	29	21	13	5
60	52	44	36	28	20	12	4
59	51	43	35	27	19	11	3
58	50	42	34	26	18	10	2
57	49	41	33	25	17	9	1

Lot=
360 acres
3/4 by 3/4
miles square

Each town contains
64 lots

Figure 7.4 Ellicott Lotting System after 1803

departures, this system became the dominant lot geometry for the remainder of the purchase (see fig. 7.3).

Ellicott adopted a flexible policy of lot subdivision that allowed settlers to purchase only portions of the surveyed 120-acre or 360-acre units. He did discourage subdivided boundaries that were not aligned with cardinal directions.[8] He also discouraged lot subdivision lines that did not extend completely across the lot because such lines made the remaining irregular parcel more difficult to sell.[9] Overall, however, settlers were remarkably free to choose the size of their own farms.

Ellicott's lot survey geometry displayed elements of two distinctive surveying traditions. Ellicott saw the virtue of employing a basic, regular pattern of 120- or 360-acre parcels across entire townships. But he also saw the value in varying the pattern where departures seemed logical and consistent with the goals of spurring settlement and maximizing company profits. This flexibility manifested itself most clearly in the use of a long lot survey geometry that adapted to particular streams, in altered lots adjacent to major roads, and in other reoriented lot patterns along lake shores. Busti agreed with Ellicott's departures, insisting that "it would not be wise to deprive a number of lots from the advantages which they may derive from roads or Water, on account of a Slavish Submission to any arbitrary rule of regularity."[10] In other words, a Cartesian grid was fine unless it interfered with the rational business of selling land.

Ellicott had a variety of reasons for adopting a long lotting strategy in the vicinity of creeks.[11] One virtue of fronting lots on creeks was that it gave more settlers accessibility to waters of the creek. Without altering the standard 120- or 360-acre lot geometries, "it would frequently happen that the Creek would pass through the Middle of a Lot and thereby give that Lot all the Water . . . consequently render those Lots deprived of the Advantage of the Water unsaleable and less valuable."[12] Ellicott therefore felt free to alter the regular pattern, laying out the lots "when there are large Creeks in such a Manner as to front on said Creeks, and not to cross them, and to extend back from the Creek 3/4 of a Mile to a Mile, and generally of the Breadth of 1/4 of a Mile" (fig. 7.5).[13]

Another motivation for long lotting was especially evident in the southern purchase, where premium lands were concentrated linearly in long, narrow alluvial valleys surrounded by steep hills. To guard against early settlers taking all their acreage only along the creeks, thereby rendering the adjacent hilly tracts less valuable, Ellicott insisted that buyers of the prime bottomlands take their acreage in the form of long lots. The lots would thus include both premium acreage along the watercourse and poorer lands in the nearby hill country. As

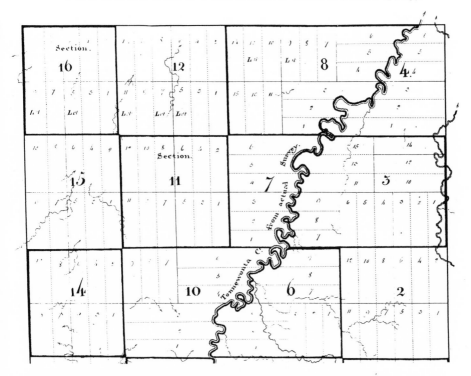

Figure 7.5 Long Lotting on the Holland Purchase, Township 11, Range 2

Ellicott explained the theory to Busti, "If they should sell the Flesh without annexing the Ribs and Back-bones thereto, I fancy it will be some Time before they will find a Purchaser for the Skeleton."[14] Thus, Ellicott's flexibility on the developer's frontier landscape effectively increased the number of valuable stream-fronting lots and raised the value of adjoining hill lands as well.

Ellicott was hardly the first American land developer to incorporate long lots along rivers, roads, and lakes.[15] The North American landscape is replete with other examples of the long lot pattern in areas ranging from the arid lands of Texas and New Mexico to the fertile lowlands of America's eastern states and of Canada's Saint Lawrence River Valley.[16] There were many examples in up-state New York.[17] In the Hudson River Valley colonial land commissioners insisted that land grants not extend along the length of a river but "into the mainland, that thereby the said Grantees may have each a convenient share of what accommodations the Said River may afford."[18] In the company's own central New York lands, both the Cazenovia and Adgate purchases contained examples of long lotting along local streams and rivers.[19]

Ellicott's decision to use long lots was significant because it contrasted, more than in the rest of the state, with the prevailing degree of conscious regularity he used in the survey of standard lot units. In both township and lot geometries, Ellicott's agency came the closest of any upstate land development to recognizing the principles of regularity and simplicity so well exemplified by the new federal system in the Ohio Country. Still, Ellicott opted to vary the pattern where he believed the departures on the landscape would increase the value of lands.

In five areas of the purchase, long lots along streams were a significant and conscious departure from the prevailing lotting systems (see fig. 7.3). There were also a number of smaller, more localized examples of stream long lotting. Long lots were probably first used along upper Tonawanda Creek in Township 11 Range 2 when the town was surveyed in 1801. In that year's annual report to his superiors, Ellicott first noted the utility of altering the prevailing lot pattern along streams.[20] The following year, a number of long lots were laid out along the Allegheny River and several of its major tributaries in the southern purchase.[21] Early lot surveying in this isolated section was necessary because Adam Hoops was anxious to purchase over twenty thousand acres in the area. In 1803, when a Baptist group settlement under the direction of Ephraim Sanford was established in Township 5 Range 1, long lots along the upper Genesee River were again used by Ellicott to sell both bottomland and upland parcels.[22]

Long lots were also used in some areas surveyed after 1803 under the new 360-acre lot system. The riverine lots continued to be of roughly the same dimensions as the long lots that had accompanied the old lotting system: one-quarter of a mile wide fronting the stream and approximately three-quarters of a mile extending into the woods. The system was used along many miles of Cattaraugus Creek in the southcentral purchase (fig. 7.3).[23] Lower Tonawanda Creek between the Tonawanda Indian Reserve and the Niagara River was lotted in similar fashion. Ellicott also provided for long lots on small portions of Connewongo Creek (Township 2 Range 10), Ellicott's Creek (Township 11 Range 7), and Black Creek (Township 12 Range 1).

Major roads were another focus of Ellicott's flexible lotting policy. For this reason, road construction and the spread of the lot surveys were clearly linked. Final lotting could not occur in some townships before the main road locations were clearly marked. In some cases, Ellicott admitted, lot surveys would need to be altered "to accommodate lots with . . . Roads that are laid out and opened after the Surveys."[24] Where possible, however, Ellicott agreed with General Agent Busti on the "usefullness of proceeding almost with equal steps in making the surveys and opening the roads."[25] Along the Buffalo Road, Ellicott delayed lotting of townships in 1801 until the road was marked.[26] When a road was laid north of Batavia, however, earlier lots laid out had "to be changed as to front on said . . . Road."[27] In all, Ellicott confined major long lot modifications on roads to the early period of surveys, altering lots only along the Genesee-Buffalo (Township 12 Ranges 1 and 7, Township 11 Range 8), Oak Orchard (Townships 12 and 13 Range 1), and Niagara (Township 14 Ranges 5 and 7) roads (see fig. 7.3). Throughout the purchase, however, where roads did not run along cardinal directions, Ellicott typically chose to make minor changes in the lot fronts adjacent to the road, causing the lot lines to border along rather than to cross the roads (fig. 7.6).

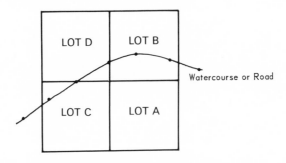

Theoretical Pattern: No variation along roads
or watercourses

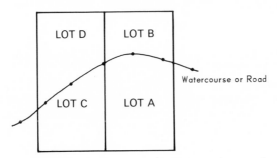

Modified Pattern: Actual variations along roads
or watercourses

Figure 7.6 Minor Lot Alterations along Watercourses and Roads

Figure 7.7 Lot Orientation near Lake Erie on McMahon Purchase

One sizable instance of lot reorientation along a lakefront occurred in
Township 3 Range 15. Ellicott allowed the deviation because it was the only way
to sell the 9,000-acre tract in a wholesale deal he arranged with two Pennsylvanian speculators, James McMahon and George Dull.[28] Ellicott wanted to bound
the tract with cardinally oriented lines, but the buyers insisted that the parcel be
surveyed "to a Southwestern or Northeastern Direction parallel to the general
Course of the Lake bounding said Township."[29] When Busti was informed of
the changes, he complained to Ellicott, telling him not to make other such
contracts. By the time Busti's complaints reached Ellicott, however, the landscape had been transformed: the angled lot pattern was in place (fig. 7.7).[30]

The Urban Lot Landscape

Just as Ellicott's lotting geometry displayed his capacity for flexibility, the urban morphology of his platted villages reflected his ability to vary plans according to the local demands of site and situation and to borrow from and adapt earlier principles of urban design that reflected well-established traditions of town founding in eastern North America and elsewhere in upstate New York.

Batavia took the shape of an unusual six-sided polygon (fig. 7.8). A series of long lots fronted on Tonawanda Creek and on a number of main roads. Typically, lots contained forty acres of land, fronted on a 330-foot strip of road or creek, and extended back for a distance of about one mile. The generous size of the lots, according to Ellicott, was "a sufficiency of Land . . . to raise Bread and support a Family."[31] It was a plan designed to produce a landscape of mixed land uses: gardens and small farms would be interspersed with and physically

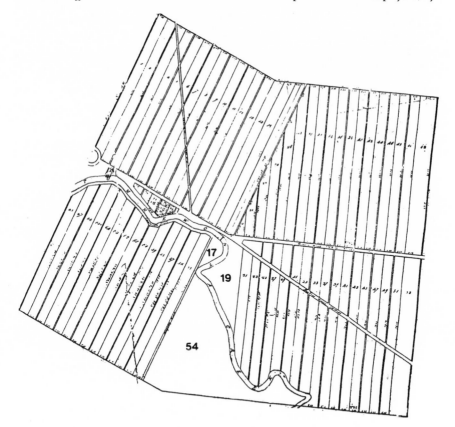

Figure 7.8 Plan of Batavia

adjacent to homes and businesses. The plat was "lain out on the Plan of Canandaigua . . . in 40-acre lots 20 Perches fronting on the Street and 320 in Depth."[32] Indeed, the village of Canandaigua east of the purchase was dominated by forty-acre long lots, although frequently the ten acres fronting on the street were subdivided into small five-acre parcels.[33] No attempt was made to orient either the village boundaries or the interior lots to the cardinal points of the compass. Because of the unusual configuration of the plat, many lots were quite irregular in shape, revealing that Ellicott was willing to sacrifice the simplicity of cardinal rectangularity for the sake of fronting the lots on the main roads that converged on the site from every direction.

Initial company-sponsored improvements shaped the landscape of the village. Ellicott set aside space for public use. A "public square" was established at a major road junction, and the designated spot soon became the site of the company-financed Genesee County courthouse.[34] Another larger area near the creek was reserved as a common grazing ground and for the development of a company mill works. In addition, Ellicott donated a few acres for a village cemetery and had the lot fenced and cleared. Main thoroughfares were also cleared at company expense, and bridges were built across Tonawanda Creek.

Street names were another element in the laying out of the village landscape. The main avenues were named Genesee Street, Big Tree Street, Allegany Road, and Ontario Road; in straightforward fashion, they indicated the significant destinations of the respective routes. The street names, as well as the entire geometry of the plan, emphasized the village's role as the center of a developing regional road network. It was an appropriate design for a center that served as the administrative focus for the purchase and a convenient stopping point for travelers and potential settlers.

If Batavia reflected the functional, practical side of Ellicott in the planning of a regional center, New Amsterdam surely revealed the more baroque leanings of his personality and development strategy. The village center focused on a series of elaborate, radiating streets, all imposed on an underlying grid (fig. 7.9).[35] For this reason, the plan has been compared to the design of Washington, D.C. In particular, the placement of outer lot 104 resembled the positioning of the White House in the nation's capital.[36] Both lots were much more prominent than surrounding parcels, and both were positioned at the center of a radial network of roads. Additional support for this comparison is suggested by the fact that Ellicott's brother Andrew contributed to the design of the capital's layout and that Ellicott himself worked on surveys of Washington, D.C., in the early 1790s before he was employed by the Dutch.[37] In New Amsterdam Ellicott noted that lot 104 occupied "the handsomest building spot in the Village, and

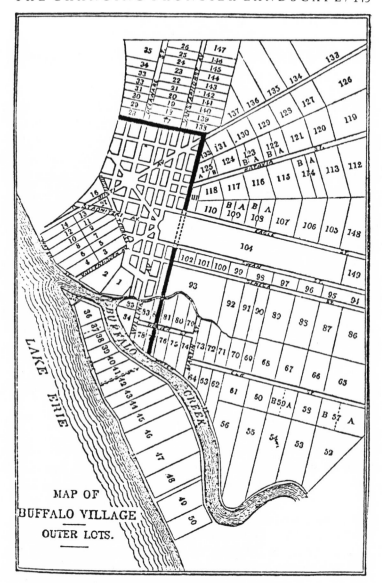

Figure 7.9 Plan of New Amsterdam, or Buffalo

the several large Avenues so directed as to intersect each other where the front of the Building ought to stand."[38] Originally, the spot was to be the home for America-bound Dutch owners, but the lot was eventually purchased at a discount by Ellicott, who hoped to operate a "tolerable Farm" there.[39]

Also enhancing the radial pattern was a public square northwest of lot 104 from which no fewer than eight roads emerged, slicing up the northern village into a variety of lotted parcels. In contrast to Batavia, Ellicott divided New Amsterdam into a series of inner and outer lots. The small size of New Amsterdam's central lots differed vastly from the parcels in Batavia. Even the outer lots of New Amsterdam averaged only fifteen to thirty acres, with the obvious exception of outer lot 104. Unlike the mixed landscape in Batavia, where settlers might produce barrels or shoes on one part of their lot and corn on another, Ellicott planned for the separation of land uses in New Amsterdam, in effect zoning the inner lots for residential and commercial purposes and the outer lots for agricultural production.[40]

A system of inner and outer lots was not uncommon in upstate New York. The system was borrowed from the traditional pattern of many New England villages, where every resident possessed an inner lot along with one or several outer lots.[41] The same pattern was suggested for western New York villages in several of the initial plans submitted to the Dutch in the 1790s. It was used in the company's village of Cazenovia.[42] Ellicott was no doubt also familiar with the inner and outer lot patterns planned around Bath, New York, home of Charles Williamson, developer of the Pulteney Purchase.[43] Ellicott was certainly also aware of the use of outer lots in the village of Erie, Pennsylvania, surveyed by his brother Andrew in the early 1790s.[44]

The first systematic clearing and surveying of New Amsterdam began in 1798 and 1799 while Ellicott used the site as his surveying headquarters.[45] During that period or shortly thereafter, Ellicott drew up a formal plan for the village and submitted it to the Dutch. Ellicott noted that the site should be named New Amsterdam, "so called from the circumstance of the facility with which all the lower part of the Town may be intersected with canals . . . as the most elevated part of the ground is not in common more than four feet above the surface of the water in the Lake."[46] The lower village was, in fact, to be intersected with a network of canals similar to its Old World counterpart. A bank of elevated land separated this lower village from the "Upper Town," to be situated north and east of Bustia and Cazenovia terraces. This portion of the village was "dry and well calculated for the erection of buildings."[47] Nearby supplies of clay, limestone, and building stone would serve as convenient sources of construction materials.

A collection of reserved lots and squares was set aside for public, or "civic," use. The large public square north of the planned canal district was designed to serve as the social center of the community. As in Philadelphia, the square would be somewhat removed from the commercial focus of the village and would provide "from its promotion of social contact . . . an increased sense of civic pride for residents of town and county alike."[48] The county courthouse was not to sit in the center of the square; rather Ellicott placed it on a reserved mound of land two blocks east of the square. Three separate lots were also reserved for schools and religion. They were distributed just south, northwest, and northeast of the square and placed on small corner parcels.

The central plat as it was laid out was very similar to Ellicott's original plan. The greatest differences were found in the "lower village," where the canals were left out of New Amsterdam.[49] Perhaps for reasons of economy, the canal district was replaced by a series of lots that filled in the lowlands between the lake and the elevated terraces. Laid mostly in 1804, the rest of the plat, with a few road and lot variations, remained as it was first planned by Ellicott. The last of the other lots was surveyed in 1808, and the unique New Amsterdam plan—minus the canals—was made a part of the western New York landscape. Part of its exterior bounds were cardinally oriented, but the complexity of its street layout created many lots that lacked rectangularity. The grid landscape apparent beneath the radial foci did reveal itself, however, especially in the many small, regularly sized parcels in the central village.

Street widths, as in Batavia, varied with their presumed importance in the plan. The process of brush clearing and tree removal also continued after the initial surveys.[50] Ellicott's planned street names in New Amsterdam were a great departure from those of Batavia, however, and they served as another indicator on the landscape of the special role the village was designed to play. One set of streets was named for Dutch agents and owners of the Holland Land Company. Unfortunately, Ellicott overlooked the fact that most of the pioneers found such names as Schimmelpennick Avenue and Stadnitski Avenue completely unpronounceable, and in later years the village changed the names of these streets. Still, it was significant that the several angled, radial avenues at the center of the plan all bore Dutch names: the most ornate dimensions of the plan were matched with the most ornate street names. The planned streets of the underlying grid were more comprehensible. Some names, such as Chippawa, Delaware, Cayuga, and Seneca, were associated with Indian tribes in the region. Other streets were named for animals. Examples included Eagle and Swan streets in the "upper Town" above the flats and Mink, Beaver, Otter, Turtle, Sturgeon, and Salmon streets closer to Lake Erie in the lower canal district.

In the southern purchase, Cattaraugus Village resembled both Batavia and Canandaigua. Most of the village was laid out in a series of long lots fronting the main road (fig. 7.10). In the village center, around a Philadelphia-type public square, lots averaged a sizable forty acres. In general size and shape, the lots

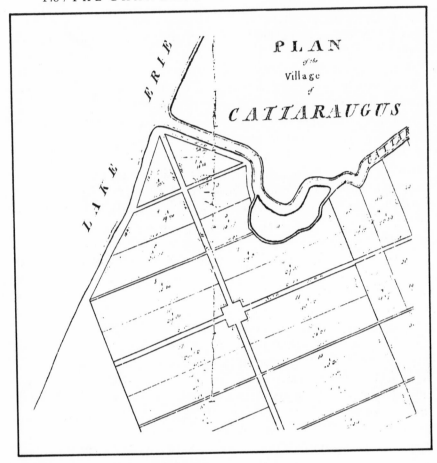

Figure 7.10 Plan of Cattaraugus Village

resembled the Batavia configuration of long lots. There was an absence of outer lots because settlers would have room for sizable garden plots on their village acreage, particularly since the original lot surveys suggested that the area's land quality was superb and dominated by rich, alluvial bottoms.[51]

Mayville was also focused on a similar public square, and long lots of fifty to eighty acres bordered its center (fig. 7.11). The center was surveyed in late 1804, but five years later a major extension to the plat more than doubled its size. Ellicott extended the northwest boundaries of the village along the all-important Portage Road because he believed that the settlers locating on the new lots would help to maintain the quality of the road. In the village center, this main thoroughfare bisected the public square, but it was removed from the heart of the planned commercial district along the lakeshore. When the village was declared the new Chautauqua County seat in 1808, the Ellicott-assisted team of commissioners designated the site of the courthouse not only to be in Mayville but specifically to be on the "Public Square."[52]

The village of Portland was platted just west of Mayville on the Lake Erie terminus of the Portage Road. Ellicott's final plan for the village revealed his increased tendency to survey his later villages in rectangular lotting patterns. Although the village was situated between an irregularly shaped harbor, the lakeshore, and a winding creek, 90 percent of the lots were rectangular. In this case, Ellicott preferred the simplicity and economy of geometrical boundaries to the irregularity of lots planned around local features. The plan encouraged a variety of land uses. Paralleling the New Amsterdam pattern, village lots were small, while larger outer lots were designed as small farm and garden parcels.

Figure 7.11 Plan of Mayville

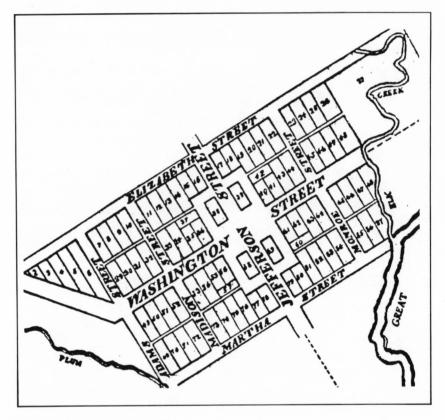

Figure 7.12 Plan of Ellicottville

Special "water lots" were surveyed along the harbor to handle the waterborne trade. A "commons" was designated near the water lots on a triangular piece of land. Finally, the "Public Square" appeared near the center of the planned village to serve as the settlement's civic focus.

Ellicott's remaining planned village was not surveyed until 1815, although the site was selected as the seat of Cattaraugus County in 1808. Ellicottville sat between three creeks near the center of the new county (fig. 7.12).[53] It was a well-chosen and desirable location for a village: the eastern sections bordering Elk Creek were the "cream of land," and other portions of the tract were described as possessing "fine rich soil and covered with all kinds of herbage peculiar to rich bottomlands."[54] Small village lots resembled the pattern at Portland. Outer lots were strung along the creek north of the village. The public square was a departure, however, from the earlier village layouts: four small, central lots, undoubtedly earmarked as sites for the county courthouse, schools, and churches, were positioned in the square.

The plats suggest that Ellicott was a talented borrower of ideas from New England, Pennsylvania, upstate New York, and elsewhere. In each plan, he took care to design a regular, systematic lotting framework. Typically this did not include orienting exterior village boundaries or interior lot lines to cardinal directions, even though cardinality was a characteristic of Ellicott's township lotting system.

Two types of village layout were evident in terms of lot size. The plans of Batavia, Cattaraugus Village, and Mayville were characterized by large village lots of forty or more acres that were oriented along main roads and that were significantly longer than they were wide. Other village landscapes combined the use of small inner lots with a series of adjoining outer lots. The diminutive size of the inner lots used by Ellicott were atypical of the pattern in New England, where inner lots of four to six acres were the norm.[55] The idea did parallel the tradition of town planning in Pennsylvania, however. Beginning with Philadelphia, Penn family land speculators saw the advantages of laying out many small lots in each center, and this tradition was repeated in other settlements platted through the postcolonial period.[56] Pittsburgh (1787) and Erie (1795), for example, contained lots under one-half acre in size that were designed for commercial and residential use rather than for agriculture.[57]

A blending of mid-Atlantic and New England planning traditions also appears evident in Ellicott's use of public space. Ellicott clearly felt that public squares, commons, and other reserved lots should be included in the plat as a service to the community and to attract new settlers. He drew both from the Philadelphia tradition of the public square and from the New England tradition of the less formal but frequently present town commons.

On the developer's frontier, village centers became focal points of landscape change. The first steps in that process were the designing and surveying of formal town plats. The size, orientation, and interior lot geometry of the plans shaped initial patterns of settlement and circulation in the village. The plats represented the formal imposition of civilization and community in a wild frontier region. Ellicott's urban landscapes revealed that his development plans and the land itself had room for a variety of urban forms, ranging from the practical design of Batavia focused on a network of converging roads, to the ornate radial avenues of New Amsterdam, to the orderly, progressively more geometrical, village plats that dotted the southern purchase.

THE ROUTE LANDSCAPE: THE TRAVELER'S VIEW

The developer's experience with landscape change was ongoing, an expression of policies and investments made over many years. The traveler's experience with the western New York scene was by its nature much more transient and fleeting. Still, the collection of contemporary travel narratives that describe the region offer a literary genre that further enriches our understanding of the area's landscape and how it evolved. Ten accounts of western New York journeys illustrate the interplay of traveler and landscape and suggest the critical aspects of the region's character that most impressed themselves on these interlopers. Five accounts set the stage by describing the pre-1800 western New York scene, while the remaining five chronicle the increasingly swift pace of change once settlement began in 1800.

One of the earliest and best-known of the seventeenth-century accounts is the journey of Louis Hennepin through the region in 1678.[58] Hennepin's travels and his description of western New York reveal the seventeenth century's fundamentally different perception of the region's orientation and function. Hennepin, characteristic of those who traveled the frontier during the French era, approached the area from Lake Ontario (and the Saint Lawrence River Valley) and traversed only the narrow stretch of land along the east bank of the Niagara River. The portage route between Lakes Ontario and Erie was "a very fine road" and was used chiefly to move furs, pelts, and other frontier goods through the Great Lakes region.[59] The famed falls were also a notable sight along the way. Hennepin displayed no conception of the region's agricultural potential. Its western extremity was simply a strategic corridor of movement, a point of least resistance in the French fur-trading network between the Upper Lakes and the Saint Lawrence River Valley. Hennepin's narrative is typical of other early French accounts, focusing on the region's peculiarly western frontier zone of European activity while leaving much of the more eastern interior in the shadows of Iroquois occupancy.

Seventy-two years later, Swedish sojourner and botanist Peter Kalm recorded his travels through the region.[60] Kalm journeyed from Albany by horseback to the British fort at Oswego on the eastern end of Lake Ontario. A small boat took him to the strategic Niagara River, still in French control. Accompanying the usual detailed descriptions of the falls were Kalm's remarks on the amount of traffic using the "carrying place" between the two lakes. He witnessed dozens of Indians loaded with furs trudging northward toward boats on Lake Ontario. In terms of Kalm's route of travel (focused on the Niagara River), his perception of the region's strategic importance (as a fur trade corridor), and his lack of commentary on the area's agricultural potential, little had changed since Hennepin's time. It was only in the last few years of the eighteenth century that travelers' experiences began to reflect the incredible transformations in eastern North America that would soon greatly accelerate the pace of landscape change.

Duncan Ingraham's 1792 trip to the Niagara country suggests some of these shifting perceptions of the region just before it fell into Dutch hands. The larger scenario had changed considerably since Kalm's voyage at midcentury. French interests had been replaced, first by British occupation and then by the extension of American sovereignty over the region after the Revolution. The British were slow to give up their strategic positions in the Niagara region, however, and they were still in the process of withdrawing from the eastern banks of the river when Ingraham arrived. Much of his narrative, because he traveled from the east, was concerned no longer with the Niagara portage but rather with detailed descriptions of the "famous Genesee flats" adjacent to the purchase. Still, Ingraham clearly distinguished that lush, fast-settling region where "cultivation is easy, and the land is grateful," from the wilderness farther west (the purchase) in which he saw "not one house or white man the whole way." His main picture of the soon-to-be acquired Dutch company lands was thus a wilderness zone still beyond the pale of the Genesee settlements in which stopping points were Indian encampments or military forts rather than country villages and friendly farmhouses.[61]

Ingraham's voyage, however, was but one of an increasing number of overland traverses of the region during the 1790s. Three years later, two Frenchmen provided their own intriguing Continental impressions of the western New York frontier. Constantin-François de Chasseboeuf, comte de Volney, passed through the area, principally to see the spectacle of Niagara Falls. Volney mentioned a characteristic of the North American backcountry that must have struck overseas travelers as an immediate contrast between Old and New worlds. Volney wrote, "To a Traveller from Europe, and especially to one accustomed, as I had been, to the naked plains of Egypt, Asia, and the coasts of the Mediterranean, the most striking feature of America is the rugged and dreary prospect of an almost universal forest."[62] What was so common as to be not worth noting by most Americans still seemed remarkable to the European eye.

Duc François-Alexandre-Frédéric de La Rochefoucauld-Liancourt, the second Frenchman journeying through the region during the period, made similar comments, noting that "in many parts, the trees are of a prodigious size and thickness." Significantly, La Rochefoucauld-Liancourt also cited the assumed relationship between such lush natural vegetation and the potential suitability of the soil for farming. In general, however, his description of the purchase focused on the dominant presence of Indians in the region. He detailed Indian farming practices as well as Indians' increasing interaction with white traders and travelers. On the map that accompanied his narrative, he carefully differentiated the Genesee Valley lands and the settled districts around Canandaigua and Geneva from the western extremity of the state, still boldly identified as "Lands of the Six Nations."[63]

By the time Rev. Lemuel Covell arrived in the region eight years later, the tract had been surveyed into townships and significant portions opened to settlement. Still, Covell's description of the area is a reminder that the actual landscape was but little transformed from its eighteenth-century state. After preaching in Batavia, still "a small village," he rode west into the Eighteenmile woods where he was "in the wilderness, without house or shelter, all the afternoon." Covell's stop at Vandeventer's tavern for the evening was typical for the traveler who journeyed through the sparsely settled district between Batavia and the Lake Erie-Niagara River region. Characteristic of such snake dens, the reverend found, to his chagrin, the local folk "in a high and merry mood . . . singing foolish songs—some laughing aloud—some swearing—and some almost helpless. All seemed to feel, more or less the effects of frolickery." Surviving his consort with the pioneers, he continued west to Buffalo Creek, where he found another "small village."[64] Covell's sojourn reveals a region being steadily transformed from La Rochefoucauld-Liancourt's "Lands of the Six Nations" to one where permanent white settlers were clearing the occasional opening in the roadside forest or slowly adding to the ranks of local village populations.

A year after Covell's missionary tour, the acerbic New Englander Timothy Dwight reconnoitered the Northeast and toured the same well-traveled path of the Genesee-Buffalo Road. Dwight directed his commentary toward the region's potential for agriculture and settlement. He considered the purchase inferior to the Genesee Valley but noted that it was still a fertile region for farming. His attention was drawn especially to a number of plains lying between Batavia and Lake Erie. He noted the probable connection to practices of Indian burning but was ambivalent about the area's potential for crops. Agreeing with other assessments of early Buffalo Creek (New Amsterdam), he noted its "indifferent houses" and its inhabitants, who were a "casual collection of adventurers" who retained "but little sense of Government, or Religion."[65] Thus Dwight, although by 1804 clearly conceiving of the purchase as an evolving region of agricultural settlement, also acknowledged its continued social primitiveness as a frontier district on the edge of the wilderness.

Robert Sutcliffe described his arrival in 1805 in western New York in his *Travels in some Parts of North America*.[66] Sutcliffe stopped in Batavia, where

Ellicott showed him the details of running a land office. Sutcliffe was impressed with Ellicott's conception of landscape revealed in the resident agent's "very neat and accurate style" of recording information on the potential quality of every lot. In his own impressions of the region, Sutcliffe remained struck by the number of Indians still on the scene. They crowded loudly into Crow's Tavern at New Amsterdam. Elsewhere, they continued to sell corn to newly arriving white settlers who had yet to master the art of raising food in the region. Along with Dwight, Sutcliffe shared a fascination with the roadside prairies between Batavia and New Amsterdam, believing that the openings were the product of purposeful Indian burning. The omnipresence of the native inhabitants suggests that the first decade of white settlement was an important transition period: the contact and interplay that bound together the two cultures before 1800 continued in a process that shaped both groups but that ultimately pushed one into the background while elevating the other to economic and social dominance.

Thomas Cooper's *Ride to Niagara* took him through the heart of the purchase in 1809. Four years had passed since Sutcliffe's journey, and Cooper's described the gradual but steady filling in of the rural landscape by farmers. He noted that the area around Batavia was "excellent land and well-settled" and that further west "there is a log cabin every mile or two." Extolling the acreage along the Genesee Road, he wrote "from Batavia, or ten miles to the east of it, to lake Erie, to lake Ontario and to Niagara is the Flanders of this part of America. . . . One continued flat country . . . all excellent land." Even with these glowing reports, Cooper was quick to add the two standard lamentations of the traveler: the taverns were indifferent at best, and the roads were poorly built and even worse maintained. Vandeventer's hostelry, home to the redoubtable Rev. Covell in 1803, had not improved, at least in Cooper's eyes. He found it to be "the only place between Batavia and Buffaloe where you can sleep, and bad enough it is." Of the region's roads, "three-fourths consist of swamps and bogholes, to say nothing of stumps innumerable."[67] Still, Cooper's western New York perceptions, like those of John Melish, who traversed the region the following year, suggest the substantial changes that occurred even between 1805 and 1810.

Melish, whose *Travels through the United States* provide a clear and detailed narrative of large portions of the new nation, described at length the western New York landscape as it appeared to him in 1810. He arrived from the west, via the Erie Road, visited Buffalo and the Niagara country, and then continued east to Batavia before leaving the purchase for Canandaigua and Geneva. Although he complained of the "excreble road" along Lake Erie, he found the land "generally pretty good" for farming. Buffalo was "rapidly increasing" in size, and Melish, unlike his predecessors, wrote optimistically on the future of the place. He described the center as "handsomely situated at the east end of Lake Erie," with buildings "mostly of wood, painted white, . . . a number of good brick homes, and some few of stone." Significantly, his comments extended the village's potential beyond that of the local agricultural center, and he acknowledged, as did Ellicott, the site's role in possible long-distance commercial trade. In his own providential prose, Melish stated, "Upon the whole, I think this is likely to become a great settlement. It already commands an immense navigation, and its increase is guaranteed by the opening of roads in all directions."[68]

Considering the gradual changes that occurred in the region between the eras of Hennepin (1678) and Ingraham (1792), the two decades that followed displayed a rapid transformation of the cultural landscape. What had been a wilderness of fur traders and Indians evolved after 1800 into a settled landscape of farmers and village folk who, though struggling with the challenges of frontier life, were rapidly altering the look of the region. By 1810, such travelers as Melish envisioned the region, especially in its incipient urban centers, as destined to be bound through long-distance commercial intercourse ever more closely with the developed East as well as with new frontiers opening even farther west. This transformation, experienced and described so vividly by the succession of travelers across the district, was also witnessed, indeed created, by the settlers themselves. Their perceptions of change, unlike those of the sojourner, however, were borne of their own slow altering of the daily scene that accompanied the development of farmstead and rural settlements.

THE EVOLVING RURAL LANDSCAPE: THE SETTLER'S VIEW

The detailed refashioning of the rural landscape was a fundamental outcome of settlement. It expressed the habits, ways of life, and economy of the frontier community. Reconstructing the minutiae of the everyday scene are impossible, for the modern landscape is a cumulative expression of continual change since the initial era of white occupancy. Still, the critical elements of that local landscape sculpted and experienced by ordinary settlers of the early nineteenth century can be appreciated and revealed to suggest something of the processes that contributed to the formation of the western New York scene.

A prospective farmer in a newly settling rural neighborhood first concerned himself with building a home. He made a small clearing and, unless a sawmill was nearby, built a log house, usually one story in height, often with the assistance of friends and neighbors. The dimensions of these initial dwellings varied, but common sizes noted during the era ranged from eighteen feet square to larger houses measuring twenty-two feet by twenty-eight feet or more.[69] Settlers fashioned roofs from bark shingles, and flooring, if any, consisted of rough-hewn pine or oak boards. Barns and smaller outbuildings added to the rural scene. Unlike villages, where the usual proximity of mills hastened the shift to frame buildings, many isolated rural farmsteads probably displayed log homes and barns for a decade or more. As mills increased in number and transportation improved, especially after the War of 1812, settlers converted to frame-board construction.

Clearing land for cultivation was another initial priority that immediately reshaped the rural scene. Productive cropping was not the only reward for these chores. Improvements clauses in land contracts issued by Ellicott awarded savings on interest payments if a stipulated number of acres, usually several per year, were chopped, cleared, and/or fenced.[70] On the other hand, if no improvements or timely cash payments were forthcoming, Ellicott reserved the right to revoke the land contract.[71] Ultimately, there surely must also have been spiritual rewards in witnessing the receding forest. The meaning of cleared land was romantically captured by traveler Francis Wright in 1818:

> The settler's first desire is to have a clear view of the heavens; when his patch of ground is completely naked, he tells you that it looks handsome. As the dense shade of the forest recedes, a tree, in his mind, becomes less associated with wolves and bears, swamps and agues, and gradually he conceives the desire that some sheltering boughs were spread between his roof and the scorching rays of July's sun.[72]

Few jobs were more tedious or time-consuming. An industrious man working alone full-time for half a year might clear between 5 and 8 acres, while large families blessed with plenty of muscle for the fields could perhaps clear over 20 acres in a year.[73] Ellicott was well aware of the effort required. He noted that land costing only two or three dollars per acre to buy would, in terms of labor inputs, require twenty or twenty-five dollars per acre to clear.[74] A comparison of the average cleared acreages per farm versus median farm sizes reveals important characteristics of the rural landscape. From the evidence, it appears that most farms before 1815 had fewer than 20 or 25 acres of cleared land.[75] Many farmers supported themselves on fewer than 15 acres, and few had over 40 or 50 acres cleared. At the same time, median farm sizes varied from 165 acres in 1804 to 120 acres in 1811.[76] Even districts that saw considerable settlement were still heavily forested. The process of extensive clearing was slow and evolutionary, only gradually transforming the landscape throughout the first half of the nineteenth century.

The process of clearing the land involved several steps.[77] Underbrushing came first; the pioneer cleared, piled, and burnt bushes and saplings. Chopping followed and involved the time-consuming job of felling the larger trees. The settler would then remove the small limbs and roll and drag the remaining logs to convenient piles to be burned. The ashes were sometimes spread over the chopped acreage to increase its fertility or leached to produce black salts used in potash and pearl ash manufacturing.[78] Often, the stumps remained in the fields, and the first year's wheat or corn crop was planted in their midst.[79] The result was hardly an idyllic country scene. The reality was probably a rather messy, unkempt rural landscape of forested tracts that, at occasional intervals, were interspersed with small, ragged clearings of partially chopped-over land. On these acres fruit orchards, grain fields, vegetable gardens, and meandering livestock were overseen by farm families living in small log or frame dwellings. Piles of logs for fuel lay stacked near the houses, while other piles of brush and felled trees littered the fields awaiting burning. A wandering fence might attempt to neaten the scene, but, overall, a rather casual and rambling display of creative, often ad hoc, frontier landscaping must have met the daily gaze of the average pioneer settler (fig. 7.13).

The crops that filled these recently cleared fields did not differ markedly from those of the famed Genesee Valley to the east.[80] The most common grains were corn and wheat. Settlers also grew rye and oats in significant quantities. Yields for corn averaged thirty to sixty bushels per acre, while yields for wheat

Figure 7.13 Basil Hall Sketch of Newly Cleared Lands in Upstate New York

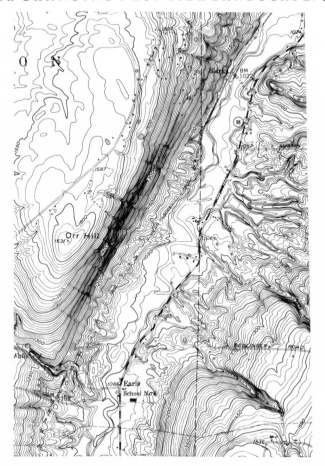

Figure 7.14 Tonawanda Creek, Wyoming County

averaged twenty-five to thirty bushels per acre.[81] Both winter and spring varieties of wheat were grown. In some cases, the grain was part of a simple two-year crop rotation in which clover or grass was used in the alternate seasons.[82] Smaller gardens contained potatoes, peas, beans, and other vegetables. While much of the food was consumed on the farm, a good deal was sold locally to other newly arriving pioneers.

The region's special proclivity for fruit crops was recognized early, and apple, peach, and cherry trees were a common sight around farms. John Stedman, a British pioneer who settled along the Niagara River after 1763, planted an orchard of apples, cherries, peaches, and pears near the site of the old French

Figure 7.15 Cultivated Bottomlands, Tonawanda Creek, Wyoming County

Figure 7.16 First Quality Uplands East of Attica, Wyoming County

Figure 7.17 "Land gently descending, soil black loam covered with nettles, richweed, ox balm," Southern Attica Township, Wyoming County

barracks close to Niagara Falls.[83] Stedman's efforts were matched by similar plantings in portions of the Genesee Valley, and it was only natural that post-1800 Holland Purchase pioneers would also try their hands at fruit grow-ing. Many succeeded; by 1810 a number of settlers reported sizable orchards of fifty to one hundred or more fruit-bearing trees.[84] Although some fruit was grown in all sections of the purchase, even by 1810 orchards were somewhat concentrated along the same environmentally favored shorelines of Lakes Erie and Ontario that support the industry today.[85]

Livestock constituted the other crucial element of the rural scene.[86] Most farms had an ox or two as draft animals, although horses were also commonly used. A cow to provide milk and a number of hogs and sheep were also the norm, along with the usual collections of geese and chickens. Some farmers raised additional cattle for commercial sale. The mobility of their animals was a distinct asset in generating long-distance trade. As Ellicott noted, "Cattle in Consequence of our Distance from Market must in a great Measure be the Staple Commodity of this Country."[87]

The annual round of work on the farm brought a continual stream of chores through the year. Settlers planted gardens in late April or early May. They cut the first hay in mid-June and made additional cuts in late summer.

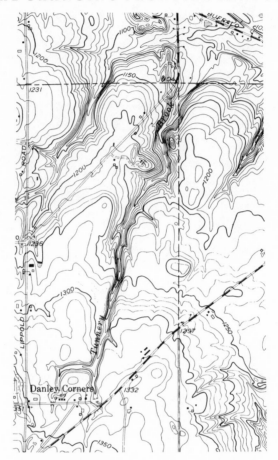

Figure 7.18 Third Quality Lands, Tunnery Brook,
Wyoming County

Corn and wheat were harvested in August and September. Autumn was a time
to prepare for winter and to plant winter wheat. Farmers stayed warm between
November and March by chopping and clearing additional acreage, keeping
firewood supplies ample, and repairing farm equipment, tools, and household
goods. Out of this steady passing of years there gradually emerged a more settled
rural landscape. Premium acreage grew increasingly open and well tended,
while marginal tracts reverted to forest or were kept for pasture.

The detailed expression of the region's evolving landscape can best be
seen by examining a particular locality. The modern township of Attica in
northern Wyoming County corresponds to Township 10 Range 2 in Ellicott's

initial surveys. In its topography and drainage, it is typical of many townships in the southern two-thirds of the purchase. Located about a dozen miles south of Batavia, Attica is mostly a rolling upland between 1,100 and 1,800 feet in elevation. The only extensive alluvial lowland borders a branch of northward-flowing Tonawanda Creek that runs through the northwestern corner of the town. In addition, several steep-sided ravines dissect the rougher, higher uplands, and a number of small swampy areas in the southeast indicate areas of poor surface drainage. This varied tract was isolated in the first years of western New York settlement; it lay off the main east-west thoroughfares that brought the bulk of pioneers into the region. By 1802, however, Ellicott built a road south from Batavia that passed through the center of the town. Thereafter, settlers began to filter in with increasing frequency.

It is impossible to reconstruct precisely the ways in which the newly arriving settlers in the town perceived the landscape they found or how they

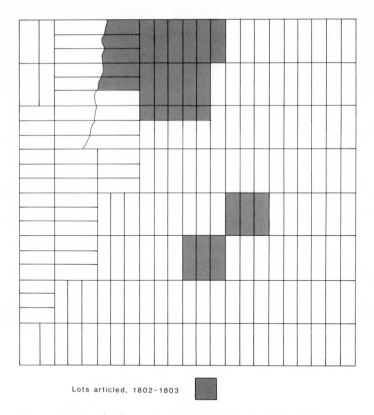

Lots articled, 1802–1803

Figure 7.19 Land Sales in Township 10, Range 2, 1802–1803

Figure 7.20 Initial Settlement in Township 10, Range 2, near Attica, Wyoming County

envisioned its potential for agricultural development. One set of clues, however, is provided in how the initial surveyors evaluated the township for settlement. After all, most were nearby settlers and were certainly schooled in the same habits of mind that shaped the decisions of pioneers. What they saw was a landscape largely suitable for cultivation.[88] Over 75 percent of the acreage along the initial township lines was judged to be first-quality land. Most of this better class of land was upland, while less than 10 percent was either bottomland or intervale land, recorded mostly along Tonawanda Creek. About 20 percent of the land was judged second-quality acreage, and only 2 percent of the land was identified as third-quality uplands or swamp.

Although the landscape has seen a great deal of change since these initial evaluations, one can still gain some understanding of those impressions by examining the sites today. Not surprisingly, the first-quality bottomlands along Tonawanda Creek are still in cultivation, while more steeply sloped second- and third-quality acreage on nearby hillsides remains in forest (figs. 7.14 and 7.15). Although the early forest cover of sugar maple, beech, and elm has been re-moved or modified, the extensive first-quality uplands in the northern township

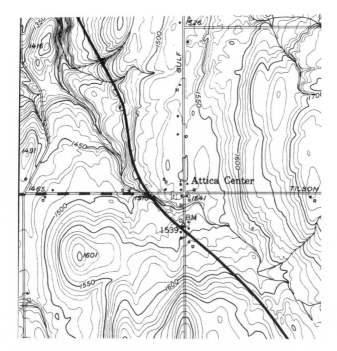

Figure 7.21 Subsequent Settlement, Attica Center

Figure 7.22 Settlement Landscape at Attica Center: First Quality Uplands, Wyoming County

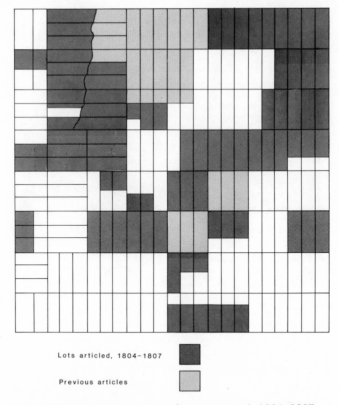

Lots articled, 1804–1807

Previous articles

Figure 7.23 Land Sales in Township 10, Range 2, 1804–1807

still display the gently rolling contours that made them highly desired lands in 1800 (fig. 7.16). To the south, surveyors commented on another site of first-quality uplands by noting "Land gently descending, soil black loam covered with nettles, richweed, ox balm" (fig. 7.17). On the other hand, the steeply sloped uplands along Tunnery Brook northeast of modern Danley Corners were judged third-quality acreage unsuitable for cultivation (fig. 7.18).

When development began in 1802, the two settlement nuclei in the township did focus on high-quality acreage. Between 1802 and 1803, Zerah Phelps, Levi Porter, Amos and Nathaniel Sprout, Stephen Crow, and Parmenio Adams purchased land in the northern township along and just east of Tonawanda Creek (fig. 7.19). The acreage included first-quality bottomlands just north of Attica that were quickly cleared for cultivation (fig. 7.20). A second nucleus of development centered on lands bought by Benjamin Porter and Stephen Crow in the south-central portion of the township. It was a good choice of acreage.

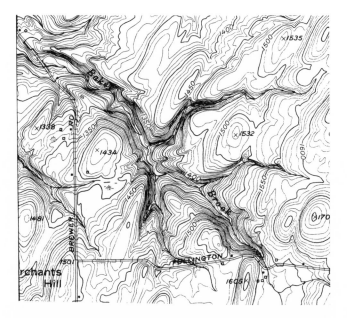

Figure 7.24 Unsettled Tracts near Baker Brook, Wyoming County

Figure 7.25 Steep Slopes, Northern Attica Township, Wyoming County

Sitting some five hundred feet higher than the tracts along Tonawanda Creek, this upland area was just southeast of the steeply dissected portions of upper Crow Creek yet just north of a ridge of high, rugged hills and northwest of the poorly drained lands of Edwards Swamp (fig. 7.21). Overall, it was an area of gently sloping first-quality uplands (fig. 7.22).

Because these settlers were the first in the township, they benefited from Ellicott's sales policy of land discounts to "first adventurers." The initial parcels sold for between $1.40 and $1.81 per acre.[89] Most early buyers purchased relatively large parcels of land: the median sales size for 1802 and 1803 was over 350 acres. Perhaps cheap land prices and the spirit of frontier enterprise— hopes for higher resale—encouraged the larger purchases. Initial cash outlays were often minimal: most contracts were made with down payments averaging 4 or 5 percent of the total purchase price. The earliest settlers came in a procession of ox carts from Connecticut, choosing the town based on the advice

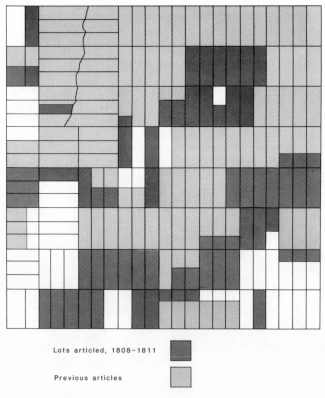

Lots articled, 1808–1811

Previous articles

Figure 7.26 Land Sales in Township 10, Range 2, 1808–1811

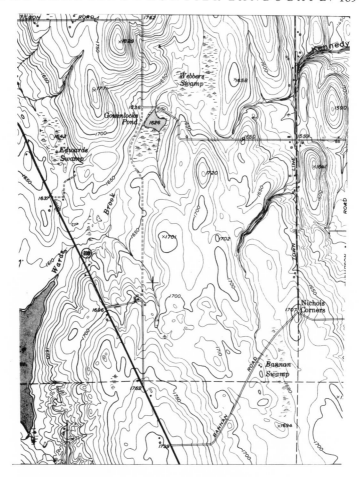

Figure 7.27 Poorly Drained Acreage, Southeastern Attica
Township, Wyoming County

of their leader, Zerah Phelps.[90] Subsequent settlers in the region also migrated predominantly from New England.

Between 1804 and the War of 1812, the pace of settlement increased. Land prices rose to a median of three dollars per acre by 1811, while the median size of parcels fell to 120 acres, the precise dimensions of the average lot in Ellicott's survey system. By 1811, over twenty contracts for land were being taken annually in the township. Settlement spread quickly from its initial concentrations in the northern and central sections. By 1807, over half the lots had been sold. The newly acquired acreage focused on or near Tonawanda Creek and, with one exception, in the north-central and northeastern portions of the township (fig.

7.23). Only along the rugged stretches of upper Baker Brook did acreage remain unsold for several more years (fig. 7.24). Several lots in that area were plagued by steeply sloped uplands, which settlers avoided in lieu of an abundance of better land in nearby areas (fig. 7.25). By 1811, after only nine years of settlement, most lots had been purchased (fig. 7.26). Unsold acreage remained in only two areas. In the far southeast, poorly drained lots, such as those around Bannon Swamp, no doubt dampened buyer enthusiasm (fig. 7.27). Above Tonawanda Creek, a series of small but deeply entrenched streams and adjacent steep slopes discouraged settlement in the far southwest (figs. 7.28 and 7.29).

Overall, settlers preferred, purchased, and improved tracts that were either premium bottomlands along Tonawanda Creek or gently sloping, well-drained uplands elsewhere in the township. Some acreage readily demonstrated

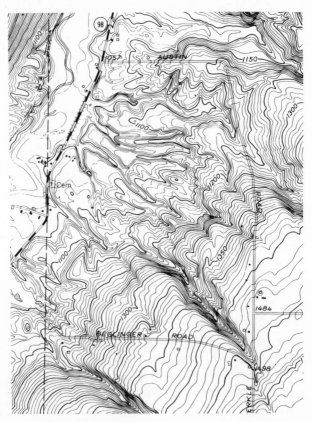

Figure 7.28 Unsettled Tracts, Southern Attica Township, Wyoming County

Figure 7.29 Steep Slopes, Southern Attica Township, Wyoming County

its fertility: Zerah Phelps noted generous early wheat yields of over forty-five bushels per acre, and he remarked that the "Crops of Corn are extraordinary."[91] The forest landscape was least altered on the less desirable steeply sloped acreage that separated better bottomlands and uplands and in poorly drained parcels that provided needless complications in the chores of initial improvement.

As communities, the villages of Attica (in the north) and Attica Center (in the central part of the town) provided increasing numbers of services to the nearby rural population.[92] Attica quickly became the dominant center. Good sites on the creek attracted both gristmills and sawmills to Attica by 1810. Two taverns, several stores, and a smithy also provided important local services. Several neighborhood distilleries quenched settlers' thirsts, while Baptist, Presbyterian, Congregational, and Methodist preachers attended to their accompanying overindulgences. Even settlers in isolated portions of the township would have a trip of only four or five miles to take advantage of these services. Once established, they no doubt attracted more settlers to the surrounding rural districts and further hastened the process of landscape change.

The evolving western New York scene was a rich repository of cultural clues that displayed the formidable and formative social and economic institutions of the time as well as a sense of the prevailing habits of mind that shaped the perceptions of developer, traveler, and settler. Planners' schemes and settlers' deeds found expression on the landscape of the western New York frontier. The rapid change that characterized the region between 1793 and the War of 1812 reflected the investments made by the Dutch developers and expressed the many individual efforts of settlers arriving from New England, Pennsylvania, and elsewhere. Certain features—chief among them the cadastral lines on the land that marked property boundaries in both rural and urban settings—were unmistakably the product of the developer's actions. The geometry of Ellicott's lot surveys was an everpresent signature of company planning etched on the land. Once established, the cadastre offered pioneers the setting necessary to begin creating their own landscape as they cleared land, built homes, and planted crops. The resulting frontier landscape was a combined effort of institutions and individuals, a synthesis in which was seen the actions and aspirations of land agents as well as pioneers.

CHAPTER 8

A Legacy on
the Landscape

*Every landscape is an accumulation. The past
endures.*

—D. W. Meinig

The western New York landscape displays a
long record of settlement and development
since the frontier was opened by Ellicott in
1800. Even so, the developer's initial imprint
has been pervasive and enduring. Many of the
developer-inspired features that characterized
the frontier period have remained to become
part of the modern scene. The remnants of the
developer's frontier are complex and fragmented, however; the landscape obscures as
well as displays the actions and intentions of
past generations. Still, in western New York,
portions of Joseph Ellicott's early marks on the
land have remained, revealing much about the
comprehensive and powerfully decisive nature
of the developer's impact on an area.

173

The developer's mark is especially bold in such linear features on the landscape as survey lines, village plats, and road networks. But even here the landscape's record is complex: although the lines on the land have remained, their function has often changed, and in some places the continuity has been broken by landscape features imposed by subsequent generations; in other places, the landscape that reveals itself as an orderly geometry and purposeful pattern from the air becomes a jumble of abandoned field lines, rutted byways, and crossroads hamlets on the ground itself. To harvest from this ordinary view a clear record of the developer's shaping influence is not an easy task, but the rewards provide an appreciation for how the developer has molded the national scene and how the landscapes of our everyday lives have come to be.

TOWNSHIP AND LOT LINES

Ellicott's township and lot survey lines had an enduring impact on later patterns of settlement and communication. Modern remnants of these lines on the land in the form of boundaries and roads remain; though they are not bold and dominating visible features, either in rural or in urban settings, their presence is pervasive and part of the fundamental underlying fabric of the landscape. The degree to which these lines have remained or been erased from the visual scene also varies significantly. Overall, there is also a clear distinction to be made between the relative durability of the township lines versus the lesser durability of the original lot lines.

In western New York and elsewhere the original township survey lines and the local road network are related. The intensity of this relationship varies in different geographical settings. In some cases, the roads that follow early survey lines make little ecological sense: they pass over steep hills and gullies to follow the geometrical patterns of the township boundaries rather than finding an easier grade that follows the natural contours of the land.[1] Not surprisingly, Norman Thrower found in Ohio that the tendency for roads to follow survey lines in a systematically surveyed area appears much stronger than in less systematically surveyed districts. In the latter, orderly townships and rectangular lots are replaced by a lack of townships altogether and by a complex mosaic of multisided lots that encourage an equally complex and confusing corresponding road network.[2]

Across the lands of the Holland Purchase the coincidence between the original lines and modern town line roads is clearly recognizable. The pattern, however, is highly fragmented: many original town lines are not a part of the modern roadscape (fig. 8.1); most modern roads do not follow original town-

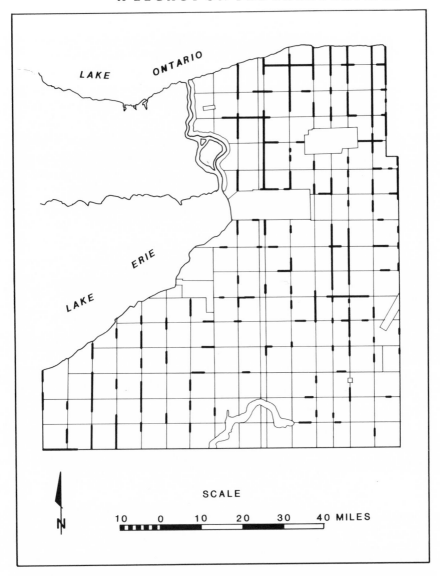

Figure 8.1 Original Survey Township Lines Coincident with Modern Town Line Roads

ship lines. In fact, many of Ellicott's earliest and most important routes failed to follow township boundaries. In western New York, unlike the public lands system in the Midwest, no general underlying pattern of section lines and associated section roads reinforced the geometry of a larger town grid.

The paucity of town line roads is particularly noteworthy in the south-central purchase, and it can perhaps be explained by the extreme steepness of the terrain in that area. Straight roads were not plausible over the rough Allegheny and Cattaraugus hills. In addition, no continuing and viable agricultural economy demanded a dense network of improved rural roads in the region. On the contrary, settlement occurred early in the northern purchase, and steadily growing rural and urban communities demanded an improved, increasingly dense road network. Relatively flat terrain did little to discourage the use of township lines for roadways. Property lines would normally not be interfered with, and the straight courses of the township lines were clearly marked in earlier surveys.

Even stronger connections are found linking the region's original survey lines and the subsequent development of modern civil township boundaries. Unlike town line roads, there is no highly visible expression of this feature on the landscape itself. Still, the political geography of township boundaries is important in determining the distribution of local services and in regulating traffic and zoning laws.[3] In western New York the original surveyed townships and later civil town boundaries correspond strongly (fig. 8.2). The degree of coincidence is especially striking in that a pattern of political boundaries designed to help perform certain public functions grew out of a pattern of private land surveys designed to sell wild acreage at a profit.

The modern pattern of approximately 150 civil townships and eight counties is the product of a process of political fragmentation that began with Ellicott's agency and was substantially in place by 1850.[4] During that half-century, an original pattern of four large townships and a single county unit was transformed into a dense network of local political units. There was a high degree of public awareness of the survey township grid, since all of the company's land deeds and sales policies were in the language of the survey system. When questions of forming a new political township arose, the familiar survey township boundaries often provided the simplest solution to planning the dimensions of the political units. Therefore, after Ellicott's initial surveys, township boundaries in the form of civil town and county lines emerged clearly.

Remnants of the lot survey pattern are also evident on the modern landscape, but in most cases the examples of persistence are highly fragmented and not so clearly displayed as are the enduring portions of the township boundaries. Ellicott's numbered lot units remain a clear part of the legal landscape of property location and identification. Deed and plat maps still use the language of Ellicott's numbered 120- and 360-acre lot units when describing the boundaries of modern ownership units. Processes of farm consolidation, farm frag-

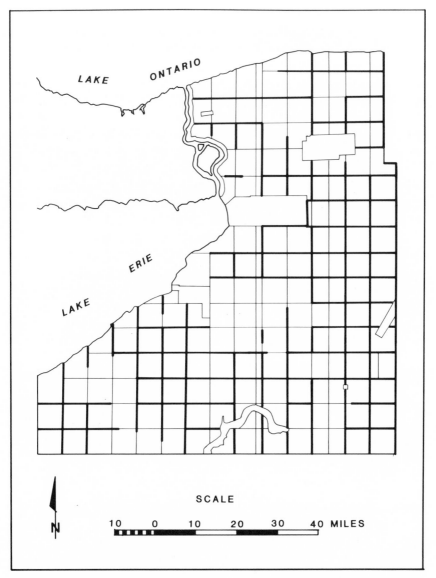

Figure 8.2 Original Survey Township Lines Coincident with Modern Civil Town Lines

mentation, and suburbanization have transformed the landscape, however, and have tended to lower the coincidence between Ellicott's lot lines and modern property lines.

From the outset, Ellicott's flexible attitude toward lot subdivision undoubtedly discouraged the persistence of lot lines on the landscape. In some cases, lots were subdivided by various owners, and in other cases, different lots were purchased by a single owner. The modern landscape reflects the complexity of these ownership patterns, and although many of Ellicott's original lot lines remain as property lines, so many subsequent property lines have subdivided the original units that today the original lines constitute only a small proportion of the total property boundaries in a given area. The visual persistence of the early lot lines is further diminished by the widespread land abandonment that characterizes much of the rural portions of the Appalachian uplands.

Long-lotted parcels have also left a varied visual legacy. The long lots surveyed along Cattaraugus Creek failed to persist because the steep and untillable terrain adjacent to the creek never encouraged sustained periods of land clearing and settlements. Aerial photos of the area reveal a thinly peopled landscape, either largely abandoned or never cultivated. Little in the modern scene mirrors the original rectangular long lot lines (fig. 8.3).[5] Where land quality was better and settlement more enduring, the long lot patterns clearly remained a part of the modern rural landscape. A north-south tributary (Fivemile Creek) of the Allegheny River was long lotted in 1803, and the surrounding valley was sufficiently broad and fertile to encourage farming and

Figure 8.3 Vanished Long Lots on Cattaraugus Creek

Figure 8.4 Enduring Long Lots on Fivemile Creek

the clearing of land. Many original lot lines (40 percent of the area's total) have endured in the form of visible features on the landscape (fig. 8.4).[6]

Similar to the township grid, the persistence of the lot landscape is best viewed from above, either in map form or through aerial photography. These marks of the developer's planning strategy do not embolden the casually viewed scene on the land surface. Qualities of cardinality and rectilinearity so readily observable from above are often lost in the landscape seen from ground level. A maze of brush and small trees in abandoned fields can obscure property lines and old farming areas. Even where the modern parcels are cleared, field and ownership lines are often a jumble of uncut trees and piles of rock on the landscape and all but invisible to the casual glance or untrained eye.

Figure 8.5 Modern Batavia

REMNANTS OF FRONTIER NUCLEI

Remnants of Ellicott's major platted villages persist on the modern landscape, and they suggest the relative success of each center after its establishment by the resident agent. Batavia is today home to about twenty thousand residents. The old Genesee Road is a broad, paved avenue that passes a mixture of strip developments, residences, small neighborhood shopping centers, and, finally, in the center of town, several blocks of commercial businesses. Remarkably, the size of the modern nucleus is such that the city limits and the edge of the built-up area correspond very closely to the boundaries of the original plat of 1801. From above, the precise original exterior boundaries are visible, especially along the northeastern edges of the village. Also remarkable is the modern road network in and around the village. The city endures as a hub, and the orientation of Ellicott's original road network, so clearly focused on the village, has shaped the pattern of circulation for almost two centuries (fig. 8.5).

New Amsterdam was an even greater success story. From a still smallish hamlet in 1811, New Amsterdam, renamed Buffalo, blossomed into one of the nation's great urbanized areas. Slightly over one million people make their home where Ellicott was convinced was "designed by nature for the grand emporium of the Western world."[7] It was indeed a strategic site on the east end of Lake Erie, made more so with the coming of the Erie Canal in 1825 and the railroads a quarter-century later. The city is the one example of an Ellicott plat that proved much too small to accommodate subsequent growth. Today, the original inner and outer lots of the village comprise only a small fraction of the city itself and even less of the entire metropolitan area. Portions of Ellicott's radial plan are still evident, however, and subsequent additions have preserved and even accentuated many of the unique elements in the city's original layout. Modern avenues, some now extended well into the suburbs, still radiate from the large public square near the lakeshore.

The square also remains highly visible and serves as the "civic center" for the city (fig. 8.6): it is bordered by the city hall, the city courthouse, the federal

Figure 8.6 Niagara Square, Buffalo

building, the state building, and one of the city's largest and oldest hotels. At the center of the traffic circle is a handsomely designed square with benches, steps, and grass that becomes the noontime meeting grounds for many downtown workers. Although Ellicott's "outlot 104" was subdivided following his death and subsequent street additions crisscross its entire length, portions of it remain a special urban space as well-used city parks. Lot space reserved by Ellicott for a courthouse, although no longer occupied by that structure, remain as Lafayette Square, another symbolic focus of the modern city. Numerous street changes and block alterations, however, have carved up the early plan, especially in its southern sections, and new harbor construction has transformed the old lakeshore area of the village.

If Buffalo displays the developer's great entrepreneurial acumen in choosing urban sites, then the villages of the southern purchase must represent the less prescient dimensions of his geographical ken. Ellicott's three portage centers—Cattaraugus Village, Portland, and Mayville—did enjoy some modest growth. All these villages, however, to varying degrees, have suffered similar fates on the modern landscape. Their value as portage points diminished with the maturing of the nineteenth century, their strategic importance evaporated by the coming of the canal and railroad. On the landscape, their present-day remnants are all smaller than the original plats. All three, however, have gained from the fact that they are located on water because the lakes offer recreational opportunities which have benefited each center.

Unlike New Amsterdam, where the city of Buffalo overwhelmed and outgrew its original platted boundaries, Cattaraugus Village never developed enough to begin to populate all of the area within the plat: the angled exterior lines of the early village stand out clearly in a still rural landscape (fig. 8.7). Interior lot and road orientations, originally focused along the northwestward-pointing Pennsylvania Road, can also still be seen within the boundaries of the plat. There is little in the way of an urban focus on the original "Public Square," however. Only a crossroads highway service hamlet marks the spot along modern U.S. Route 20. Near the lake, a small residential area is focused on a boat marina at the mouth of Cattaraugus Creek. Similarly, the village of Portland, today called Barcelona, is a tiny fishing and boating resort. Some road orientations near the lake conform to the original plan, but the public square has disappeared: even before 1836, the square had been replaced by a new lotting arrangement.[8]

Mayville is still the largest of the three portage centers, and, with a population of between fifteen hundred and two thousand, it also remains the Chautauqua County seat. The modern village boundaries, however, are much smaller

Figure 8.7 Modern Site of Cattaraugus Village

than the extended Mayville plat surveyed after 1809 and resemble, to a much greater degree, the original, smaller plat. The built-up portion of the village is even smaller than either the early plat or the modern village bounds. The angled outlines of the original plat have remained on the rural landscape surrounding the village and southwest to northeast trending tree, and field lines reveal many of the interior long lots that still lead back from the old Portage Road (fig. 8.8). The original "Public Square" remains a central feature on the modern scene: it serves as a major highway junction point, and located on the site are the county courthouse, a small park, and the offices of the local newspaper.

Ellicottville, the resident agent's last platted village, is home today to about one thousand residents. Modern village limits are slightly larger than

Figure 8.8 Modern Mayville

those platted by Ellicott, but the built-up portions of the village correspond closely to the original plat. The village outer lots also clearly remain part of the modern scene. The original public square, although somewhat altered in form, is the functioning social and civic center of the village: lining the square are a local school, the public library, a church, the town offices, and the local historical society.

ROUTE LANDSCAPES

The developer's commitment to improved transportation remains on the landscape in the form of modern roads and in the field and property lines that have been shaped by the original network of frontier routes. As with the township and lot lines and the frontier villages, the early roads have been preserved in piecemeal fashion: whole routes have vanished while others remain, some as major, well-traveled highways, others in a state barely improved since Ellicott's time. The remnants of the road system are scattered throughout the region (fig. 8.9). Passable roads, some paved, others with dirt and gravel surfaces, follow closely almost three-quarters of the original company network.

Best preserved have been Ellicott's earliest routes. The network surrounding Batavia has been especially enduring. Once a route was in place, improved, and performing a viable function in the frontier circulation system, its very

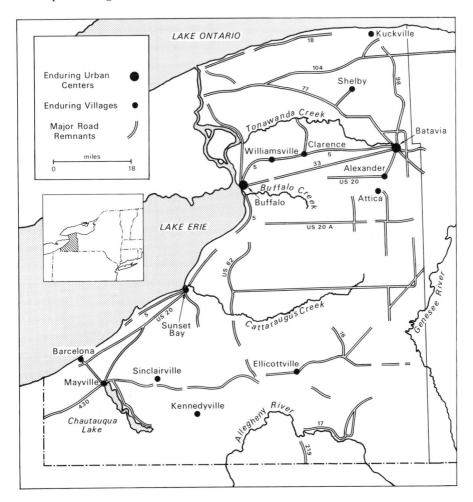

Figure 8.9 Road and Village Remnants

existence encouraged the construction of connecting secondary roads, which further enhanced the development of adjacent farms and villages and led also to further widening and improvement in later years as traffic increased and economic demands changed.

As landscape features, the developer's routeways have left their mark in highly varied linear forms that range from multilane highways to overgrown backroads to the mere fence-and-tree lines that denote the alignments of routes now entirely vanished. Particularly in areas of considerable local relief, persisting sections of Ellicott's network have become highly fragmented, adding to the complexity of the modern landscape.

Along and near the Genesee-Buffalo Road and west near Lake Erie, much of Ellicott's road system is preserved in broad paved highways. Development in these areas came early, and sustained economic growth continually targeted investment into the road network of this region. Such thoroughfares as U.S. Route 20 and New York State Route 5 carry considerable local traffic and enjoy a high degree of maintenance and improvement (fig. 8.10). Other paved but

Figure 8.10 Modern Buffalo Road—Route 5

Figure 8.11 Modern Niagara Road—Route 63

clearly more secondary routes have preserved remnants of the developer's frontier landscape. Less maintenance and investment along these routes has meant a generally rougher surface, narrower shoulders, and slower traffic patterns. Sections of U.S. Route 62 south of Buffalo and sizeable stretches of secondary roads running northeast and southwest of Mayville in the southern purchase are major examples of this landscape feature. In the northern purchase, the original Niagara Road northwest of Batavia, for example, is followed today by New York State Route 63, a paved but hardly high-speed thoroughfare (fig. 8.11).

More confined to the rugged and isolated southern purchase are the unpaved and gravel remnants of Ellicott's enduring route landscape. Consider-

Figure 8.12 Modern Southern Road, Chautauqua County

Figure 8.13 Middle Road, Wyoming County

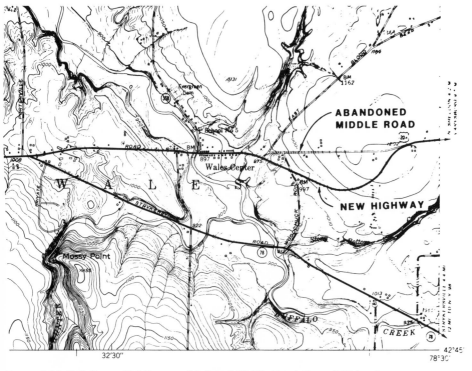

Figure 8.14 U.S. Route 20A Bypass of Original Middle Road, East of Wales Center

able portions of the two most important routes in the south, the Southern Road and the Pennsylvania Road, are preserved as local, unpaved rural routes. Sections of the Southern Road near Sinclairville, for example, have been maintained, but they are almost precisely of the same one-rod width originally financed by Ellicott (fig. 8.12). Even less conspicuous on the landscape are route remnants that have entirely ceased to be roads. Some thoroughfares, such as the old Middle Road near Warsaw in Wyoming County, are preserved only in the form of field and vegetation lines on the distant hills (fig. 8.13). The linear landscape is still apparent, a reflection of both the original route and the original lotting patterns in the area. Portions of many routes have vanished. Where excessive grades have made following the original track impractical, modern highways have bypassed the Ellicott routes. Near Wales Center in Erie County, for example, the original route, still partially preserved as a local farm road, continues directly up a steep hill east of the village, while the modern section of U.S. Route 20A avoids the grade by curving widely to the south (fig. 8.14).

THE LOCAL SCENE

Every township in the region felt the imprint of these initial developer investments. How they combined with the precise site and situation of a given locality
was a function of physical geography and their subsequent use and alteration by
succeeding generations of settlers. Attica Township (Township 10 Range 2)
illustrates some of the varied expressions of these frontier investments on the
modern scene. Filtered through almost two centuries of subsequent settlement,
these signatures on the land are pervasive but often undramatic and usually
unrecognized components of the everyday scene.

The original township perimeter line remains as the modern civil town-
ship boundary of Attica (fig. 8.15). In fact, all but a small fraction of Wyoming
County's civil township lines correspond exactly to the original Holland Land
Company survey boundaries. In addition, most of the eastern boundary of
Attica township is coincident with a town line road that runs south from Vernal
Corners (fig. 8.16). Hardly a major thoroughfare, the route serves local farm

Figure 8.15 Attica Township Line, Wyoming County

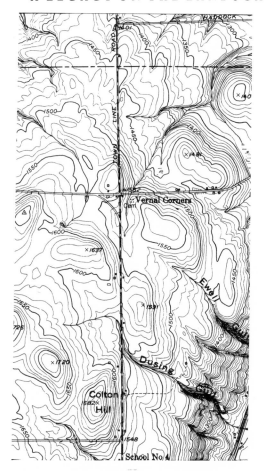

Figure 8.16 Town Line Road, East Edge of Attica
Township, Wyoming County

traffic in the hilly terrain east of Attica. Still, it remains on the Attica landscape
as a legacy of the developer and the township system (fig. 8.17).

The lotting pattern, similar to the circumstances elsewhere on the purchase, is less completely revealed on the modern scene. A typical rural view in
the town would undoubtedly reveal identifiable legal and visual fragments of
the original lot system. Commonly, however, cultivated fields or pasture alternate in irregular fashion with wood lots and abandoned land, and the result is a
contemporary landscape devoid of an orderly checkerboard pattern of cleared
lots and farmsteads that correspond to Ellicott's initial 120-acre lotting geometry (fig. 8.18). In general, land first settled, usually the better acreage for farm-

Figure 8.17 Town Line Route Landscape, East Edge of Attica
Township, Wyoming County

ing, is still in agricultural use and therefore cleared, often as feed corn or pasture
land used in local dairying operations (fig. 8.19).

Economically, the village of Attica is closely tied to the infamous state
prison of the same name located just southeast of town (fig. 8.20). The site of the
village, however, is precisely where Zerah Phelps, with Ellicott's assistance,
established a pioneer milling center in the first years of settlement. The modern
downtown thus sits where the initial cluster of taverns, stores, and artisans'
shops assembled once milling operations commenced (fig. 8.21). The mills
themselves have departed: the modern setting along Tonawanda Creek has

Figure 8.18 Fragmented Lot Line and Field Landscape, Attica Township, Wyoming County

Figure 8.19 Cultivated Land in Attica Township, Wyoming County

Figure 8.20 Village of Attica, Wyoming County

turned its back on the site and is now bordered by the usual parking lots and accumulated refuse found behind taverns, cafes, and retailing establishments (fig. 8.22).

In addition to the impact of the Town Line Road on the eastern perimeter, Attica's modern route landscape also retains an expression of Ellicott's larger regional investments in the frontier road network. The north–south-trending Allegany Road, constructed after 1801, ran from Batavia to Township 6 Range 2, where it joined with other routes to the Allegheny River in the southern purchase. The Allegany Road's path took it through the center of Attica Township along a route today traversed by McGrath and Nesbitt roads. The modern byway passes through the historical settlement focus of Attica Center, today an unincorporated crossroads hamlet amounting to several farmhouses, and then up into the rougher hill country of the southern township (fig. 8.23). It remains as yet another silent remnant of the developer's impact on the ordinary western New York scene.

THE DEVELOPER'S ROLE

The process of making the western New York landscape did not begin on the land itself. It originated within the imaginations of those given the task of planning its development. Understanding how the developer envisioned the land and its potential is fundamental to understanding how he changed it in the ways he did. In western New York, Ellicott's initially sketchy perceptions of the region's environment were replaced with more detailed and systematic evaluations based on the township and lot surveys and on the experience he gained simply by living within and traveling about the purchase over an extended period. Ellicott also possessed definite notions about the "geographical situation" of the purchase and its relation to distant cities and markets. Before the first trees were marked to locate a lot and before the first brush was cleared to make way for a road, Ellicott conceived of these actions as part of a larger strategy for regional development.

Figure 8.21 Village Landscape, Attica, Wyoming County

Figure 8.22 Mill Site, Attica Village, Wyoming County

Resident Agent Ellicott brought many virtues to the job. Above all, he was a practical man, schooled since childhood in the ways of the frontier. His development policies were consistently characterized by a simplicity that assumed that a rational and balanced approach would certainly yield profitable results for the Holland Land Company. When desirable sales failed to materialize, Ellicott felt free to adapt to changing conditions, sometimes even before confirming policy alterations with his superiors. This flexibility was another asset in the unpredictable physical and economic environment of the frontier. Ellicott possessed the imagination necessary to plan for future change or growth, but he was hardly a visionary with a self-conscious sense of destiny or power. The degree of order he helped to create in the region's settlement system was no reflection of a utopian mission or grand design; rather, it mirrored his commonsense notions of promoting settlements via new surveys, village centers, and roads. Given the investments he made, typically prudent and frugal, he expected a reasonable return for the Dutch in the form of profitable sales to incoming settlers.

Compared to his colleagues, such as Williamson, Lincklaen, Boon, and others, Ellicott's approach was rather successful in balancing the necessary expenditures with the actual sales revenues that were eventually generated as parcels were sold to retail and wholesale purchasers. Several of these other land agents became well known for their liberal spending policies. Ellicott never suffered from such problems. In fact, he was frequently encouraged by potential settlers and entrepreneurs to spend more on building towns, roads, mills, taverns, stores, schools, and other services. Typically, however, Ellicott chose to be in scrupulous control of the company's expenditures, a fact that certainly endeared him more to the Dutch than to the common settler in western New York. Even so, he was able to encourage a system of land sales and surveys, a sprinkling of towns and mills, and a comprehensive network of roads that, though lacking any pretense of princely grandeur, proved remarkably functional in meeting the needs of the thousands of new settlers that arrived during his first decade as resident agent.

The endeavors of the Dutch and their resident agent were part of a larger developer's frontier that constituted an important chapter in the postrevolutionary movement into the interior. It was as characteristically "American" as the Turnerian frontier of the eastern Tennessee backcountry or the federal

Figure 8.23 Modern Allegany Road just South of Attica Center, Wyoming County

frontier of the Seven Ranges District in eastern Ohio. It expressed complex American impulses that were a curious mix of a speculative quest for riches and an almost paternalistic concern for the viability and durability of a frontier community. Profit was surely the motive to those developing such a frontier, but profits were a possibility only after careful and often expensive assessments of the wilderness environment were made and only after a program of planned development was adopted to attract potential buyers. Without the developer on the scene, many of the improvements and much of the economic growth on such frontiers would surely have been delayed or redirected.

The timing of the opening of western New York proved especially crucial in guaranteeing the key role of the developer in the region. The fortunes of many American speculators and land agents had both soared and soured in the decade that followed the signing of the Constitution and preceded the formal opening of the Holland Purchase (1789–99). The late 1780s and early 1790s saw an explosion in the sale of wild lands in America. Typically, this generation of promoters was interested in turning a quick profit on the sale of large parcels. Why make costly improvements in a tract if a greater fool could be found to buy the acreage still wild at twice the price?

The speculative fever subsided sharply in the late 1790s. This placed the Dutch investors and their western New York lands in an unusual position. Although the Dutch purchased the 3.3 million acres through Theophile Cazenove during the height of the speculative binge, they did not open the purchase for sale until after the buying activity had subsided. Perhaps the investors would have been delighted if Cazenove had quickly sold all of their land to other capitalists in a few years for a fast profit, but the changing economic climate made that impossible. The Dutch, with the help of Ellicott, were forced to take a different course. Their hope of selling the tract at a profit became directly linked to the ability of their agent—Ellicott—to develop the parcel and thereby make it attractive to small retail purchasers. Ellicott's role as agent-developer thus became quite distinct from the land speculators of the earlier decade. His approach and the changes he brought to the region made sense in an economic environment in which only a low or moderate demand for wild land existed. Ultimately, Ellicott had to appeal to a class of pioneers more impressed with the practical virtues of handy mills and passable roads than they were with hazily defined notions of certain profits in distant lands. Although it can be argued that Ellicott's ultimate aims and those of the short-term speculator were the same—profits—the timing of expected returns on each investment created vastly different development strategies that had profound consequences for regional change and for the transformation of the landscape.

Ellicott's strategy for development succeeded in transforming the Holland Purchase, an arbitrary block of varied ground, into part of a larger, well-defined region that included other adjacent private land-selling efforts in the Massachusetts Pre-emption tract of upstate New York and in nearby portions of northern and western Pennsylvania. The settlement of all of these parcels was strongly shaped by the actions of particular agents and developers who directed surveys, town founding, and road construction.

Certainly physical geography did little to unify particular land agencies. Natural features helped to make Ellicott's job of developing the purchase more complex. No single waterway connected the tract in a clear fashion to other areas. If drainage basins had been used to define the boundaries of land-selling ventures, the purchase surely would have split into a half-dozen or more parcels. The southernmost reaches would have clearly belonged to a Pennsylvanian entrepreneur who might easily have seen the Allegheny and its tributaries in New York as simply a northern extension of the larger Ohio River basin. On the other hand, some portions of the southeastern purchase lay near tributaries of the Susquehanna, while other sections were linked to the Genesee River, which flowed almost due north from the Pennsylvania border to Lake Ontario. Still other waterways oriented western portions of the purchase to Lake Erie, northwest sections to the Niagara River, and northernmost tracts to Lake Ontario and the distant Saint Lawrence River.

Where physical geography failed, Ellicott's actions, other varied institutional influences, the area's relative location, and the mix of settlers succeeded in better defining its distinctive character. Similar to other land development ventures in upstate New York and in northwestern Pennsylvania, the purchase was distinguished by the fact that it was part of a frontier that was already within the boundary of an existing state. As such, its development and sale were linked from the earliest period to state political and judicial institutions. This placed it in a far different situation from the classic Turnerian frontier in which ad hoc institutions were created by isolated pioneers in an area completely divorced from the effective political control of a state government. What might have characterized the upland south was not the case on the Holland Purchase. The presence of government—local, state, and federal—from the first days of settlement supplied a variety of established institutional officials that ranged from Indian agents and postmasters to local tax collectors, legislators, and judges.

The overriding importance of private institutions, particularly the land company itself, is also illustrated by the Ellicott example. Throughout upstate New York and northwestern Pennsylvania, private land developing institutions were closely managing and manipulating frontier settlement systems. This presence of early authority, by providing an infrastructure of initial surveys, village sites, frontier services, roads, and organized sales policies molded the whole area into a recognizable region bound together by its heritage of related institutions.

The very real functional links between different land agencies also made the region more cohesive. Most obviously, some coordination was necessary in terms of integrating the road networks of different land agencies. There was no problem when the same land company owned different agencies. Such was the case with the coordinated construction of the Pennsylvania Road, which extended from Dutch company lands in north central Pennsylvania to the shores of Lake Erie in their western New York tract. Company employees in the two states jointly planned and executed the project. In other cases, however, conflicts sometimes resulted when different land agents developed their own plans for improving the region's road system. Nearby land agents, for example, often put pressure on Ellicott to support various turnpike schemes that he did not think particularly necessary. Many times, however, agents readily agreed on the need for coordination in building roads, and several of Ellicott's east-west routes were functionally connected to larger regional networks.

The New York agents were also bound by the fact that they were all tied to the dictates of the same state government policies. The same situation was true for the agents in Pennsylvania and elsewhere. All of the promoters habitually competed for their own agency's interests in the state legislature. They also competed for the same limited number of potential settlers that moved through the region in search of new lands. These common economic and political conditions shared by all of the land agents further defined the distinctive character of the region.

The regional identity of the purchase was complicated by its complex relationship to distant markets and by Ellicott's strategy for linking them to the purchase. As did other land agents in the area, Ellicott believed that the ultimate prosperity of the purchase could be guaranteed only if the channels of long-distance trade could be opened to cities and to markets far beyond the boundaries of the purchase. This idea was expressed in a decade of experimentation and testing in which Ellicott explored the various prospects for commercial expansion. He helped to establish the early divergent orientations to Philadelphia, Pittsburgh, Upper Canada, Montreal, Albany, and New York. After the War of 1812, he was also instrumental in encouraging the increasingly east-west component of trade and commerce between the purchase and the Hudson-Mohawk axis. The entire evolutionary process through which the area's regional commercial orientation was established was guided by the resident agent; he helped to create the larger regional economic context of western New York's settlement system, then and now.

In just a few short years, the Holland Purchase became a distinctive example of the developer's frontier in which private land agents exerted their special institutional influence over the structure of the settlement system. It also came to bear the mark of its resident agent, Joseph Ellicott, whose strategy for developing its forests, fields, and streams reached out for a new commercial prosperity and so by doing set the framework of orderly settlement for decades to come.

The developer's frontier impressed a new order on the land of western New York. Where only Indian villages and narrow paths once existed, a pattern of farms, settlements, and roads emerged. Every dimension of Ellicott's regional development strategy was reflected on the land itself. The new structure of surveys, villages, and roads arose from Ellicott's skill at borrowing from various planning traditions and combining them within the particular context of a western New York setting. Clearly, the new order impressed on the land represented a variegated mix of upstate New York, New England, and Pennsylvanian influences that contributed to new national patterns emerging during the period.

Obviously, Ellicott had more impact on some features than he did on others. His chief influence in shaping the regional geography came in projects that demanded the most centralized authority and the greatest degree of coordination. Chief among such features were the regular township and lot surveys laid out by Ellicott. The need for an integrated road network also placed much of the responsibility of establishing this element in the settlement landscape with Ellicott, although surveyors did enjoy more freedom in altering local routes than they did in altering township or lot patterns. Local residents also contributed their own road-building efforts, which added to the density and connectivity of the Ellicott network. The formal platting of villages was another ordering feature imposed on the land from above, but much of the townscape produced after Ellicott's platting was the product of individual settlers, some assisted by Ellicott, others unassisted. Ellicott's encouragement of mills can be seen from a similar perspective. The mills were a product both of Ellicott's knowledge and funding as well as of the entrepreneurs who conducted the day-to-day business of the mill.

At the most local level, Ellicott's impact on the frontier was evident but still more limited. Lot patterns influenced property boundaries and farm sizes, but Ellicott's flexibility in subdividing lots reduced the importance of the original 120- or 360-acre units. Ellicott's sales requirements regarding the prompt construction of a house, the clearing and planting of fields, and the fencing of lands also had an impact on the farm, but it was left to the predilections and resources of particular farmers to fashion the details of the rural landscape. Ellicott was continually frustrated by pioneers' notions of frontier settlement, which did not always parallel his own policies for development. The result was a landscape jointly created by the planned hand of the developer and by the sometimes capricious spirit of the settler. Still, in every county and in every township, Ellicott helped to establish a new frontier settlement system; in so doing, he changed the western New York landscape in fundamental ways.

Not only was the developer's impact on western New York pervasive and direct, it was also enduring. It is a reminder that certain stages in the process of making a landscape are of great importance. Ellicott's role as the initial land agent in the region meant that his decisions on original surveys, villages, mills, and roads would set the pattern and provide the foundation for future landscapes. The fragmentary nature of the remnants demonstrates, however, that the survival of the developer's imprint has been selective. Typically, those elements of the developer's frontier design that played a continuing functional role in later generations were much more apt to be preserved. Where survey lines, villages, or roadways ceased to be of use, they either disappeared or became obscure relics amid a landscape of more recent creation. The features that do remain, however, are a vivid visual display of both human greed and human ingenuity. As part of the ordinary landscape, they reveal the extraordinary impact of the land developer on the American scene, both in 1800 and today.

Notes

ABBREVIATIONS

AMS   Municipal Archives of Amsterdam
BHS   Buffalo and Erie County Historical Society, Buffalo, New York
HLC   Holland Land Company Collection
NYSL   New York State Library Archives, Albany
Range   "Field Notes of Survey of Township Lines in Various Ranges, Joseph
Books   Ellicott, Surveyor," 16 volumes
RG   Record Group
RJE 1   *Reports of Joseph Ellicott,* vol. 1, ed. Robert Warwick Bingham (Buffalo,
     N.Y.: Buffalo Historical Society, 1937)
RJE 2   *Reports of Joseph Ellicott,* vol. 2, ed. Robert Warwick Bingham (Buffalo,
     N.Y.: Buffalo Historical Society, 1941)
USGS   United States Geological Survey

CHAPTER 1: THE DEVELOPER'S FRONTIER

1. An excellent overview of the company's operations is provided by Paul D. Evans, *The Holland Land Company* (Buffalo, N.Y.: Buffalo Historical Society, 1924).

2. For a biography of Ellicott, see William Chazanof, *Joseph Ellicott and the Holland Land Company* (Syracuse, N.Y.: Syracuse University Press, 1970).

3. The interpretation of the everyday landscape is the subject of D. W. Meinig, ed., *The Interpretation of Ordinary Landscapes* (New York: Oxford University Press, 1979).

4. Promotional activities of the railroads are discussed in David Emmons, *Garden in the Grasslands* (Lincoln, Nebr.: University of Nebraska Press, 1971), and in Robert G. Athearn, *Rebel of the Rockies: A History of the Denver and Rio Grande Western Railroad* (New Haven, Conn.: Yale University Press, 1962).

5. For some examples, see Jerome Fellman, "Pre-Building Growth Patterns of Chicago," *Annals of the Association of American Geographers* 47 (1957): 59–82, and Sam Bass Warner, *Streetcar Suburbs: The Process of Growth in Boston, 1870–1900* (Cambridge, Mass.: Harvard University Press, 1962).

6. Frederick Jackson Turner, *The Frontier in American History* (New York: Henry Holt, 1947): 1–38.

7. Ibid., p. 20.

8. Ray Allan Billington, *Westward Expansion* (New York: Macmillan, 1949), and Frederick Merk, *History of the Westward Movement* (New York: Alfred A. Knopf, 1978).

9. Richard Hofstadter and Seymour Martin Lipset, eds., *Turner and the Sociology of the Frontier* (New York: Basic Books, 1968).

10. Billington, *Westward Expansion,* pp. 160–61, 173–74, and Ralph Brown, *Historical Geography of the United States* (New York: Harcourt Brace and World, 1948), pp. 183–89.

11. Robert Mitchell, "The Formation of Early American Cultural Regions: An Interpretation," in *European Settlement and Development in North America: Essays on Geographical Change in Honour and Memory of A. H. Clark,* ed. James R. Gibson (Toronto: University of Toronto Press, 1978), pp. 71–72.

12. Excellent studies that examine different dimensions of the public land system are Hildegard Binder Johnson, *Order upon the Land* (New York: Oxford University Press, 1976); William D. Pattison, *Beginnings of the American Rectangular Land Survey System, 1784–1800,* University of Chicago, Department of Geography Research Paper no. 50 (Chicago, 1957); and Malcolm G. Rohrbough, *The Land Office Business: The Settlement and Administration of American Public Lands, 1789–1837* (New York: Oxford University Press, 1968).

13. Paul Wallace Gates, *The Illinois Central Railroad and Its Colonization Work* (New York: Johnson Reprint Corporation, 1968), p. 119.

14. David M. Ellis, ed., *The Frontier in American Development: Essays in Honor of Paul Wallace Gates* (Ithaca, N.Y.: Cornell University Press, 1969), pp. 407–10.

15. Aaron Morton Sakolski, *The Great American Land Bubble* (New York: Harper Brothers, 1932).

16. Douglass C. North, "Location Theory and Regional Economic Growth," in *Regional Policy: Readings in Theory and Applications,* ed. John Friedmann and William Alonso (Cambridge, Mass.: MIT Press, 1975), pp. 332–47.

17. Mitchell, "Formation of Early American Cultural Regions," p. 71.

18. See, for example, John Reps, *The Making of Urban America* (Princeton, N.J.: Princeton University Press, 1965), and Richard C. Wade, *The Urban Frontier: The Rise of Western Cities, 1790–1830* (Cambridge, Mass.: Harvard University Press, 1959).

19. James E. Vance, *The Merchant's World: The Geography of Wholesaling* (Englewood-Cliffs, N.J.: Prentice-Hall, 1970).

20. The role of particular individuals in shaping the landscape is assessed by Marwyn Samuels, "The Biography of Landscape: Cause and Culpability," in Meinig, ed., *Interpretation of Ordinary Landscapes,* pp. 51–88.

21. Joseph S. Wood, "Village and Community in Early Colonial New England," *Journal of Historical Geography* 8 (1982): 335.

22. Ibid., p. 341; Douglas McManis, *Colonial New England: A Historical Geography* (New York: Oxford University Press, 1975), p. 123; Merk, *Westward Movement,* p. 117.

23. An excellent assessment of a number of Hudson Valley manors is provided by Sung Bok Kim, *Landlord and Tenant in Colonial New York: Manorial Society, 1664–1775* (Chapel Hill, N.C.: University of North Carolina Press, 1978).

24. Ibid., pp. 142, 165–69, 171–72.

25. Ibid., p. 126.

26. Wadsworth's land dealings are detailed in Neil McNall, *An Agricultural History of the Genesee Valley, 1790–1860* (Philadelphia: University of Pennsylvania Press, 1952).

27. Sakolski, *American Land Bubble,* pp. 1–28.

28. L. H. Butterfield, "Judge William Cooper (1754–1809): A Sketch of His Character and Accomplishment," *New York History* 30 (1949): 385–408, and John Thompson, ed., *Geography of New York State* (Syracuse, N.Y.: Syracuse University Press, 1977), p. 148.

29. William Cooper, *A Guide in the Wilderness* (Dublin: Gilbert and Hodges, 1810).

30. Ibid., p. 7.

31. Ibid.
32. Billington, *Westward Expansion,* pp. 208–15; Brown, *Historical Geography,* pp. 215–18.
33. Billington, *Westward Expansion,* p. 213.
34. Ibid., p. 214; Brown, *Historical Geography,* pp. 218–20; Shaw Livermore, *Early American Land Companies* (New York: Octagon Books, 1968), pp. 134–46.
35. Billington, *Westward Expansion,* p. 254; Brown, *Historical Geography,* pp. 220–27; Harlan Hatcher, *The Western Reserve* (Indianapolis, Ind.: Bobbs-Merrill, 1949).
36. An overview of land development ventures is offered by D. W. Meinig in Thompson, ed., *New York State,* pp. 140–71.
37. Evans, *Holland Land Company,* pp. 37–86.
38. G. M. Craig, *Upper Canada: The Formative Years, 1784–1861* (London: McClelland and Stewart, 1963); L. F. Gates, *Land Policies of Upper Canada* (Toronto: University of Toronto Press, 1968); J. D. Wood, "Grand Design on the Fringes of Empire: New Towns for British North America," *Canadian Geographer* 26 (1982): 243–55.
39. J. M. Cameron, "The Canada Company and Land Settlement as Resource Development in the Guelph Block," in *Perspectives on Landscape and Settlement in Nineteenth Century Ontario,* ed. J. D. Wood (Toronto: McClelland and Stewart, 1975); F. C. Hamil, *Lake Erie Baron: The Story of Colonel Thomas Talbot* (Toronto: Macmillan, 1955); G. Scott, *The Settlement of Huron County* (Toronto: Ryerson Press, 1966).
40. James Lemon, *The Best Poor Man's Country: A Geographical Study of Early Southeastern Pennsylvania* (New York: W. W. Norton, 1976), p. 55; Harry Roy Merrens, *Colonial North Carolina in the Eighteenth Century* (Chapel Hill, N.C.: University of North Carolina Press, 1964), p. 25; Robert Mitchell, *Commercialism and Frontier: Perspectives on the Early Shenandoah Valley* (Charlottesville, Va.: University of Virginia Press, 1977), pp. 29–30, 44.
41. Johnson, *Order upon the Land,* pp. 53–64.
42. McNall, *Agricultural History;* Helen Cowan, *Charles Williamson: Genesee Promoter* (Rochester, N.Y.: Rochester Historical Society, 1944); William Herbert Siles, "A Vision of Wealth: Speculators and Settlers in the Genesee Country of New York, 1788–1800" (Ph.D. diss., University of Massachusetts, 1978).
43. Early land transactions are discussed in Barbara Chernow, "Robert Morris: Genesee Land Speculator," *New York History* 58 (1977): 194–220.
44. Siles, "Vision of Wealth."
45. Evans, *Holland Land Company,* pp. 3–35.
46. Ibid.
47. Charles W. Evans, *Biographical and Historical Accounts of the Fox, Ellicott, and Evans Families* (Buffalo, N.Y.: Baker, Jones, 1887), pp. 166–77.
48. C. V. C. Matthews, *Andrew Ellicott: His Life and Letters* (New York: Grafton Press, 1908), pp. 31–42.
49. Joseph Ellicott to Theophile Cazenove, 29 February 1794, RG 140–10, HLC-AMS.
50. Joseph Ellicott to Theophile Cazenove, 3 November 1795, 8:263, HLC-BHS.
51. Joseph Ellicott to Thomas Mifflin, 1796, 8:233, HLC-BHS.
52. Thompson, *New York State,* pp. 25–33.
53. Ibid., pp. 104–10.
54. Ibid., pp. 90–103. Vegetation patterns were also reconstructed through the use of the Range Books.
55. Thompson, *New York State,* pp. 113–20.
56. Blake McKelvey, *Rochester: The Water-Power City* (Cambridge, Mass.: Harvard University Press, 1945), p. 15.
57. "Account of the Census of the Seneca Indians within the District of the Genesee Country Taken 1795," RG 81–18–64, HLC-AMS.

58. Gordon M. Day, "The Indian as an Ecological Factor in the Northeastern Forests," *Ecology* 34 (1953): 329–46.

59. De La Rochefoucault Liancourt, *Travels through the United States of North America in the Years 1795, 1796, and 1797* (London: R. Phillips, 1799), p. 175.

60. Day, "Ecological Factor," p. 334; Robert Sutcliffe, *Travels in Some Parts of North America in the Years 1804, 1805, 1806* (Philadelphia: B. and T. Kite, 1812), p. 147.

61. "Original Books of Field Notes," vol. 59, HLC-NYSL; Benjamin Ellicott to Joseph Ellicott, 6 July 1798, 8:59, HLC-BHS; Reading Howell, "A Map of the State of Pennsylvania" (Philadelphia, 1791); Samuel Lewis, "The State of New York" (1795).

62. Andrew F. Burghardt, "The Origin and Development of the Road Network of the Niagara Peninsula, Ontario, 1770–1851," *Annals of the Association of American Geographers* 59 (1969): 417–40.

63. Thompson, *New York State,* p. 118.

64. De La Rochefoucault Liancourt, *Travels through the United States,* p. 177.

CHAPTER 2: THE TOWNSHIP SURVEYS OF 1797–1799

1. Amelia C. Ford, *Colonial Precedents of Our National Land System as It Existed in 1800* (Madison, Wis.: University of Wisconsin Press, 1910), p. 14; Carville Earle, *The Evolution of a Tidewater Settlement System: All Hallow's Parish, Maryland, 1650–1783,* University of Chicago, Department of Geography Research Paper no. 170 (Chicago, 1975), pp. 182–93; James Lemon, *The Best Poor Man's Country: A Geographical Study of Early Southeastern Pennsylvania* (New York: W. W. Norton, 1976), p. 55.

2. Hildegard Binder Johnson, *Order upon the Land* (New York: Oxford University Press, 1976), pp. 28–31, 46–47; James E. Vance, Jr., *This Scene of Man* (New York: Harper and Row, 1977), pp. 55–56.

3. Ford, *Colonial Precedents,* p. 42; Marshall Harris, *Origin of the Land Tenure System in the United States* (Ames, Iowa: Iowa State College Press, 1953), pp. 278–79; Douglas R. McManis, *Colonial New England: A Historical Geography* (New York: Oxford University Press, 1975), pp. 63–66.

4. Paul Evans, *The Holland Land Company* (Buffalo, N.Y.: Buffalo Historical Society, 1924), pp. 22–23, 39–40; "Plan of the Province of Main," RG 479–47, HLC-AMS.

5. Clarence Edwin Carter, ed., *The Territorial Papers of the United States,* vol. 2: *The Territory Northwest of the River Ohio, 1787–1803* (Washington, D.C.: U.S. Government Printing Office, 1934), pp. 12–18, 552–57; William D. Pattison, *Beginnings of the American Rectangular Land Survey System, 1784–1800,* University of Chicago, Department of Geography Research Paper no. 50 (Chicago, 1957).

6. "Items Concerning Companies and Negotiations Dealing with Land in the United States of America," RG 267–268, HLC-AMS.

7. John Thompson, ed., *Geography of New York State* (Syracuse, N.Y.: Syracuse University Press, 1977), pp. 149–50; "A Map of the Military Lands and 20 Townships in the Western Part of the State of New York," RG 479–24, HLC-AMS.

8. William Herbert Siles, "A Vision of Wealth: Speculators and Settlers in the Genesee Country of New York, 1788–1800" (Ph.D. diss., University of Massachusetts, 1978), p. 57.

9. R. Louis Gentilcore, "The Beginning of Settlement in the Niagara Peninsula," *Canadian Geographer* 7 (1963): 76–77; R. Louis Gentilcore and Kate Donkin, "Land Surveys of Southern Ontario: An Introduction and Index to the Field Notebooks of the Ontario Land Surveyors, 1784–1859," *Canadian Cartographer* 10 (1973): suppl. 2, pp. 2–4.

10. "Explanation B," RG 143–1–6, HLC-AMS.

11. William Morris to Theophile Cazenove, 23 January 1793, RG 130–3, HLC-AMS.

12. Joseph Ellicott to Theophile Cazenove, 3 May 1798, RG 130–10, HLC-AMS; William Morris to Cazenove, 23 January 1793, RG 130–3, HLC-AMS.

13. Thomas Morris, "Proposals," 28 December 1797, RG 130–9, HLC-AMS.

14. William Morris to Theophile Cazenove, 23 January 1793, RG 130–3, HLC-AMS.

15. James Wadsworth to John Lincklaen, 30 January 1796, RG 130–7, HLC-AMS.

16. Theophile Cazenove to Joseph Ellicott, 6 October 1797, 8:205, HLC-BHS.

17. The variety of supplies is described in "Report and Bill of Surveying in the Genesee Lands of J. Ellicott, 1798–1800," RG 414, HLC-AMS.

18. Details of life on the survey are provided in Ellicott's correspondence in vols. 8–9, HLC-BHS.

19. John Thomson to Joseph Ellicott, 16 September 1798, 8:79, HLC-BHS.

20. Evans, *Holland Land Company,* pp. 186–95; "Big Tree Treaty," September 1797, RG 81–11, HLC-AMS.

21. F. M. L. Thompson, *Chartered Surveyors: The Growth of a Profession* (London: Routledge and Kegan Paul, 1968), pp. 1–108; Silvio Bedini, *Thinkers and Tinkers: Early American Men of Science* (New York: Charles Scribner's Sons, 1975), pp. 128–29; William and Mabel Smallwood, *Natural History and the American Mind* (New York: Columbia University Press, 1941), pp. 21–23; Raymond Stearns, *Science in the British Colonies of America* (Urbana, Ill.: University of Illinois Press, 1970), pp. 305–15, 535–39, 564–66.

22. Carter, *Territorial Papers,* 2:554.

23. "East Allegheny—Original Field Notes," RG 593–5, HLC-AMS.

24. Major Hoops to Robert Morris, 20 April 1798, 8:39, HLC-BHS.

25. Joseph Ellicott to Ebenezar Cary, 31 May 1805, 3b:351, HLC-BHS.

26. Range Books, HLC-NYSL.

27. Alexander Autrechy, "Map of the Several Tracts of Land Belonging to the Holland Company" (1799), RG 219–11, HLC-AMS.

28. William Morris to Theophile Cazenove, 23 January 1793, RG 130–3, HLC-AMS, and William Vance, "Field Notes," 29 April 1795, 8:251, HLC-BHS.

29. Figures were calculated from all the surveyed township perimeters assessed in the Range Books.

30. Joseph Ellicott to James Dewey, 1 July 1800, 8:771, HLC-BHS.

31. Ibid.

32. Noah Webster, *An American Dictionary of the English Language,* 2 vols. (1828; reprint, New York: Johnson Reprint Corporation, 1970).

33. Charles Williamson, "Description of the Genesee Country in the State of New York in a Series of Letters from a Gentleman to His Friend," in *Documentary History of the State of New York,* vol. 2, ed. E. B. O'Callaghan (Albany, N.Y.: Weed, Parsons, 1849), p. 1146.

34. John Melish, *Travels in the United States of America in the Years 1806 and 1807, and 1809, 1810, and 1811* (1812; reprint, New York: Johnson Reprint Corporation, 1970), p. 512.

35. Joseph Ellicott to Paul Busti, 30 June 1808, 4a:205, HLC-BHS, and John Lincklaen to Busti, 25 October 1802, RG 131–9, HLC-AMS.

36. William Morris to John Lincklaen, 8 July 1793, RG 130–3, HLC-AMS.

37. Christian Schultz, *Travels on an Inland Voyage through the States of New York . . . in the Years 1807 and 1808* (New York: Isaac Riley, 1810), pp. 104–5.

38. Joseph Ellicott to Paul Busti, 6 January 1809, 4a:235, HLC-BHS.

39. Mary Dobson, "'Marsh Fever': The Geography of Malaria in England," *Journal of Historical Geography* 6 (1980): 357–89.

40. Joseph Ellicott to Paul Busti, n.d., RG 143–1–3, item 3, HLC-AMS.

41. Kenneth Kelly, "The Evaluation of Land for Wheat Cultivation in Early Nineteenth Century Ontario," *Ontario History* 62 (1970): 63; Clayton Mau, *The Development of Central and Western New York* (Rochester, N.Y.: Dubois Press, 1944), p. 212; Webster, *American Dictionary.*

42. Range Books, vols. 7-8, HLC-NYSL.

43. Donald Steila, *The Geography of Soils* (Englewood-Cliffs, N.J.: Prentice-Hall, 1976), p. 36–38; Melish, *Travels,* p. 510.

44. Joseph Ellicott to David Ogden, 2 February 1811, 4b:53, HLC-BHS.

45. Evans, *Holland Land Company,* pp. 63–85; Gilbert Imlay, "A Topographical Description of the Western Territory of North America" in *Documentary History of New York,* vol. 2, ed. O'Callaghan, pp. 1111–25.
46. William Cooper, *Guide in the Wilderness* (Dublin: Gilbert and Hodges, 1810), pp. 34–36; Robert Munro, "A Description of the Genesee Country," in *Documentary History of New York,* vol. 2, ed. O'Callaghan, p. 1173.
47. Jabish Warner to Joseph Ellicott, 16 April 1810, 16:317, HLC-BHS.
48. By contrast, William Cooper noted that hemlock indicated a good soil when it was found along with other hardwoods (*Guide,* pp. 34–36).
49. Bernard C. Peters, "Changing Ideas about the Use of Vegetation as an Indicator of Soil Quality: Examples of New York and Michigan," *Journal of Geography* 72, no. 2 (1973): 19; J. B. Bicker to Theophile Cazenove, 1 September 1797, RG 81–30–33, HLC-AMS.
50. William Morris to Theophile Cazenove, 30 July 1793, RG 130–3, HLC-AMS.
51. James Brisbane to Joseph Ellicott, 5 September 1798, 8:77, HLC-BHS.
52. Isaac Weld, *Travels through the States of North America,* vol. 2 (1799; reprint, New York: Johnson Reprint Corporation, 1968), p. 315.
53. Williamson, "Description of the Genesee Country," p. 1147.
54. Robert Sutcliffe, *Travels in Some Parts of North America in the Years 1804, 1805, 1806* (Philadelphia: B. and T. Kite, 1812), p. 147.
55. Joseph Ellicott to Paul Busti, 3 June 1799, 8:635, HLC-BHS.
56. RJE 2, p. 207; Joseph Ellicott to Paul Busti, 19 September 1809, 4a:269, HLC-BHS.
57. Thomas Cooper, *Some Information respecting America* (1793; reprint, New York: A. M. Kelly, 1969), p. 14; Joseph Ellicott to Paul Busti, 29 August 1799, RG 405, HLC-AMS.
58. Thomas Cooper, *A Ride to Niagara* (1814), p. 300.

CHAPTER 3: OPENING THE PURCHASE

1. William Morris to Theophile Cazenove, 23 January, 30 July 1793, RG 130–3, HLC-AMS; Joseph Ellicott to Cazenove, 3 May 1798, Ellicott to Cazenove and Paul Busti, 15 May 1799, and Ellicott to Busti, 26 March 1800, RG 130–10, HLC-AMS.
2. James Wadsworth to John Lincklaen, 30 January 1796, and Wadsworth to Theophile Cazenove, 14 January 1800, RG 130–7, HLC-AMS.
3. Charles Williamson, "Observations on New Settlements," 30 December 1796, RG 130–8, HLC-AMS.
4. Thomas Morris, "Proposals," 28 December 1797, RG 130–9, HLC-AMS.
5. Gerritt Boon to Theophile Cazenove, 20 April 1797, RG 130–6, HLC-AMS.
6. "Plan Proposed by J. Lincklaen," April 1798, RG 130–5, HLC-AMS; Lincklaen, "A Few Observations respecting Mr. Wadsworth's Plan of Settlement," December 1796, RG 130–7, HLC-AMS; Lincklaen, "Observations respecting Mr. Williamson's Plan of Settlement," 21 January 1797, RG 130–8, HLC-AMS; and Lincklaen to Theophile Cazenove, 17 November 1800, RG 130–5, HLC-AMS.
7. Charles-Maurice de Talleyrand-Périgord, Prince de Bénévent, "Observations on Speculation in Lands in the United States of America," in *Talleyrand in America as a Financial Promoter: 1794–1798: Unpublished Letters and Memoirs,* ed. and trans. Hans Huth and Wilma Pugh (Washington, D.C.: U.S. Government Printing Office, 1942), pp. 137–75.
8. Ibid., p. 168.
9. Ibid., p. 170.
10. Ibid., p. 169.
11. Marshall Harris, *Origin of the Land Tenure System in the United States* (Ames, Iowa: Iowa State

College Press, 1953), pp. 278–85; Douglas McManis, *Colonial New England: A Historical Geography* (New York: Oxford University Press, 1975), pp. 53–63; John Reps, *Town Planning in Frontier America* (Princeton, N.J.: Princeton University Press, 1969), pp. 147–49, 183.

12. William Morris to Theophile Cazenove, 30 July 1793, RG 130–3, HLC-AMS.

13. Williamson, "Observations on New Settlements."

14. Gerritt Boon to Theophile Cazenove, 20 April 1797, RG 130–6, HLC-AMS.

15. Ibid.; Morris, "Proposals."

16. Paul Evans, *The Holland Land Company* (Buffalo, N.Y.: Buffalo Historical Society, 1924), p. 220; Theophile Cazenove, "Lands of the Genesee," 16 January 1800, RG 167–Da4, HLC-AMS.

17. Joseph Ellicott to Theophile Cazenove and Paul Busti, 15 May 1799, RG 130–10, HLC-AMS.

18. Joseph Ellicott, 3 June 1799, 8:635, HLC-BHS.

19. Theophile Cazenove to Joseph Ellicott, 1 June 1799, RG 167–Da5, HLC-AMS.

20. Joseph Ellicott to Theophile Cazenove, 3 May 1798, RG 130–10, HLC-AMS.

21. Theophile Cazenove to Joseph Ellicott, 4 April 1799, 8:535, HLC-BHS.

22. Joseph Ellicott to Paul Busti, 15 May 1800, RG 751–10, HLC-AMS.

23. Theophile Cazenove, "Terres du Genesee," 16 January 1800, RG 167–Da4, HLC-AMS; Paul Busti to Joseph Ellicott, 15 August 1800, RG 167–Da9, HLC-AMS.

24. Paul Busti to Joseph Ellicott, RG 167–Da9, HLC-AMS.

25. Ibid.

26. Joseph Ellicott to James Dewey, 29 June, 1 July 1800, 8:767, 771, HLC-BHS.

27. Joseph Ellicott to Benjamin Ellicott, 18 March 1801, 3a:38, HLC-BHS.

28. RJE 1, pp. 104, 182.

29. Joseph Ellicott to Paul Busti, 8 September 1801, 3a:109, HLC-BHS.

30. RJE 1, p. 148; Joseph Ellicott, "Journal," 29:113, HLC-BHS; "Annual Settlement of Accounts with the General Agent, 1800–1810," p. 6, RG 779, HLC-AMS; Ellicott to Paul Busti, 8 September 1801, 3a:109, HLC-BHS.

31. RJE 1, pp. 152, 277.

32. Joseph Ellicott to Benjamin Ellicott, 18 March 1801, 3a:38, HLC-BHS; Joseph Ellicott to John Thomson, 14 July 1801, 3a:78, HLC-BHS; Joseph Ellicott, "Journal," 29:196–97, 226, HLC-BHS.

33. Joseph Ellicott, "Journal," 29:13, 73, 99, 108, 116, 123, 197, 219, 226.

34. Ibid., pp. 99, 197; RJE 1, p. 144.

35. Joseph Ellicott to James Wilkinson, 22 May 1801, 3a:59, HLC-BHS.

36. Joseph Ellicott to Alexander Rea, 4 March 1801, 3a:27, HLC-BHS; "Annual Settlement of Accounts, 1800–1810," p. 15; "Accounts and Receipts Belonging to the Annual Settlement of Accounts with the General Agent, 1800–1802," RG 782, HLC-AMS.

37. Joseph Ellicott to James Gould, 30 September 1803, 3b:153, HLC-BHS; Paul Busti to Joseph Ellicott, 23 October 1804, 6:601, HLC-BHS.

38. Joseph Ellicott to Paul Busti, 7 June 1805, 3b:356, HLC-BHS; Ellicott to Busti, 24 December 1808, 4a:233, HLC-BHS.

39. Joseph Ellicott to Paul Busti, 15 July 1803, 3b:90, HLC-BHS; Ellicott to James Gould, 30 September 1803, 3b:153, HLC-BHS; Gould and Post to Ellicott, 9 October 1803, 11a:90, HLC-BHS; "Annual Settlement of Accounts, 1800–1810," p. 58.

40. Samuel Brown to Joseph Ellicott, 2 February 1801, 9:19, HLC-BHS; William Stark to Ellicott, 18 September 1803, 11a:75, HLC-BHS.

41. Thomas Kennedy to Joseph Ellicott, 15 March 1804, 12:21, HLC-BHS.

42. Specific agreements with surrogate agents are found in Ellicott's correspondence and copy books in vols. 3–4, 6–9, 11–17, 21–23, and 29, HLC-BHS.

43. Joseph Ellicott to Jacob Taylor, 25 October, 25 November 1805, 4a:20, 30, HLC-BHS; Taylor to Ellicott, 4 November 1806, 15:42, HLC-BHS.

44. RJE 2, pp. 67–74, 207–12, 397–404.
45. Williamson, "Observations on New Settlements."
46. RJE 1, p. 104.
47. Joseph Ellicott, "Private Day Book," vol. 26, HLC-BHS.
48. Joseph Ellicott to Paul Busti, 7 June 1805, 3b:356, HLC-BHS.
49. Joseph Ellicott to Paul Busti, 15 September 1810, 4a:309, HLC-BHS.
50. Joseph Ellicott to A. M. Grosvenor, 15 July 1811, 4b:113, HLC-BHS.
51. Joseph Ellicott to Paul Busti, 21 July 1801, 3a:89, HLC-BHS.
52. Joseph Ellicott to Paul Busti, 14 July 1801, 3a:80, HLC-BHS.
53. Joseph Ellicott to Parmenio Adams, 13 August 1808, 4a:227, HLC-BHS.

CHAPTER 4: SETTLEMENT POLICY ON THE DEVLOPER'S FRONTIER

1. Joseph Ellicott, "Journal," 29:40, HLC-BHS; Paul Busti to Ellicott, 15 August 1800, RG 167–Da9, HLC-AMS.
2. Ellicott's lobbying efforts can be followed in his correspondence with Busti in 1801 and 1802. See 3a:80–248, HLC-BHS.
3. Joseph Ellicott to Paul Busti, 21 July 1801, 3a:89, HLC-BHS.
4. Paul Busti to Joseph Ellicott, 21 April 1803, 6:389, HLC-BHS; Ellicott to Busti, 2 July 1803, 3b:79, HLC-BHS.
5. RJE 1, p. 301; Joseph Ellicott to Paul Busti, 10 November 1802, and Ellicott to Adam Hoops, 10 July 1804, 3b:11, 256, HLC-BHS.
6. Joseph Ellicott to Paul Busti, 8 June 1804, 3b:236, HLC-BHS.
7. Joseph Ellicott to Joseph McClure, 17 June 1805, 4a:2, HLC-BHS.
8. RJE 1, p. 307.
9. Paul Busti to Joseph Ellicott, 18 July 1810, 7:713, HLC-BHS.
10. The price of any parcel was a function of many variables, and it expressed an overall assessment of the parcel by Ellicott using "contemporary ideas on land values." See R. L. Heathcote, *Back of Bourke: A Study of Land Appraisal and Settlement in Semi-Arid Australia* (London: Melbourne University Press, 1965), pp. 62–66.
11. Joseph Ellicott to Theophile Cazenove and Paul Busti, 15 May 1799, RG 130–10, HLC-AMS; Robert Silsby, "Mortgage Credit in the Phelps-Gorham Purchase," *New York History* 41 (1960): 7.
12. Joseph Ellicott to Paul Busti, 17 February 1801, 3a:12, HLC-BHS.
13. Joseph Ellicott to Theophile Cazenove and Paul Busti, 15 May 1799, RG 130–10, HLC-AMS; James Wadsworth to Cazenove, 4 June 1799, RG 267–29–5, HLC-AMS; Curtis P. Nettels, *The Emergence of a National Economy, 1775–1815* (New York: Holt, Rinehart, and Winston, 1962), p. 148.
14. Paul Busti to Joseph Ellicott, 15 August 1800, RG 167–Da9, HLC-AMS.
15. Joseph Ellicott, "Table of Terms and Conditions of Sale," 1801, RG 167–Da15, HLC-AMS.
16. William Morris to John Lincklaen, 8 July 1793, RG 130–3, HLC-AMS; James Wadsworth to Theophile Cazenove, 4 January 1799, RG 267–29–5, HLC-AMS.
17. Nettels, *Emergence of a National Economy,* p. 4.
18. RJE 1, p. 164.
19. William Herbert Siles, "A Vision of Wealth: Speculators and Settlers in the Genesee Country of New York, 1788–1800" (Ph.D. diss., University of Massachusetts, 1978), p. 182.
20. These 1801 policy shifts can be followed in 3a:12–100, HLC-BHS.
21. Joseph Ellicott to Paul Busti, 10 November 1802, and Ellicott to Alexander McConnell, 11 December 1802, 3b:11, 85, HLC-BHS.
22. Joseph Ellicott to Paul Busti, 17 July 1802, 3a:243, HLC-BHS.

23. Data on land sales are from "Report of Land Tables, 1804," RG 484, HLC-AMS.

24. Data on land sales are from "Report of Land Tables, 1811, 1812," RG 489, 490, HLC-AMS.

25. Paul Busti to Joseph Ellicott, 22 June, 18 July 1810, 7:665, 713, HLC-BHS.

26. Joseph Ellicott to Paul Busti, 3 November 1810, and Ellicott to William Peacock [1810], 4b:9, 1, HLC-BHS.

27. Joseph Ellicott to Ebenezer Cary, 3 September 1804, 3b:284, HLC-BHS.

28. Joseph Ellicott to William Peacock, 28 October 1811, 4b:128, HLC-BHS.

29. Joseph Ellicott to Paul Busti, 9 July, 19 September 1807, 4a:123, 269, HLC-BHS.

30. Joseph Ellicott to Paul Busti, 15 December 1803, 3b:178, HLC-BHS.

31. Joseph Ellicott to Paul Busti, 17 November 1803, 3b:173, HLC-BHS.

32. Joseph Ellicott to Paul Busti, 4 June 1802, 3a:215, HLC-BHS.

33. Joseph Ellicott to Paul Busti, 30 December 1805, 4a:42, HLC-BHS.

34. Joseph Ellicott to Paul Busti, 4 June, 7 July 1802, 3a:215, 235, HLC-BHS; Busti to Ellicott, 20 April 1803, 6:379, HLC-BHS.

35. Such an "entrepôt alignment" in frontier areas is described in James Vance, *The Merchant's World: The Geography of Wholesaling* (Englewood-Cliffs, N.J.: Prentice-Hall, 1970), pp. 157–59.

36. Joseph Ellicott to Paul Busti, 30 May 1801, 3a:64, HLC-BHS.

37. Joseph Ellicott to Paul Busti, 3 June 1799, 8:635, HLC-BHS.

38. "Cumulative causation" is described in Allan R. Pred, *The Spatial Dynamics of U.S. Urban-Industrial Growth, 1800–1914: Interpretative and Theoretical Essays* (Cambridge, Mass.: MIT Press, 1966), pp. 177–78.

39. Joseph Ellicott, "Proposed Plan for a Town at the East End of Lake Erie Called New Amsterdam," RG 480–8, HLC-AMS.

40. Joseph Ellicott to Paul Busti, 21 July 1801, 3a:89, HLC-BHS.

41. Paul Busti to Joseph Ellicott, 20 April 1803, 6:379, HLC-BHS; Joseph Ellicott to Adam Hoops, 24 August 1804, 3b:273, HLC-BHS.

42. Andrew Ellicott to Sarah Ellicott, 13 September 1787, Papers of Andrew Ellicott, Manuscripts Division, Library of Congress.

43. RJE 1, pp. 279–80.

44. Joseph Ellicott to Paul Busti, 7 June 1805, 3b:356, HLC-BHS; Busti to Ellicott, 9 June 1804, 6:371, HLC-BHS.

45. Joseph Ellicott to Paul Busti, 27 February 1808, 4a:181, HLC-BHS; James Stevens to Ellicott, 17 November 1808, 9:637, HLC-BHS.

46. Ibid.

47. Joseph Ellicott to Paul Busti, 7 June 1805, 3b:356, HLC-BHS.

48. RJE 1, p. 330.

49. Joseph Ellicott to Paul Busti, 21 July 1801, 3a:89, HLC-BHS.

50. RJE 1, p. 330.

51. Joseph A. Durrenberger, *Turnpikes* (Cos Cob, Conn.: John E. Edwards, 1960), pp. 14–15.

52. RJE 1, p. 143; Joseph Ellicott to James Brookes, 6 March 1801, 3a:35, HLC-BHS.

53. Paul Busti to Joseph Ellicott, 4 September 1806, 6:159, HLC-BHS; Ellicott to Busti, 17 October 1806, 4a:84, HLC-BHS.

54. Joseph Ellicott to Benjamin Riggs, 6 September 1806, 4a:76, HLC-BHS.

55. Joseph Ellicott to Paul Busti, 12 August 1803, Ellicott to Jacob Taylor, 7 July 1804, 3b:117, 255, HLC-BHS; "Annual Settlement of Accounts with the General Agent, 1800–1810," p. 177, RG 779, HLC-AMS.

56. Joseph Ellicott to James Wilkinson, 22 May 1801, 3a:59, HLC-BHS; "Annual Settlement of Accounts, 1800–1810," pp. 29, 177; Ellicott to Eli Griffith, 30 August 1808, 4a:221, HLC-BHS; Ellicott to Paul Busti, 30 August 1811, 4b:116, HLC-BHS.

57. William Adams, *Historical Gazetteer and Biographical Memorial of Cattaraugus County* (Syracuse, N.Y.: Lyman, Horton and Co., 1893), p. 1142; "Records," Town of Clarence (Willinks), vols. 1, 3, and 7, Town Clerk's Office, Clarence Center, N.Y.; "Records," Town of Hamburg, vol. 1, Town Clerk's Office, Hamburg, N.Y.

58. Matthew Prendergast to Joseph Ellicott, 18 June 1808, 13:256, HLC-BHS; various references to road construction are noted in 4a:204–27, HLC-BHS.

59. Andrew White Young, *History of Chautauqua County* (Buffalo, N.Y.: Matthews and Warren, 1875), p. 332; Robert Hoops to Joseph Ellicott, 27 January 1806, 15:290, HLC-BHS; "Annual Settlement of Accounts, 1800–1810," p. 78.

60. Durrenberger, *Turnpikes,* pp. 11–12; Andrew F. Burghardt, "The Origin and Development of the Road Network of the Niagara Peninsula, Ontario, 1770–1851," *Annals of the Association of American Geographers* 59 (1969): 426–27.

61. Ebenezar Cary to Joseph Ellicott, 12 July 1804, 12:54, HLC-BHS; "Lot Field Books," vol. 80, 126, HLC-NYSL.

62. Joseph Ellicott to Paul Busti, 29 August 1799, RG 405, HLC-AMS; "Holland Land Company Lot Survey Notes," vol. 5, Erie County Clerk's Office, Buffalo, N.Y.; Joseph Ellicott to Benjamin Ellicott, 18 March 1801, 3a:38, HLC-BHS.

63. Thomas Cooper, *A Ride to Niagara* (1814), p. 60; G. T. Hopkins, "Visit of Gerald T. Hopkins," *Publications of the Buffalo Historical Society* 6 (1903): 221; John Melish, *Travels in the United States of America* (1812; reprint, New York: Johnson Reprint Corporation, 1970), p. 511.

64. Joseph Ellicott to Alexander Rea, 14 February 1805, 3b:325, HLC-BHS.

65. RJE 1, pp. 272, 332–33.

CHAPTER 5: COMMERCIAL POLICY ON THE DEVELOPER'S FRONTIER

1. Cornelius Van Dyck to Joseph Ellicott, 24 April 1805, 14:4, HLC-BHS.

2. RJE 1, pp. 343–44; "Annual Settlement of Accounts with the General Agent, 1800–1810," p. 113, RG 779, HLC-AMS; "Annual Settlement of Accounts with the General Agent, 1810–1822," RG 780, p. 51, HLC-AMS.

3. RJE 1, p. 149.

4. "Accounts and Receipts Belonging to the Annual Settlement of Accounts with the General Agent, 1803," pts. A and B, RG 783, HLC-AMS.

5. RJE 1, p. 152.

6. Ibid., pp. 277, 358–89; "Annual Settlement of Accounts, 1800–1810," p. 92.

7. Joseph Ellicott to Paul Busti, 8 May 1802, 3a:199, HLC-BHS; Busti to Ellicott, 20 April 1803, 6:379, HLC-BHS.

8. RJE 1, p. 342; Paul Busti to Joseph Ellicott, 1 June 1808, RG 168–DA–32–1, HLC-AMS; "Annual Settlement of Accounts, 1800–1810," p. 184.

9. Simeon Cummings to Joseph Ellicott, 21 March 1811, 17:421, HLC-BHS.

10. RJE 1, pp. 181, 198.

11. Joseph Ellicott to Paul Busti, 20 September 1804, 3b:291, HLC-BHS.

12. Joseph Ellicott to Paul Busti, 8 September 1801, 3a:109, HLC-BHS.

13. Joseph Ellicott to Louis Le Couteulx, 16 July 1803, 3b:93, HLC-BHS.

14. Joseph Ellicott to David Ogden, 25 February 1802, 3a:180, HLC-BHS.

15. Joseph Ellicott to Paul Busti, 30 May 1801, 3a:64, HLC-BHS.

16. Joseph Ellicott to Paul Busti, 12 August, 20 October 1803, 3b:117, 197, HLC-BHS.

17. William Chazanof, *Joseph Ellicott and the Holland Land Company* (Syracuse, N.Y.: Syracuse University Press, 1970), pp. 50–52; Joseph Ellicott to Dudley Saltonstall, 24 February 1802, 3a:179, HLC-BHS.

18. Joseph Ellicott to Paul Busti, 27 March, 8 May 1802, 3a:189, 199, HLC-BHS.

19. "The Transcript of the Act Separating Genesee from Ontario County, Passed 30 March 1802," vol. 27, HLC-BHS.

20. Joseph Ellicott to Paul Busti, 7 August 1802, 3a:260, HLC-BHS.

21. "Act Separating Genesee from Ontario County."

22. Chazanof, *Joseph Ellicott,* pp. 106–7.

23. Joseph Ellicott to Paul Busti, 9 January 1807, and Ellicott to the New York State Legislature, February 1808, 4a:112, 179, HLC-BHS.

24. Chazanof, *Joseph Ellicott,* p. 108.

25. Joseph Ellicott to Paul Busti, 30 June 1808, 4a:205, HLC-BHS.

26. Joseph Ellicott to Daniel Tompkins, 4 June 1808, 4a:201, HLC-BHS.

27. Chazanof, *Joseph Ellicott,* pp. 55–59. Further details of local governmental structure and responsibilities can be found in local records; see, for example, Elial Foote, *Abstract of the Proceedings of the Board of Supervisors of the County of Chautauqua* (Fredonia, N.Y.: W. McKinstry and Son, 1868); Chautauqua County, New York, Board of Supervisors, *Laws and Resolutions* (Ripley, N.Y., 1945); "Original Records of the Town of Batavia from 1803 and the Laws of the State of New York . . . ," vol. 27, HLC-BHS; "Proceedings of the Board of Supervisors, Genesee County, 1803–1807," Hollinger Box 2, file 5, HLC-BHS; and "Records," Town of Clarence (Willinks), vols. 1, 3, and 7, Town Clerk's Office, Clarence Center, N.Y.

28. Foote, *Proceedings;* "Original Records of the Town of Batavia"; "Records," Town of Clarence (Willinks), vols. 1, 3, and 7.

29. Joseph Ellicott, 19 April 1803, 11a:2, HLC-BHS; Ellicott to Busti, 17 November 1803, 3b:173, HLC-BHS; Joseph Ellicott to Paul Busti, 22 June 1804, 3b:242, HLC-BHS.

30. "Records of 1st Annual Town Meeting," 1803, vol: 27, HLC-BHS.

31. Adam Hoops to Joseph Ellicott, 22 January 1806, 13:19, HLC-BHS; Ellicott to Mr. Alsop and Mr. Brannan, 6 August 1808, 4a:225, HLC-BHS.

32. Foote, *Proceedings,* p. 16.

33. Pitt Petri, *The Postal History of Western New York: Its Post Offices and Post Masters* (Buffalo, N.Y., 1960); Joseph Ellicott to Seth Pease, 15 May 1802, and Ellicott to Gideon Granger, 15 May 1802, 3a:208, 210, HLC-BHS.

34. Joseph Ellicott to Calendar Irvine, 31 August 1802, 3a:284, HLC-BHS.

35. Ibid.

36. Joseph Ellicott to Paul Busti, 28 March 1804, 3b:220, HLC-BHS.

37. R. L. Garff, "Social and Economic Conditions in the Genesee Country, 1787–1813" (Ph.D. diss., Northwestern University, 1939), pp. 344–52.

38. William Wyckoff, "Frontier Milling in Western New York," *Geographical Review* 76 (1986): 90–91.

39. RJE 1, p. 148.

40. Ibid.

41. Eric Sloane, *Our Vanishing Landscape* (New York: Wilfred Funk, 1955), p. 38; Martha and Murray Zimiles, *Early American Mills* (New York: Bramhall House, 1973), p. 6.

42. "Remarks on Joseph Ellicott's Plan," 8:819, HLC-BHS; Paul Busti to Joseph Ellicott, 21 April 1803, 6:389, HLC-BHS.

43. Joseph Ellicott to Paul Busti, 30 June 1808, 4a:205, HLC-BHS.

44. RJE 1, pp. 148–49, 190, 250–51, 274–76.

45. H. Perry Smith, *History of the City of Buffalo and Erie County,* 2 vols. (Syracuse, N.Y.: D. Mason, 1884), 1:398.

46. Joseph Ellicott to Paul Busti, 14 May 1804, 3b:226, HLC-BHS.

47. Arad Thomas, *Pioneer History of Orleans County* (Albion, N.Y.: H. A. Brunner, 1871), p. 378.

48. RJE 1, p. 275; Joseph Ellicott to Paul Busti, 20 October 1803, 3b:157, HLC-BHS; Land Deeds of Cattaraugus County, Cattaraugus County Clerk's Office, Little Valley, N.Y.

49. Land Deeds of Allegany County, Allegany County Clerk's Office, Belmont, N.Y.

50. Andrew White Young, *History of Chautauqua County* (Buffalo, N.Y.: Matthews and Warren, 1875), p. 332.

51. RJE 1, pp. 370, 386; "Annual Settlement of Accounts, 1800–1810," pp. 6, 66, 196; Joseph Ellicott to Asa Ransom, 25 July 1803, 3b:106, HLC-BHS; Ellicott to Paul Busti, 30 June 1808, 4a:205, HLC-BHS; William Peacock to Ellicott, 27 May, 17 June 1811, vol. 18, HLC-BHS.

52. Edward K. Muller, "Selective Urban Growth in the Middle Ohio Valley, 1800–1860," *Geographical Review* 66 (1976): 178–79.

53. Charles Mason Dow, *Anthology and Bibliography of Niagara Falls,* vol. 1 (Albany, N.Y.: T. B. Lyon, 1921), p. 55; Marvin Rapp, "New York's Trade on the Great Lakes, 1800–1840," *New York History* 39 (1958): 23–24; Frank H. Severance, *Old Trails on the Niagara Frontier* (Cleveland, Ohio: Burrows Brothers, 1903), p. 142.

54. Frank H. Severance, ed., "The Dobbins Papers," *Publications of the Buffalo Historical Society* 8 (1905): 283–85.

55. Thomas Cooper, *Some Information respecting America* (1793; reprint, New York: A. M. Kelley, 1969), pp. 12–13.

56. Charles Williamson, "Description of the Settlement of the Genesee Country," in *Documentary History of the State of New York,* vol. 2, ed. E. B. O'Callaghan (Albany, N.Y.: Weed, Parsons, 1849), pp. 1144–49.

57. Robert Troup to Joseph Ellicott, 27 December 1806, RG 406, HLC-AMS.

58. Joseph Ellicott to Paul Busti, 16 February 1802, 3a:163, HLC-BHS; Ellicott to Busti, 16 October 1802, 20 September 1804, 3b:1, 291, HLC-BHS; James Green to Ellicott, 8 December 1807, 13:58, HLC-BHS; Ellicott to Busti, 8 March 1810, 4a:309, HLC-BHS.

59. Solon Justus Buck and Elizabeth Hawthorn Buck, *The Planting of Civilization in Western Pennsylvania* (Pittsburgh, Pa.: University of Pittsburgh Press, 1939).

60. Joseph Ellicott to Thomas Kennedy, 2 December 1805, 4a:31, HLC-BHS.

61. Joseph Ellicott to Paul Busti, 7 July 1802, 3a:235, HLC-BHS; Thomas Cooper, *A Ride to Niagara* (1814), p. 60.

62. Paul Busti to Joseph Ellicott, 20 June 1804, 6:575, HLC-BHS.

63. Thomas Kennedy to Joseph Ellicott, 12 October 1809, 9:725, HLC-BHS.

64. Details of annual salt shipments through Erie were compiled from "Ship Manifest Records, Presque Isle, 1800–1814," 2 vols., Dobbins Papers, BHS.

65. Severance, "Dobbins Papers," p. 293; Augustus Porter Collection, RG 202, BHS.

66. RJE 1, p. 166; Paul Busti to Joseph Ellicott, March 1802, 6:173, HLC-BHS; "Accounts and Receipts Belonging to the Annual Settlement of Accounts with the General Agent, 1803," RG 783–84, HLC-AMS.

67. RJE 1, pp. 283–85; Joseph Ellicott to Paul Busti, 28 August 1804, 3b:276, HLC-BHS; Busti to Ellicott, 30 October 1811, 7:899, HLC-BHS.

68. Paul Busti to Joseph Ellicott, 20 April 1803, 6:379, HLC-BHS; Ellicott to Thomas Kennedy, 15 December 1803, 3b:180, HLC-BHS.

69. Joseph Ellicott to Paul Busti, 19 September 1809, 4a:269, HLC-BHS; William Peacock to Ellicott, 29 July 1811, vol. 18, HLC-BHS.

70. RJE 1, pp. 145, 150; Smith, *History of Buffalo,* 2:22; Joseph Ellicott to Mr. Tiffany, 10 August 1802, 3a:269, HLC-BHS; Ellicott to Mr. Church, 12 August 1803, 3b:123, HLC-BHS; Ellicott, "Journal," 29:20, HLC-BHS.

71. Richard P. Casey, "North Country Nemesis: The Potash Rebellion and the Embargo of 1807–1809," *New-York Historical Society Quarterly* 64 (1980): 30–49.

72. Joseph Ellicott to Paul Busti, 10 February 1809, RG 406, HLC-AMS.

73. Casey, "North Country Nemesis," p. 36.

74. RJE 2, p. 85.

75. Ibid., pp. 35–36, 81.

76. Joseph Ellicott to Paul Busti, 15 December 1810, 30 August 1811, 4b:25, 116, HLC-BHS.

77. Joseph Ellicott to Paul Busti, 15 December 1810, 4b:25, HLC-BHS.

78. Joseph Ellicott to Paul Busti, 7 January 1803, 3b:43, HLC-BHS.

79. Alexander Rea to Joseph Ellicott, 3 February 1805, 21:4, HLC-BHS; Robert Troup to Joseph Ellicott, December 1806, RG 406, HLC-AMS.

80. Ellicott, "Journal," p. 28; Norton and Richards to Ellicott, 6 November 1803, 11a:113, HLC-BHS.

81. LeRoy, Bayard, and McEvers to Joseph Ellicott, 19 October 1803, 11a:99, HLC-BHS; Ellicott to Paul Busti, 19 August 1809, RG 406, HLC-AMS; Ellicott to Busti, 30 August 1811, 4b:116, HLC-BHS.

82. Frederick Walther to Joseph Ellicott, 11 February 1800, 8:689, HLC-BHS.

83. Joseph Ellicott to Paul Busti, 9 July 1807, 4a:123, HLC-BHS.

84. James Vance, *The Merchant's World: The Geography of Wholesaling* (Englewood Cliffs, N.J.: Prentice-Hall, 1970), pp. 81–85, 157–58.

85. Joseph Ellicott to Paul Busti, 16 July 1808, 4a:207, HLC-BHS.

86. John Melish, *Travels in the United States of America in the Years 1806 and 1807, and 1809, 1810, and 1811* (1812; reprint, New York: Johnson Reprint Corporation, 1970), p. 513.

87. Paul Busti to Joseph Ellicott, 14 August 1810, 7:729, HLC-BHS.

CHAPTER 6: SETTLERS ON THE DEVELOPER'S FRONTIER

1. Joseph Ellicott to Paul Busti, 19 September 1809, 4a:269, HLC-BHS.

2. James Cochran to Joseph Ellicott, 13 June 1804, 13:14, HLC-BHS.

3. James P. Allen, "Changes in the American Propensity to Migrate," *Annals of the Association of American Geographers* 67 (1977): 584.

4. Joseph Ellicott to Paul Busti, 16 March 1806, 4a:54, HLC-BHS.

5. Royal Lovell Garff, "Social and Economic Conditions in the Genesee Country, 1787–1813" (Ph.D. diss., Northwestern University, 1939), p. 64.

6. "Map from Adlum and Wallis's Large Map," 1791(?), RG 219–9, HLC-AMS; Samuel Lewis, "The State of New York" (Philadelphia, 1795).

7. William Morris to John Lincklaen, 8 July 1793, RG 130–3, HLC-AMS.

8. J. and Polly Clark to Joseph Ellicott, 13 January 1808, 13:31, HLC-BHS.

9. Stoughton Morr to Joseph Ellicott, 19 August 1810, 17:158, HLC-BHS.

10. Lawton Richmond to Joseph Ellicott, 25 May 1810, 16:387, HLC-BHS.

11. David Eddy to Joseph Ellicott, 29 July 1808, 9:469, HLC-BHS.

12. David Eddy to Joseph Ellicott, 20 July 1810, 17:206, HLC-BHS.

13. Lemuel Chipman to Joseph Ellicott, 15 April 1804, 12:3, HLC-BHS.

14. John McMahon to Joseph Ellicott, 7 May 1802, 11:31, HLC-BHS.

15. Jan O. M. Broek and John W. Webb, *A Geography of Mankind* (New York: McGraw-Hill, 1978), p. 395.

16. Arthur Getis, Judith Getis, and Jerome Fellman, *Human Geography: Culture and Environment* (New York: Macmillan, 1985), p. 44.

17. John Williams and Robert Andrews to Joseph Ellicott, 13 June 1808, 13:262, HLC-BHS.

18. Robert Dodge and Matthew Nealy to Joseph Ellicott, 17 March 1810, 16:279, HLC-BHS.

19. Joseph Ellicott to Paul Busti, 22 July 1803, 27 July 1804, 3b:95, 263, HLC-BHS.

20. Joseph Ellicott to Paul Busti, 23 March 1804, 3b:217, HLC-BHS; Ellicott to Busti, 25 February 1809, 4a:239, HLC-BHS.

21. Stanley Lebergott, "Migration within the United States, 1800–1860: Some New Estimates," *Journal of Economic History* 30 (1970): 839–47.

22. Lois Kimball Mathews, *The Expansion of New England* (Boston: Houghton Mifflin, 1909), pp. 139–70; Wilbur Zelinsky, *The Cultural Geography of the United States* (Englewood-Cliffs, N.J.: Prentice-Hall, 1973), pp. 118–19.

23. Garff, "Social and Economic Conditions," pp. 65–66; Mathews, *Expansion of New England,* pp. 139–70.

24. The Reverend Joseph Avery, "Visit of Reverend Joseph Avery," *Publications of the Buffalo Historical Society* 6 (1903): 228; John Melish, *Travels in the United States of America in the Years 1806 and 1807, and 1809, 1810, and 1811* (1812; reprint, New York: Johnson Reprint Corporation, 1970), pp. 485–86, 513; J. U. Niemciwiez, "Journey to Niagara, 1805," *New-York Historical Society Quarterly* 44 (1960): 103.

25. Joseph Ellicott to Paul Busti, 7 June 1805, 3b:356, HLC-BHS; Ellicott to Busti, 22 May 1807, 4a:118, HLC-BHS.

26. Joseph Ellicott to Paul Busti, 7 June 1805, 3b:356, HLC-BHS; Ellicott to Busti, 22 May 1807, 4a:118, HLC-BHS.

27. William Adams, *Historical Gazetteer and Biographical Memorial of Cattaraugus County* (Syracuse, N.Y.: Lyman, Horton, 1893), p. 674; J. T. Horton, E. T. Williams, and H. S. Douglas, *History of Northwestern New York* (New York: Lewis Historical Publishing, 1947), p. 503; David Eddy to Joseph Ellicott, 29 July 1808, 9:469, HLC-BHS; Robert Dodge and Matthew Nealy to Ellicott, 17 March 1810, 16:279, HLC-BHS; David Eddy to Ellicott, 20 July 1810, and Edward Putnam to Ellicott, 25 August 1810, 17:206, 420, HLC-BHS; William Peacock to Ellicott, 18 June 1811, vol. 18, HLC-BHS.

28. John Thompson, ed., *The Geography of New York State* (Syracuse, N.Y.: Syracuse University Press, 1977), pp. 146–47.

29. Data on settler inquiries were gathered from vols. 3–4, 8–9, 11–17, 21–23, and 29, HLC-BHS.

30. Names and residences of participating surveyors and laborers were usually noted on the front page of the original township survey field notebooks. See Original Books of Field Notes of Survey of Holland Land Company Lands, HLC-NYSL.

31. Joseph Ellicott to Paul Busti, 14 May 1804, 3b:226, HLC-BHS; Thomas Kennedy to Ellicott, 3 August, 19 September 1804, 16 August 1806, 21:9, 10, 70, HLC-BHS.

32. John McMahon to Joseph Ellicott, 7 May 1802, 17 May 1804, 11:31, 184, HLC-BHS.

33. Jacob Taylor to Joseph Ellicott, 28 July 1804, 12:51, HLC-BHS; Ellicott to Stephan Hazeltine, 8 June 1808, 9:499, HLC-BHS.

34. Melish, *Travels,* p. 510; Joseph Ellicott to Paul Busti, 30 September 1809, 4a:282, HLC-BHS.

35. Paul Busti to Joseph Ellicott, 9 June 1804, 6:571, HLC-BHS.

36. Joseph Ellicott to Paul Busti, 24 December 1808, 4a:233, HLC-BHS.

37. Joseph Ellicott to Paul Busti, 7 June 1805, 3b:356, HLC-BHS.

38. Joseph Ellicott to Paul Busti, 28 May 1808, 4a:197, HLC-BHS.

39. Joseph Ellicott to John Thomson, 9 March 1802, 3a:186, HLC-BHS.

40. *History of Niagara County, New York* (New York: Sanford, 1878), p. 382; William Pool, ed., *Landmarks of Niagara County* (Syracuse, N.Y.: D. Mason, 1897), pp. 260, 303–5, 323; Orasmus Turner, *Pioneer History of the Holland Purchase* (Buffalo, N.Y.: George H. Derby, 1850), pp. 548–49; Joseph Ellicott to Paul Busti, 16 February 1802, 3a:163, HLC-BHS.

41. Turner, *Pioneer History,* pp. 453–54, 522–25; Jean Rumsey, "Family History of Colonel William Rumsey (1774–1820)" (typescript, 1968, HLC, Genesee County Historical Society, Batavia, N.Y.).

42. Turner, *Pioneer History,* p. 476.

43. Andrew Hill Clark, "Suggestions for the Geographical Study of Agricultural Change in the United States, 1790–1840," *Agricultural History* 46 (1972): 155–72.

44. *History of Niagara County,* pp. 382–86; Turner, *Pioneer History,* pp. 548–50.

45. R. Cole Harris and John Warkentin, *Canada before Confederation* (New York: Oxford University Press, 1974), p. 116.

46. Turner, *Pioneer History*, pp. 487–88.

47. Ibid., pp. 469–70.

48. General discussions on mapping the spread of settlement include Michael Williams, "Delimiting the Spread of Settlement: An Examination of Evidence in Southern Australia," *Economic Geography* 42 (1966): 336–55, and David Wishart, "The Changing Position of the Frontier of Settlement on the Eastern Margins of the Central and Northern Great Plains, 1854–1900," *Professional Geographer* 21 (1969): 153–57.

49. Data on initial settlement were from "Annual Report to the General Agent, 1801–1820," RG 756–57, 758, 759, HLC-AMS.

50. The pickup in sales can be followed in Ellicott's letterbooks. See entries for 1803 and 1804 in 3b:74–207, HLC-BHS.

51. The increased sales in 1805 and 1806 can be followed in Ellicott's letterbooks. See entries in 4a:24–54 and RJE 1, p. 305.

52. RJE 2, p. 57; Joseph Ellicott to Paul Busti, 16 March 1811, 4b:64, HLC-BHS.

53. Joseph Ellicott to Paul Busti, 30 March, 13 April 1811, 4b:69, 72, HLC-BHS.

54. John A. McGaraty, *The American Nation* (New York: Harper and Row, 1971), p. 238; RJE 2, pp. 78–79; Joseph Ellicott to Paul Busti, 6 August 1808, 4a:224, HLC-BHS.

55. Data on land sales were from "Report of Land Tables, 1811, 1812," RG 489, 490, HLC-AMS.

56. F. W. Beers, *History of Wyoming County, New York* (New York: F. W. Beers, 1880), pp. 126–37.

57. RJE 2, pp. 78–79.

58. There were no sales that year in Township 13 Range 5, three sales in Township 13 Range 6, two sales in Township 13 Range 7, and one sale in Township 13 Range 8.

59. David Eddy to Joseph Ellicott, 29 April 1807, 9:367, HLC-BHS; Eddy to Ellicott, 27 January 1808, 13:35, HLC-BHS.

60. Nathaniel Sheldon to Joseph Ellicott, 20 December 1807, 13:20, HLC-BHS; Randal Baker to Obadiah Baker, 15 April 1810, 16:337, HLC-BHS; Ebenezar Pike to Ellicott, 24 September 1810, 17:379, HLC-BHS.

61. Jacob Taylor to Joseph Ellicott, 25 June 1806, 14:35, HLC-BHS; Taylor to Ellicott, 17 June 1809, 22:170, HLC-BHS.

62. H. G. Spafford, *Gazetteer of the State of New York* (Albany, N.Y.: H. C. Southwick, 1813), pp. 67–68.

63. Joseph Ellicott to Paul Busti, 25 May, 12 August 1809, 4a:249, 258.

64. Joseph Ellicott to John Thomson, 20 February 1802, 3a:177, HLC-BHS.

65. Paul Busti to Joseph Ellicott, 11 March 1802, 11:43, HLC-BHS.

66. RJE 1, p. 277; Joseph Ellicott to Paul Busti, 7 June 1805, 3b:356, HLC-BHS.

67. "Annual Settlement of Accounts with the General Agent, 1800–1810," p. 123, RG 779, HLC-AMS.

68. Melish, *Travels*, pp. 513–14; Niemciwiez, "Journey," p. 102.

69. Melish, *Travels*, pp. 511–13.

70. RJE 2, p. 42.

71. Garff, "Social and Economic Conditions," pp. 134–45.

72. RJE 1, p. 199.

73. Garff, "Social and Economic Conditions," p. 167.

74. Ibid., pp. 141–42.

75. Ibid., pp. 145–52; Ulysses Prentice Hedrick, *A History of Agriculture in the State of New York* (New York: Hill and Wang, 1966), pp. 217–35; Joseph Ellicott, "Private Day Book," 3 August 1804, vol. 26, HLC-BHS.

76. RJE 2, p. 45.

77. Garff, "Social and Economic Conditions," pp. 237–38; Hedrick, *History of Agriculture,* pp. 200–203.

78. William Seaver, *A Historical Sketch of the Village of Batavia* (Batavia, N.Y.: William Seaver and Son, 1849), pp. 49–50; Joseph Ellicott to Dudley Walsh, 21 January 1804, 3b:194, HLC-BHS.

79. Joseph Ellicott to Paul Busti, 20 September 1804, 3b:291, HLC-BHS.

80. Seaver, *Historical Sketch,* pp. 49–50.

81. RJE 2, p. 43.

82. William Wyckoff, "Frontier Milling in Western New York," *Geographical Review* 76 (1986): 77.

83. Seaver, *Historical Sketch,* pp. 18–20; Ezra Waite to Joseph Ellicott, 10 May 1802, 11:35, HLC-BHS.

84. Seaver, *Historical Sketch,* pp. 15–17.

85. Hedrick, *History of Agriculture,* pp. 233–35.

86. Garff, "Social and Economic Conditions," p. 344; "Town Records," vols. 1, 3, and 7, Town of Clarence Clerk's Office, Clarence Center, N.Y.

87. Seaver, *Historical Sketch,* pp. 18–19.

88. "Accounts and Receipts Belonging to the Annual Settlement of Accounts with the General Agent, 1803," RG 783–A, HLC-AMS.

89. Melish, *Travels,* pp. 511–13; RJE 2, pp. 43–44.

90. Seaver, *Historical Sketch,* pp. 117–18.

91. RJE 1, p. 342.

92. Seaver, *Historical Sketch,* pp. 19–20.

93. Ibid., pp. 44–45; Simeon Cummings to Joseph Ellicott, 21 March 1811, 17:421, HLC-BHS.

94. Turner, *Pioneer History,* p. 580.

95. RJE 2, pp. 43–45.

96. James H. Hotchkin, *A History of the Purchase and Settlement of Western New York and the Rise, Progress, and Present State of the Presbyterian Church in That Section* (New York: M. W. Dodd, 1848), p. 78.

97. Avery, "Visit," p. 226.

98. The Reverend Roswell Burrows, "Visit to Buffalo," *Publications of the Buffalo Historical Society* 6 (1903): 235.

99. Paul Busti to Joseph Ellicott, 30 October 1811, 7:899, HLC-BHS.

100. Safford E. North, ed., *Our Country and Its People: A Descriptive and Biographical Record of Genesee County, New York* (Boston: Boston History Co., 1899), p. 89.

101. RJE 1, p. 200.

102. Hedrick, *History of Agriculture,* p. 198.

103. Garff, "Social and Economic Conditions," pp. 334–38.

CHAPTER 7: THE CHANGING FRONTIER LANDSCAPE

1. Paul Busti to Joseph Ellicott, 22 May 1804, 6:273, HLC-BHS.

2. Joseph Ellicott, "Surveys-Rules and Directions," n.d., RG 140–7b, HLC-AMS.

3. "Genesee Townships," RG 219–17, HLC-AMS.

4. R. Louis Gentilcore and Kate Donkin, "Land Surveys of Southern Ontario: An Introduction and Index to the Field Notebooks of the Ontario Land Surveyors, 1784–1859," *Canadian Cartographer* 10 (1973): suppl. 2, pp. 4–10.

5. RJE 2, p. 6.

6. RJE 1, p. 186; Joseph Ellicott to B. Gorham, 27 August 1802, 3a:277, HLC-BHS.

7. Paul Busti to Joseph Ellicott, 20 April 1803, 6:379, HLC-BHS.

8. Joseph Ellicott to Adam Hoops, 19 September 1804, 3b:289, HLC-BHS.

9. Joseph Ellicott to George Colvin, 30 March 1805, 12:164, HLC-BHS.
10. Paul Busti to Joseph Ellicott, 22 September 1803, 6:451, HLC-BHS.
11. Alvar Carlson, "Long Lots in the Rio Arriba," *Annals of the Association of American Geographers* 65 (1975): 48–57; Cole Harris, *The Seigneurial System in Early Canada: A Geographical Study* (Madison, Wis.: University of Wisconsin Press, 1968); Terry Jordan, "Antecedents of the Long Lot in Texas," *Annals of the Association of American Geographers* 64 (1974): 70–86; Peter Wacker, *Land and People* (New Brunswick, N.J.: Rutgers University Press, 1975), pp. 317–19.
12. RJE 1, p. 176.
13. Ibid., pp. 176–77.
14. Joseph Ellicott to Paul Busti, 10 November 1802, 3b:11, HLC-BHS.
15. Jordan, "Antecedents of the Long Lot."
16. Carlson, "Long Lots"; Wacker, *Land and People,* pp. 317–19.
17. For example, evidence of long lotting can be found on the Cayuga and Onondaga Reservation parcels surveyed in 1795; see "A Map of the Late Cayuga Reservation," 1795, and "A Map of the Late Onondaga Reservation," 1795, RG 479–33, HLC-AMS.
18. Ruth L. Higgins, *Expansion in New York* (Columbus, Ohio: Ohio State University Press, 1931), p. 29.
19. Alexander Autrechy, "A Map of Adgate's Patent," n.d., RG 479–65, HLC-AMS; Autrechy, "A Map of the City of Cazenovia, and the Out Lots," n.d., RG 480–12, HLC-AMS.
20. RJE 1, pp. 176–77.
21. "Deed Atlas MOPQ," RG 519, HLC-AMS.
22. Joseph Ellicott to Alexander Rea, 14 May 1804, 3b:70, HLC-BHS.
23. "Maps of Territory H," RG 525, HLC-AMS.
24. RJE 1, p. 185.
25. Paul Busti to Joseph Ellicott, 20 April 1803, 6:379, HLC-BHS.
26. Joseph Ellicott to Alexander Rea, 6 March 1801, 29:73, HLC-BHS.
27. Joseph Ellicott to John Thomson, 9 March 1802, 3a:186, HLC-BHS.
28. Joseph Ellicott to Paul Busti, 31 August 1803, 3b:128, HLC-BHS.
29. Joseph Ellicott to Paul Busti, 7 July 1803, RG 406, HLC-AMS.
30. Paul Busti to Joseph Ellicott, 27 July 1803, 6:419, HLC-BHS; "Survey Field Books of Chautauqua County," vol. 199, Chautauqua County Clerk's Office, Mayville, N.Y.
31. Joseph Ellicott to Paul Busti, 30 May 1801, 3a:64, HLC-BHS.
32. Joseph Ellicott to Calendar Irvine, 31 August 1802, 3a:284, HLC-BHS.
33. William Herbert Siles, "A Vision of Wealth: Speculators and Settlers in the Genesee Country of New York, 1788–1800" (Ph.D. diss., University of Massachusetts, 1978), pp. 72, 87.
34. Joseph Ellicott to Ezra Waite, 6 March 1801, 3a:34, HLC-BHS.
35. Turpin C. Bannister, "Early Town Planning in New York State," *New York History* 24 (1943): 191–92.
36. Ibid.; John Reps, *Cities of the American West: A History of Frontier Urban Planning* (Princeton, N.J.: Princeton University Press, 1979), pp. 8–9; "Plan of the City of Washington," 1792, RG 480, HLC-AMS.
37. C. V. C. Matthews, *Andrew Ellicott: His Life and Letters* (New York: Grafton Press, 1908), p. 105.
38. Joseph Ellicott to Paul Busti, 20 September 1804, 3b:291, HLC-BHS.
39. Paul Busti to Joseph Ellicott, 24 October 1804, 6:601, HLC-BHS; Ellicott to Busti, 21 November 1804, 3b:308, HLC-BHS.
40. Joseph Ellicott to Louis Le Couteulx, 16 July 1803, 3b:93, HLC-BHS.
41. Marshall Harris, *Origin of the Land Tenure System in the United States* (Ames, Iowa: Iowa State College Press, 1953), pp. 279–85; Douglas McManis, *Colonial New England: A Historical Geography* (New York: Oxford University Press, 1969), pp. 147–49, 183.
42. Autrechy, "Map of the City of Cazenovia."

43. "Extract from a Letter Wrote December, 1792, by C. Williamson to the Company in London to Explain His Plan for the Improvement of the Genesee," RG 267–26–13, HLC-AMS.

44. Thomas Forster, "Map of the Borough of Erie," 1836, RG 480–10, HLC-AMS.

45. Joseph Ellicott to Paul Busti, 7 February 1800, RG 405, HLC-AMS; Ellicott to Busti, 29 September 1803, 3b:148, HLC-BHS.

46. Joseph Ellicott, "Proposed Plan for a Town at the East End of Lake Erie Called New Amsterdam," n.d., RG 480–8, HLC-AMS.

47. Ibid.

48. Edward T. Price, "The Central Courthouse Square in the American County Seat," *Geographical Review* 58 (1968): 58–59.

49. Joseph Ellicott, "Plan of the Village of New Amsterdam," n.d., RG H8000011, HLC-AMS.

50. Louis Le Couteulx to Joseph Ellicott, 8 November 1809, 17:177, HLC-BHS.

51. Joseph Ellicott to Adam Hoops, 24 August 1804, 3b:273, HLC-BHS; "Survey Field Books of Chautauqua County," vols. 213, 214, 312, Chautauqua County Clerk's Office, Mayville, N.Y.

52. James Stevens to Joseph Ellicott, 17 November 1808, 9:637, HLC-BHS.

53. "Ellicottville, Village Plans," 1913, Land Contract Book—Village of Ellicottville, 1818, HLC, Cornell University, Ithaca, N.Y.

54. "Field Books of Cattaraugus County," vol. 1, Cattaraugus County Clerk's Office, Little Valley, N.Y.

55. McManis, *New England*, p. 55.

56. James Vance, *This Scene of Man* (New York: Harper's College Press, 1977), pp. 257–61.

57. John Reps, *Town Planning in Frontier America* (Princeton, N.J.: Princeton University Press, 1969), p. 262; F. Molineux, "Plan of the Town of Erie and Lake Erie," n.d., RG 480–10, HLC-AMS.

58. Charles Mason Dow, *Anthology and Bibliography of Niagara Falls* (Albany, N.Y.: J. B. Lyon, 1921), pp. 23–29.

59. Ibid., p. 23.

60. Frank Severance, *Studies of the Niagara Frontier* (Buffalo, N.Y.: Buffalo and Erie County Historical Society, 1911), pp. 324–34.

61. Duncan Ingraham, "Description of the Country between Albany and Niagara in 1802," in *Documentary History of the State of New York,* vol. 2, ed. E. B. O'Callaghan (Albany, N.Y.: Weed, Parsons, 1849), pp. 1105–10, quotations on pp. 1107–8.

62. C. F. Volney, *A View of the Soil and Climate of the United States of America* (Philadelphia: T. and G. Palmer, 1804), p. 6.

63. De La Rochefoucault Liancourt, *Travels through the United States of North America in the Years 1795, 1796, and 1797* (London: R. Phillips, 1799), p. 166.

64. The Reverend Lemuel Covell, *A Narrative of a Missionary Tour through the Western Settlements of the State of New York and into the Southwestern Parts of the Province of Upper Canada* (Troy, N.Y.: Moffitt and Lyon, 1804), pp. 8–9.

65. Timothy Dwight, *Travels in New England and New York,* vol. 4 (New Haven, Conn.: Timothy Dwight, 1821–22), quotation on p. 67.

66. Robert Sutcliffe, *Travels in Some Parts of North America in the Years 1804, 1805, and 1806* (Philadelphia: B. and T. Kite, 1812).

67. Thomas Cooper, *A Ride to Niagara* (1814), quotations from pp. 58–60, 300, 49, and 168.

68. John Melish, *Travels in the United States of America in the Years 1806 and 1807, and 1809, 1810, and 1811* (1812; reprint, New York: Johnson Reprint Corporation, 1970), quotations from pp. 485–88.

69. Royal Lovell Garff, "Social and Economic Conditions in the Genesee Country, 1787–1813" (Ph.D. diss., Northwestern University, 1939), p. 98; O. Pattengell, Summer Warren, et al., to Joseph Ellicott, 16 February 1810, 16:244, HLC-BHS; John Scott and John Mayhall to Joseph Ellicott, 27 October 1810, 17:404, HLC-BHS.

70. Joseph Ellicott to John Thomson, 9 March 1802, 3a:186, HLC-BHS; Joseph Ellicott to William Ellis, 7 June 1806, 4a:58, HLC-BHS; O. Pattengell, Summer Warren et al. to Joseph Ellicott, 16 February 1810, 16:244, HLC-BHS.

71. Joseph Ellicott to William Updegraff, 1 October 1802, 3a:293, HLC-BHS; Joseph Ellicott to Gardner Spooner, 23 August 1803, 3b:126, HLC-BHS.

72. Francis Wright, *Views of Society and Manners in America* (New York: E. Bliss and E. White, 1821), p. 104.

73. Garff, "Social and Economic Conditions," pp. 166–68.

74. Joseph Ellicott to Paul Busti, 14 July 1801, 3a:80, HLC-BHS.

75. Garff, "Social and Economic Conditions," p. 98; O. Pattengell, Summer Warren, et al., to Joseph Ellicott, 16 February 1810, 16:244, HLC-BHS; Robert Lee, John Brown, and Elijah Doty to Joseph Ellicott, 15 February 1810, 17:3, HLC-BHS; Amos Webster et al. to Joseph Ellicott, 13 September 1810, 17:313, HLC-BHS; John Scott and John Mayhall to Joseph Ellicott, 27 October 1810, 17:403, HLC-BHS.

76. Data on median farm sizes were from "Report on Land Tables, 1804, 1811, 1812," RG 484, 489, 490, HLC-AMS.

77. Garff, "Social and Economic Conditions," p. 168; J. T. Horton, E. T. Williams, and H. S. Douglas, *History of Northwestern New York,* vol. 1 (New York: Lewis Historical Publishing, 1947), pp. 518–19; Andrew White Young, *History of Chautauqua County* (Buffalo, N.Y.: Matthews and Warren, 1875), pp. 80–81.

78. F. W. Beers, *History of Wyoming County, New York* (New York: F. W. Beers, 1880), p. 64; Garff, "Social and Economic Conditions," pp. 194–205; Jared van Wagenen, Jr., *The Golden Age of Homespun* (New York: Hill and Wang, 1963), pp. 166–67.

79. Arad Thomas, *Pioneer History of Orleans County* (Albion: H. A. Bruner, 1871), p. 43; John Scott and John Mayhall to Joseph Ellicott, 27 October 1810, 17:403, HLC-BHS.

80. J. B. Bicker to T. Cazenove, 1 September 1797, RG 81–30–33, HLC-AMS; William Morris to John Lincklaen, 8 July 1793, RG 130–3, HLC-AMS.

81. Garff, "Social and Economic Conditions," p. 183; Thomas, *History of Orleans County;* Joseph Ellicott to Bayard and McEvers, 7 May 1801, 3a:45, HLC-BHS; Ellicott to Paul Busti, 20 September 1804, 3b:291, HLC-BHS; Ellicott to Busti, 12 August 1809, 4a:258, HLC-BHS.

82. Horton, *History of Northwestern New York,* 1:518–19.

83. Henry Howland, "The Niagara Portage and Its First Attempted Settlement under British Rule," *Publications of the Buffalo Historical Society* 6 (1903): 35–45; Orasmus Turner, *Pioneer History of the Holland Purchase of Western New York* (Buffalo, N.Y.: George H. Derby, 1850), p. 490; Joseph Ellicott, "Field Notes," Fall 1797, HLC-BHS.

84. Thomas Brown, Elijah Doty, et al., to Joseph Ellicott, 14 February 1810, and O. Pattengell, Sumner Warren, et al., 16 February 1810, 16:244, 263, HLC-BHS; Christopher Vansicklen to Joseph Ellicott, 12 December 1810, 9:1233, HLC-BHS.

85. Isaac Signor, ed., *Landmarks of Orleans County* (Syracuse, N.Y.: D. Mason, 1894), pp. 638–39, 649; Thomas Robinson to Joseph Ellicott, 2 August 1805, 14:118, HLC-BHS; E. Rose to Benjamin Ellicott, 7 May 1807, 15:209, HLC-BHS; Elijah Pertry to Joseph Ellicott, 23 January 1810, and Thomas Brown, Elijah Doty, et al., to Joseph Ellicott, 16:206, 263, HLC-BHS; William Peacock to Joseph Ellicott, 7 May 1811, vol. 18, HLC-BHS.

86. Garff, "Social and Economic Conditions," p. 184.

87. Joseph Ellicott to Paul Busti, 19 September 1809, 4a:269, HLC-BHS.

88. Range Books, HLC-NYSL.

89. "Genesee County Land Office Records, Township 10, Range 2, volume 1, 1802–1840," Holland Land Company Collection, Holland Land Office Library, Batavia, N.Y.

90. Beers, *History of Wyoming County,* pp. 59–72, 126–45; Lockwood Doty, ed., *History of the Genesee Country* (Chicago: S. J. Clarke, 1925), 2:1209–11; Horton, *History of Northwestern New York,* 1:513.

91. Joseph Ellicott to Paul Busti, 20 September 1804, 3b:291, HLC-BHS.
92. Beers, *History of Wyoming County,* pp. 59–72, 126–45; Doty, *Genesee Country,* 2:1209–11.

CHAPTER 8: A LEGACY ON THE LANDSCAPE

1. Hildegard Binder Johnson, *Order upon the Land* (New York: Oxford University Press, 1976), pp. 166–67.
2. Norman Thrower, *Original Survey and Land Subdivision* (Chicago: Association of American Geographers, 1966), pp. 86–101.
3. Karl B. Raitz and John Fraser Hart, *Cultural Geography on Topographic Maps* (New York: John Wiley and Sons, 1975), p. 91.
4. Township patterns in 1850 are shown in Orasmus Turner, *Pioneer History of the Holland Purchase of Western New York* (Buffalo, N.Y.: George H. Derby, 1850), pp. 570–83.
5. The corresponding area is mapped in USGS, 1:24,000 series, Collins Center, N.Y., 1963.
6. The corresponding area is mapped in USGS, 1:24,000 series, Humphrey, N.Y., 1961.
7. RJE 1, p. 53.
8. T. J. Simpson, "Map of Portland Harbor," 1838, RG A7, 119, Iconography Collection, BHS.

Selected Bibliography

PUBLISHED SOURCES

New York State

Adams, William, ed. *Historical Gazetteer and Biographical Memorial of Cattaraugus County, New York.* Syracuse, N.Y.: Lyman, Horton, 1893.

Avery, Reverend Joseph. "Visit of Reverend Joseph Avery." *Publications of the Buffalo Historical Society* 6 (1903): 223–30.

Bannister, Turpin C. "Early Town Planning in New York State." *New York History* 24 (1943): 185–95.

Beers, D. G. and Beers, S. N. *New Topographic Atlas of Genesee and Wyoming Counties, New York.* Philadelphia: Stone and Stewart, 1866.

Beers, F. W. *Gazetteer and Biographical Record of Genesee County, New York, 1788–1890.* Syracuse, N.Y.: J. W. Vose, 1890.

———. *History of Allegany County, New York.* New York: F. W. Beers, 1879.

———. *History of Wyoming County, New York.* New York: F. W. Beers, 1880.

Bingham, Robert W. *The Cradle of the Queen City.* Buffalo, N.Y.: Buffalo Historical Society, 1931.

———, ed. *Reports of Joseph Ellicott,* 2 vols. Buffalo, N.Y.: Buffalo Historical Society, 1937, 1941.

Buffalo Historical Society. "Buffalo and Black Rock Harbor Papers." *Publications of the Buffalo Historical Society* 14 (1910): 309–88.

———. "The Holland Land Company and Canal Construction in Western New York." *Publications of the Buffalo Historical Society* 14 (1910); 3–185.

Burr, David. *An Atlas of the State of New York.* New York: D. H. Burr, 1829.

Butterfield, L. H. "Judge William Cooper (1754–1809): A Sketch of His Character and Accomplishments." *New York History* 30 (1949): 385–408.

Campbell, Patrick. *Travels in the Interior Inhabited Parts of North America in the Years 1791 and 1792.* Toronto: Champlain Society, 1937.

Casey, Richard P. "North Country Nemesis: The Potash Rebellion and the Embargo of 1807–1809." *New-York Historical Society Quarterly* 64 (1980); 130–49.

Chazanof, William. *Joseph Ellicott and the Holland Land Company.* Syracuse, N.Y.: Syracuse University Press, 1970.

————. "The Van Eeghen Collection." *Niagara Frontier* 15 (1968): 80–85.

Chernow, Barbara. "Robert Morris: Genesee Land Speculator." *New York History* 58 (1977): 195–220.

Cooper, Thomas. *A Ride to Niagara.* 1814.

Cooper, William. *Guide in the Wilderness.* Dublin: Gilbert and Hodges, 1810.

Covell, Reverend Lemuel. *A Narrative of a Missionary Tour through the Western Settlements of the State of New York and into the Southwestern Parts of the Province of Upper Canada.* Troy, N.Y.: Moffitt and Lyon, 1804.

Cowan, Helen. *Charles Williamson: Genesee Promoter, Friend of Anglo-American Rapprochement.* Rochester, N.Y.: Rochester Historical Society, 1941.

Darby, William. *A Tour from the City of New York, to Detroit, in the Michigan Territory.* New York: Kirk and Mercein, 1819.

Deusen, John G. van. "Robert Troup: Agent of the Pulteney Estate." *New York History* 23 (1942): 166–80.

De Witt, Benjamin. "A Sketch of the Turnpike Roads in the State of New York." *Society for the Promotion of Useful Arts* 2 (1807): 190–204.

Doty, Lockwood, ed. *History of the Genesee Country,* 4 vols. Chicago: S. J. Clarke, 1925.

Dow, Charles Mason. *Anthology and Bibliography of Niagara Falls,* vol. 1. Albany, N.Y.: J. B. Lyon, 1921.

Dwight, Timothy. *Travels in New England and New York,* 4 vols. New Haven, Conn.: Timothy Dwight, 1821–22.

Edson, Obed. *History of Chautauqua County, New York.* Boston: W. A. Ferguson, 1894.

Elkinton, Joseph. "The Quaker Mission among the Indians of New York State." *Publications of the Buffalo Historical Society* 18 (1914): 169–89.

Ellis, David M., et al. *A Short History of New York State.* Ithaca, N.Y.: Cornell University Press, 1957.

Evans, Paul D. *The Holland Land Company.* Buffalo, N.Y.: Buffalo Historical Society, 1924.

————. "The Pulteney Purchase." *Proceedings of the New York State Historical Society* 20 (1922): 83–103.

Everts, L. H. *History of Cattaraugus County, New York.* Philadelphia: J. B. Lippincott, 1879.

Flick, Alexander, ed. *History of the State of New York,* 10 vols. New York: Columbia University Press, 1933.

Follett, Frederick. *History of the Press in Western New York.* Harrison, N.Y.: Harbor Hill Books, 1973.

Foreman, Edward R. "Crown Grants and Early Land Claims Affecting the Rochester Region." *Rochester Historical Society Publications* 10 (1931): 111–27.

Fox, Dixon Ryan. *Yankees and Yorkers.* New York: New York University Press, 1940.

French, J. H. *Gazetteer of the State of New York.* Syracuse, N.Y., 1860.

Frese, Joseph R., and Jacob Judd, eds. *Business Enterprise in Early New York.* Tarrytown, N.Y.: Sleepy Hollow Press, 1979.

Hall, Basil. *Forty Etchings from Sketches Made with the Camera Lucida in North America.* Edinburgh: Cadell, 1830.

Hatfield, Joseph. *An Englishman in America, 1785, Being the Diary of Joseph Hatfield,* ed. D. S. Robertson. Toronto: Hunter Rose, 1933.

Hazeltine, G. W. *The Early History of the Town of Ellicott.* Jamestown, N.Y.: Journal Printing, 1887.

Hedrick, Ulysses P. *A History of Agriculture in the State of New York.* Albany, N.Y.: New York State Agricultural Society, 1933.

Higgins, Ruth. *Expansion in New York.* Columbus, Ohio: Ohio State University Press, 1931.

Historical Records Survey. *Guide to Depositories of Manuscript Collections in New York State,* vol. 1. Albany, N.Y.: Work Project Administration, 1941.

———. *Inventory of the County Archives of New York State, No. 4, Cattaraugus County.* Albany, N.Y.: Historical Records Survey, 1939.

———. *Inventory of Maps.* Albany, N.Y.: Work Project Administration, 1942.

Horton, J. T., E. T. Williams, and H. S. Douglas. *History of Northwestern New York.* 2 vols. New York: Lewis Historical Publishing, 1947.

Hotchkin, Rev. James H. *A History of the Purchase and Settlement of Western New York and of the Rise, Progress and Present State of the Presbyterian Church in That Section.* New York: M. W. Dodd, 1848.

Houghton, Frederick. "The History of Buffalo Creek Reservation." *Publications of the Buffalo Historical Society* 24 (1920): 3–181.

Imlay, Gilbert. "A Topographical Description of the Western Territory of North America." In *Documentary History of the State of New York,* 2:1111–25. Ed. E. B. O'Callaghan. Albany, N.Y.: Weed, Parsons, 1849.

Ingraham, Duncan. "Description of the Country between Albany and Niagara in 1792." In *Documentary History of the State of New York,* 2:1105–10. Ed. E. B. O'Callaghan. Albany, N.Y.: Weed, Parsons, 1849.

Johnson, Crisfield. *Centennial History of Erie County.* Buffalo, N.Y.: Matthews and Warren, 1876.

Kass, Alvin. *Politics in New York State, 1800–1830.* Syracuse, N.Y.: Syracuse University Press, 1965.

Ketchum, William. *History of Buffalo.* Buffalo, N.Y.: Rockwell, Baker, and Hill, 1865.

Kim, Sung Bok. *Landlord and Tenant in Colonial New York: Manorial Society, 1664–1775.* Chapel Hill, N.C.: University of North Carolina Press, 1978.

Larned, J. N. *A History of Buffalo.* 2 vols. New York: Progress of the Empire State, 1911.

Lindley, Jacob. "Journal." *Publications of the Buffalo Historical Society* 6 (1903): 169–82.

McKelvey, Blake. *Rochester: The Water-Power City, 1812–1854.* Cambridge: Harvard University Press, 1945.

———, ed. "Foreign Traveler's Notes on Rochester and the Genesee Country before 1840." *Rochester Historical Society Publications* 18 (1940): 1–117.

McNall, Neil. *An Agricultural History of the Genesee Valley, 1790–1860.* Philadelphia: University of Pennsylvania Press, 1952.

Mau, Clayton. *The Development of Central and Western New York.* Rochester, N.Y.: DuBois Press, 1944.

Melish, John. *Travels in the United States of America in the Years 1806 and 1807, and 1809, 1810, and 1811.* 1812; reprint, New York: Johnson Reprint Corporation, 1970.

Niemcewicz, J. U. "Journey to Niagara." *New-York Historical Society Quarterly* 44 (1960): 73–113.

North, Safford E. *Our County and Its People: A Description and Biographical Record of Genesee County, New York.* Boston: Boston Historical Co., 1899.

O'Callaghan, E. B., ed. *Documentary History of the State of New York,* vol. 2. Albany, N.Y.: Weed, Parsons, 1849.

Palmer, R. F. *The Old Line Mail: Stagecoaching Days in Upstate New York.* Lakemont, N.Y.: North Country Books, 1977.

Parker, Arthur C. "Charles Williamson: Builder of the Genesee Country." *Rochester Historical Society Publications* 6 (1927): 1–34.

Petri, Pitt. *The Postal History of Western New York: Its Post Offices and Postmasters.* Buffalo, N.Y., 1960.

Pool, William, ed. *Landmarks of Niagara County.* Syracuse, N.Y.: D. Mason, 1897.

Rapp, Marvin A. "New York's Trade on the Great Lakes, 1800–1840." *New York History* 39 (1958): 22–33.

Rayback, Robert J., ed. *Richard's Atlas of New York State.* Phoenix, N.Y.: F. E. Richards, 1965.

Rochefoucault Liancourt, [Duke] De La. *Travels through the United States of North America.* London: R. Phillips, 1799.

Schultz, Christian. *Travels on an Inland Voyage through the States of New York . . . in the Years 1807 and 1808.* New York: Isaac Riley, 1810.

Severance, Frank. *Old Trails on the Niagara Frontier.* Cleveland, Ohio: Burrows Brothers, 1903.

———, ed. "The Dobbins Papers." *Publications of the Buffalo Historical Society* 8 (1905): 257–379.

———, ed. "Narratives and Journals of Pioneer Surveyors." *Publications of the Buffalo Historical Society* 7 (1904): 229–376.

———, ed. "Narratives of Eighteenth Century Visitors to Niagara." *Publications of the Buffalo Historical Society* 15 (1911): 315–400.

———, ed. *The Picture Book of Early Buffalo.* Buffalo, N.Y.: Buffalo Historical Society, 1912.

Signor, Isaac S. *Landmarks of Orleans County.* Syracuse, N.Y.: D. Mason, 1894.

Silsby, Robert W. "Mortgage Credit in the Phelps-Gorham Purchase." *New York History* 41 (1960): 3–34.

Smith, H. Perry. *History of the City of Buffalo and Erie County,* 2 vols. Syracuse, N.Y.: D. Mason, 1884.

Spafford, H. G. *Gazetteer of the State of New York.* Albany, N.Y.: H. C. Southwick, 1813.

Stewart, William. *New Topographical Atlas of Chautauqua County, New York.* Philadelphia: William Stewart, 1867.

Sutcliffe, Robert. *Travels in Some Parts of North America in the Years 1804, 1805, 1806.* Philadelphia: B. and T. Kite, 1812.

Thomas, Arad. *Pioneer History of Orleans County.* Albion, N.Y.: H. A. Brunner, 1871.

Thompson, John, ed. *The Geography of New York State.* Syracuse, N.Y.: Syracuse University Press, 1977.

Todd, C. Lafayette. "Some Nineteenth Century European Travelers in New York State." *New York History* 43 (1962): 336–70.

Turner, Orasmus. *History of Phelps and Gorham's Purchase.* Rochester, N.Y.: William Alling, 1851.

————. *Pioneer History of the Holland Purchase of Western New York.* Buffalo, N.Y.: George H. Derby, 1850.

Walters, Raymond, and Philip G. Walters. "David Parrish: York Land Promoter." *New York History* 26 (1945): 146–61.

Weld, Isaac. *Travels through the States of North America.* 1799; reprint, New York: Johnson Reprint Corporation, 1968.

White, Truman C. *Our County and Its People: A Descriptive Work on Erie County, New York.* 2 vols. Boston: Boston Historical Co., 1898.

Williams, Clara. *Joseph Ellicott and Stories of the Holland Purchase.* N.p.: Clara Williams, 1936.

Williamson, Chilton. "New York's Impact on the Canadian Economy." *New York History* 24 (1943): 24–38.

Work Project Administration. *New York.* New York: Oxford University Press, 1940.

Wyckoff, William. "Frontier Milling in Western New York." *Geographical Review* 76 (1986): 73–93.

————. "Original Surveys and Land Subdivision in Western New York State." *Journal of Historical Geography* 12 (1986): 142–61.

Young, Andrew White. *History of Chautauqua County.* Buffalo, N.Y.: Matthews and Warren, 1875.

General

Adams, Ian H. "The Land Surveyor and His Influence on the Scottish Rural Landscape." *Scottish Geographical Magazine* 84 (1968): 248–55.

Agnew, Dwight L. "The Government Land Surveyor as a Pioneer." *Mississippi Valley Historical Review* 28 (1941): 369–82.

Bartlett, G. Hunter. "Andrew and Joseph Ellicott." *Publications of the Buffalo Historical Society* 26 (1922): 3–48.

Bedini, Silvio. "Andrew Ellicott, Surveyor of the Wilderness." *Surveying and Mapping* 36 (1976): 113–35.

Billington, Ray Allen. *Westward Expansion.* New York: Macmillan, 1949.

Brown, Ralph. *Historical Geography of the United States.* New York: Harcourt Brace and World, 1948.

Buck, Solon Justus, and Elizabeth Hawthorn Buck. *The Planting of Civilization in Western Pennsylvania.* Pittsburgh, Pa: University of Pittsburgh Press, 1939.

Burghardt, Andrew F. "The Origin and Development of the Road Network of the Niagara Peninsula, Ontario, 1770–1851." *Annals of the Association of American Geographers* 59 (1969): 417–40.

Carlson, Alvar. "Long Lots in the Rio Arriba." *Annals of the Association of American Geographers* 65 (1975): 48–57.

Commager, Henry Steele. *Jefferson, Nationalism, and the Enlightenment.* New York: George Braziller, 1975.

Craig, G. M. *Upper Canada: The Formative Years, 1784–1861.* London: McClelland and Stewart, 1963.

Day, Gordon M. "The Indian as an Ecological Factor in the Northeastern Forests." *Ecology* 34 (1953): 329–46.

Durrenberger, Joseph. *Turnpikes.* Cos Cob, Conn.: John E. Edwards, 1968.

Earle, Alice Morse. *Stage-Coach and Tavern Days*. New York: Macmillan, 1927.

Earle, Carville. *The Evolution of a Tidewater Settlement System: All Hallow's Parish, Maryland, 1650–1783*. University of Chicago, Department of Geography, Research Paper no. 170. Chicago, 1975.

Ellicott, Andrew. *The Journal of Andrew Ellicott*. Philadelphia: Budd and Bartram, 1803.

Ellis, David M. *The Frontier in American Development: Essays in Honor of Paul Wallace Gates*. Ithaca, N.Y.: Cornell University Press, 1969.

Evans, Charles W. *Biographical and Historical Accounts of the Fox, Ellicott, and Evans Families*. Buffalo, N.Y.: Press of Baker, Jones, and Co., 1882.

Ford, Amelia Clewley. *Colonial Precedents of Our National Land System as It Existed in 1800*. Madison, Wis.: University of Wisconsin Press, 1910.

Gates, L. F. *Land Policies of Upper Canada*. Toronto: University of Toronto Press, 1968.

Gates, Paul Wallace. "The Role of the Land Speculator in Western Development." *Pennsylvania Magazine of History and Biography* 66 (1942): 314–33.

Gentilcore, R. Louis. "The Beginnings of Settlement in the Niagara Peninsula (1782–1792)." *Canadian Geographer* 7 (1962): 72–82.

Gentilcore, R. Louis, and Kate Donkin. "Land Surveys of Southern Ontario: An Introduction and Index to the Field Notebooks of the Ontario Land Surveyors, 1784–1859." *Canadian Cartographer* 10 (1973): suppl. 2.

Gibson, Robert. *A Treatise of Practical Surveying*. New York: William Davis, 1798.

Harris, R. Cole. "The Historical Mind and the Practice of Geography." In *Humanistic Geography*, pp. 123–37. Ed. David Ley and Marwyn Samuels. Chicago: Maaroufa Press, 1978.

———. *The Seigneurial System in Early Canada: A Geographical Study*. Madison, Wis.: University of Wisconsin Press, 1968.

———. "Theory and Synthesis in Historical Geography." *Canadian Geographer* 15 (1971): 157–72.

Harris, R. Cole, and John Warkentin. *Canada before Confederation: A Study in Historical Geography*. New York: Oxford University Press, 1974.

Harris, Marshall. *Origin of the Land Tenure System in the United States*. Ames, Iowa: Iowa State College Press, 1953.

Hatcher, Harlan. *The Western Reserve: The Story of New Connecticut in Ohio*. New York: Bobbs-Merrill, 1949.

Heathcote, R. L. *Back of Bourke: A Study of Land Appraisal and Settlement in Semi-Arid Australia*. London: Melbourne University Press, 1965.

Hofstadter, Richard, and Seymour Martin Lipset, eds. *Turner and the Sociology of the Frontier*. New York: Basic Books, 1968.

Jakle, John. *Images of the Ohio River Valley*. New York: Oxford University Press, 1977.

———. "Salt on the Ohio Valley Frontier, 1770–1820." *Annals of the Association of American Geographers* 59 (1969): 687–709.

Johnson, Hildegard Binder. *Order upon the Land*. New York: Oxford University Press, 1976.

Jordan, Terry. "Antecedents of the Long Lot in Texas." *Annals of the Association of American Geographers* 64 (1974): 70–86.

Kelly, Kenneth. "The Evaluation of Land for Wheat Cultivation in Early Nineteenth Century Ontario." *Ontario History* 62 (1970): 57–64.

Lane, Wheaton J. *From Indian Trail to Iron Horse: Travel and Transportation in New Jersey, 1620–1860.* Princeton, N.J.: Princeton University Press, 1939.

Lemon, James. *The Best Poor Man's Country: A Geographical Study of Early Southeastern Pennsylvania.* New York: W. W. Norton, 1976.

Livermore, Shaw. *Early American Land Companies.* New York: Oxford University Press, 1939.

McManis, Douglas. *Colonial New England: A Historical Geography.* New York: Oxford University Press, 1975.

―――. *The Initial Evaluation and Utilization of the Illinois Prairies, 1815–1840.* University of Chicago, Department of Geography, Research Paper no. 94. Chicago, 1964.

Matthews, Catherine Van Cortlandt. *Andrew Ellicott: His Life and Letters.* New York: Grafton Press, 1908.

Meinig, D. W. "The Continuous Shaping of America: A Prospectus for Geographers and Historians." *American Historical Review* 83 (1978): 1186–1205.

―――. "Environmental Appreciation: Localities as a Humane Art." *Western Humanities Review* 25 (1971): 1–11.

―――, ed. *The Interpretation of Ordinary Landscapes.* New York: Oxford University Press, 1979.

Merrens, Harry Roy. *Colonial North Carolina in the Eighteenth Century.* Chapel Hill, N.C.: University of North Carolina Press, 1964.

Mitchell, R. D. *Commercialism and Frontier: Perspectives on the Early Shenandoah Valley.* Charlottesville, Va: University of Virginia Press, 1977.

―――. "The Formation of Early American Cultural Regions: An Interpretation." In *European Settlement and Development in North America,* pp. 66–90. Ed. James R. Gibson. Toronto: University of Toronto Press, 1978.

Muller, Edward K. "Selective Urban Growth in the Middle Ohio Valley, 1800–1860." *Geographical Review* 66 (1976): 178–99.

―――. "Regional Urbanization and the Selective Growth of Towns in North American Regions." *Journal of Historical Geography* 3 (1977): 21–39.

Nettels, Curtis P. *The Emergence of a National Economy: 1775–1815.* New York: Holt, Rinehart, and Winston, 1962.

Newton, Milton. "Route Geography and the Routes of St. Helena Parish, Louisiana." *Annals of the Association of American Geographers* 60 (1970): 134–52.

Nye, Russel Blaine. *The Cultural Life of the New Nation, 1776–1830.* New York: Harper and Row, 1960.

Paterson, J. H. "Writing Regional Geography: Problems and Progress in the Anglo-American Realm." *Progress in Geography* 6 (1975): 1–26.

Pattison, William D. *Beginnings of the American Rectangular Land Survey System, 1784–1800.* University of Chicago, Department of Geography, Research Paper no. 50. Chicago, 1957.

―――. "Use of the Public Land Survey Plats and Notes as Descriptive Sources." *Professional Geographer* 8 (1956): 10–14.

Peters, Bernard C. "Changing Ideas about the Use of Vegetation as an Indicator of Soil Quality: Example of New York and Michigan." *Journal of Geography* 72, no. 2 (1973): 18–28.

Pillsbury, Richard. "The Urban Street Pattern as a Culture Indicator." *Annals of the Association of American Geographers* 60 (1970): 428–46.

Pred, Allen R. *The Spatial Dynamics of U.S. Urban-Industrial Growth, 1800–1914: Interpretive and Theoretical Essays.* Cambridge, Mass.: MIT Press, 1966.

Price, E. T. "The Central Courthouse Square in the American County Seat." *Geographical Review* 58 (1968): 28–60.

Reps, John. *Monumental Washington.* Princeton, N.J.: Princeton University Press, 1967.

———. *Town Planning in Frontier America.* Princeton, N.J.: Princeton University Press, 1969.

Rohrbough, Malcolm G. *The Land Office Business: The Settlement and Administration of American Public Lands, 1789–1837.* New York: Oxford University Press, 1968.

Sakolski, Aaron Morton. *The Great American Land Bubble.* New York: Harper Brothers, 1932.

Sloane, Eric. *Our Vanishing Landscape.* New York: Wilfred Funk, 1955.

Smart, Charles E. *The Makers of Surveying Instruments in America since 1700.* Troy, N.Y.: Regal Art Press, 1962.

Stearns, Raymond Phineas. *Science in the British Colonies of America.* Urbana, Ill.: University of Illinois Press, 1970.

Thompson, Francis M. L. *Chartered Surveyors: The Growth of a Profession.* London: Routeledge and Kegan Paul, 1968.

Thrower, Norman. *Original Survey and Land Subdivision.* Chicago: Association of American Geographers Monograph Series 4, 1966.

Turner, Frederick Jackson. *The Frontier in American History.* New York: Henry Holt, 1947.

Vance, James E. *The Merchant's World: The Geography of Wholesaling.* Englewood-Cliffs, N.J.: Prentice-Hall, 1970.

Wacker, Peter O. *Land and People: A Cultural Geography of Preindustrial New Jersey: Origins and Settlement Patterns.* New Brunswick, N.J.: Rutgers University Press, 1975.

Wade, Richard C. *The Urban Frontier: The Rise of Western Cities, 1790–1830.* Cambridge, Mass.: Harvard University Press, 1959.

Watson, J. W. "The Influence of the Frontier on Niagara Settlements." *Geographical Review* 38 (1948): 113–19.

Williams, Michael. "Delimiting the Spread of Settlement: An Examination of Evidence in South Australia." *Economic Geography* 42 (1966): 336–55.

———. *The Making of the South Australian Landscape: A Study in the Historical Geography of Australia.* New York: Academic Press, 1974.

Wood, J. D., ed. *Perspectives on Landscape and Settlement in Nineteenth Century Ontario.* Toronto: McClelland and Stewart, 1975.

Wood, Joseph S. "Village and Community in Early Colonial New England." *Journal of Historical Geography* 8 (1982): 333–46.

Zelinsky, Wilbur. *The Cultural Geography of the United States.* Englewood-Cliffs, N.J.: Prentice-Hall, 1973.

Zimiles, Martha, and Murray Zimiles. *Early American Mills.* New York: Bramhall House, 1973.

Zube, Ervin H., ed. *Landscapes: Selected Writings of J. B. Jackson.* Amherst, Mass.: University of Massachusetts Press, 1970.

UNPUBLISHED SOURCES

Theses and Dissertations

Chazanof, William. "The Political Influence of Joseph Ellicott in Western New York, 1800–1821." Ph.D. diss., Syracuse University, 1955.

Garff, Royal Lovell. "Social and Economic Conditions in the Genesee Country, 1787–1813." Ph.D. diss., Northwestern University, 1939.

Gimigliano, Michael N. "Experiences along the Cherry Valley Turnpike: The Education of a Traveler." Ph.D. diss., Syracuse University, 1979.

Hugill, Peter. "A Small Town Landscape as Sustained Gesture on the Part of a Dominant Social Group: Cazenovia, New York: 1794–1976." Ph.D. diss., Syracuse University, 1977.

Mogavero, I. Frank. "Peter Porter, Citizen and Statesman." Ph.D. diss., Ottawa University, 1950.

Rose, Robert S. "The Military Tract of Central New York." M.A. thesis, Syracuse University, 1935.

Siles, William Herbert. "A Vision of Wealth: Speculators and Settlers in the Genesee Country of New York, 1788–1800." Ph.D. diss., University of Massachusetts, 1978.

Manuscript Collections

Albany, N.Y. New York State Library. Holland Land Company Collection.

Amsterdam, The Netherlands. Municipal Archives of Amsterdam. Holland Land Company Collection.

Batavia, N.Y. Genesee County Clerk's Office. Deed Records.

———. Genesee County Historical Society Land Office Museum. Holland Land Company Collection.

Belmont, N.Y. Allegany County Clerk's Office. Deed Records.

Buffalo, N.Y. Buffalo and Erie County Historical Society. Dobbins Papers, Holland Land Company Collection, Seth Pease Papers, Augustus Porter Papers.

———. Erie County Clerk's Office. Deed Records, Holland Land Company Lot Survey Notes.

Clarence Center, N.Y. Town of Clarence Clerk's Office. Town Records, vols. 1, 3, and 7.

Hamburg, N.Y. Town of Hamburg Clerk's Office. Town Records, vol. 1.

Ithaca, N.Y. Cornell University. Holland Land Company Collection.

Little Valley, N.Y. Cattaraugus County Clerk's Office. Deed Records. Field Books of Cattaraugus County.

Lockport, N.Y. Niagara County Clerk's Office. Deed Records.

Mayville, N.Y. Chautauqua County Clerk's Office. Deed Records, Survey Field Books of Chautauqua County.

Syracuse, N.Y. Syracuse University. Spaulding Papers.

Washington, D.C. National Archives. Papers of Andrew Ellicott.

Westfield, N.Y. Patterson Library. Holland Land Company Collection.

Index

Accessibility, 44, 53; commerce and, 83–102; frontier theories and, 4–16; land prices and, 74–75; planning for, 50–51; village locations and, 75–78. *See also* Canals; Commerce; Roads; Urban centers

Adgate Purchase, 139

Adlum, John, 106

Advertisements, 14, 59–60

Agriculture: annual round of, 161–62; corn, 116, 126, 158–59, 171; fruit, 159–61; grain, 57, 116, 126, 158–59, 170–71; Indians and, 21–22; oats, 57; potential for, 30–41; village gardens and, 61–62, 126; wheat, 101, 170–71. *See also* Economy; Farms; Land: assessment of; Land: clearing of; Livestock; Pioneers; Soils

Ague, 35, 129; near Lake Ontario, 40, 122

Albany: commercial links with, 94–95, 101–2

Alcoholic beverages, 127–29. *See also* Taverns

Allegany County: created, 88; land assessed in, 38–41; land prices in, 69–75; lotting in, 65–69, 136; mills in, 92; planned commerce of, 97–99; planned roads in, 76, 78–′ 82; road remnants in, 184–89; settlement in, 119–25; township remnants in, 174–77. *See also* Local government

Allegany Road. *See* Roads: Allegany

Allegheny (East and West) land agencies, 12, 18–19, 200

Allegheny River, 21; bottomlands on, 72; Hoops' acreage and, 67; Indian settlement and, 22, 30; long lots on, 140; trade and, 98

Allegheny River Indian Reservation, 30. *See also* Indian reservations

American Revolution, 22, 106

Architecture. *See* Buildings; Housing

Artisans, 48–49. *See also* Blacksmiths

Attica Center, 171; initial site selection of, 166–68; modern setting of, 194

Attica Township: landscape of, 162–72, 190–94

Attica Village, 124; initial site selection of, 166; modern setting of, 192–94; services in, 171

Avery, Joseph, 109, 130

Barcelona. *See* Portland

Batavia Township, 87. *See also* Genesee County; Local government

Batavia Village, 126–31, 154–56; company assistance to, 57, 60–62, 65, 84–85; initial etablishment of, 56, 58, 75, 143–44; land prices in, 86; remnants of, 180; services in, 57, 87, 127–31. *See also* Genesee County

Bath, 12, 16; commercial development, 81, 97, 180; survey of, 146

Big Tree Road. *See* Roads: Big Tree

Black Rock, 100. *See also* Niagara River

Blacksmiths: company assistance to, 48–49, 57–58, 85; function of, 128

Boon, Gerritt, 43–52

Bridges: cost of, 80

Brisbane, James, 85, 127–28

British Canada. *See* Montreal; Upper Canada

Buffalo: burning of, 123; Ellicott property in, 145; land prices in, 86; landscape of, 62, 180–82; plan of, 144–47; services in, 88, 96, 154–56; site of, 56, 75–77; subagency in, 61. *See also* Erie County

Buffalo Creek, 21, 53; site of Indian settlement, 53

Buffalo Road. *See* Roads: Buffalo

Buildings, 62, 118, 125–27, 156–57. *See also* Housing

Burt, Timothy, 128

Busti, Paul, 17, 53, 55, 66–68, 70–71, 102, 137

Cadastral patterns. *See* Land: Survey of; Lot surveys; Townships

Cambria Township, 118

Canada. *See* Montreal; Upper Canada

Canada Company, 13

Canals: commercial activity and, 96; land prices and, 102. *See also* Accessibility

Canandaigua, 12, 16, 17, 87, 101; plat as model for Batavia, 144

Carpenters, 128

Cary, Ebenezar, 90

Cattaraugus County: county seat of, 78; created, 88; initial lotting in, 65–69, 136; land assessed in, 38–41, 68; land prices in, 69–75; mills in, 92; planned commerce of, 97–99; planned roads in, 76, 78–82; planned urban centers in, 78; settlement in, 119–25. *See also* Local government

Cattaraugus Creek: Indian settlement on, 22; long lots of, 140, 178

Cattaraugus Road. *See* Roads: Cattaraugus

Cattaraugus Village, 77, 81, 147–48, 182

Cattle, 97–98, 100, 161

Causewaying, 80

Cazenove, Theophile, 17, 24–25, 27–28, 43–45, 51–52, 54–55

Cazenovia, 12, 18, 139, 146

Chain migration, 106–7

Chautauqua County: created, 88, 90; demand for land in, 122; initial lotting in, 65–69, 136, 142; land prices in, 69–75; land quality of, 38–41, 106–7; mills in, 92–93; planned commerce of, 97–99; planned roads in, 76, 78–82; planned urban centers in, 77–78; road remnants in, 184–89; settlement in, 119–25; township remnants in,

174–77; travel in, 155. *See also* Chautauqua Township; Local government; Portland

Chautauqua Lake. *See* Mayville; Roads: Portage

Chautauqua Township, 88. *See also* Chautauqua County; Local government

Chipman, Samuel, 107

Churches, 44, 48–49, 171. *See also* Religion

Cities. *See* Urban centers

Clarence. *See* Ransom, Asa; Ransoms

Class structure, 108

Clinton-Sullivan campaign, 106

Commerce: frontier economy and, 8, 15, 79, 94–102; Indians and, 22–23, 152–55; landscape change and, 195; village location and, 75–78. *See also* Accessibility; Economy; Roads; Urban centers

Commercialism: policy in developer's frontier, 50–52, 83–102, 200–201

Commons. *See* Public squares

Communities, 125–31; planning for, 44–52. *See also* Families; Urban centers

"Company farm," 61–62

Connecticut Land Company, 26, 70

Connewongo Creek, 21, 77, 92, 140

Cooper, Judge William, 11

Cooperstown, 11

Corn. *See* Agriculture: corn

County government. *See* Local government *and particular counties*

Covell, Lemuel, 154

Credit sales. *See* Land: sale of

Crops. *See* Agriculture; Farms

Crow's tavern, 155

Cummings, Simeon, 85, 129

Developer's frontier, 9–16, 195–202; commercial policy on, 83–102; planned for in western New York, 42–52; remnants of, 173–202; settlement policy on, 64–82. *See also* Ellicott, Joseph; Frontier

Diet, 127

Disease. *See* Ague; Physicians

Distilleries, 127

Doctors. *See* Physicians

Drainage patterns: western New York, 20–21, 94–95, 199

Dull, George, 142

Dutch investors, 17–18, 42–43. *See also* Busti, Paul; Cazenove, Theophile